6/04

ON SACRED GROUND

The Spirit of Place
in Pacific Northwest Literature

ON SACRED GROUND

The Spirit of Place
in Pacific Northwest Literature

NICHOLAS O'CONNELL

UNIVERSITY OF WASHINGTON PRESS

Seattle and London

Library of Congress Cataloging-in-Publication Data
O'Connell, Nicholas.
On sacred ground : the spirit of place in Pacific Northwest
literature / Nicholas O'Connell.
p. cm.
Includes bibliographical references and index.
ISBN 0-295-98346-9 (cloth : alk. paper)
1. American literature—Northwest, Pacific—History and criticism.
2. Northwest, Pacific—Intellectual life.
3. Northwest, Pacific—In literature.
4. Place (Philosophy) in literature.
5. Regionalism in literature.
6. Local color in literature.
I. Title.
PS282 .O266 2003   810.9'9795—dc21   2003010732

To my teachers, especially Charles Johnson,

Jack Brenner, George Dillon, Miceal Vaughan,

Father Emmett Carroll, Society of Jesus,

and Father John Foster, Society of Jesus

CONTENTS

PREFACE ix

ACKNOWLEDGMENTS xv

1 / Early Native American Stories 3

2 / Journals of Exploration and Settlement 15

3 / Romantic Movement 33

4 / Realistic Writing 47

5 / The Northwest School 97

6 / Contemporary Northwest Literature 140

REFERENCES 181

ADDITIONAL SOURCES 197

INDEX 201

PREFACE

WHEN I WAS A STUDENT at Amherst College in Massachusetts, a friend invited me to spend a weekend at his family's ski cabin in the White Mountains of New Hampshire. I eagerly accepted, as I wanted to see New England's mountains.

On a cold, clear Friday afternoon in February, we drove north on Interstate 91 through western Massachusetts. The sun shone, thin and metallic, in the western sky. The dark trunks of birch trees stood out starkly against the snow-covered fields. The road snaked through a patchwork of farms, forests, and New England towns, a pastoral landscape so different from the rugged Western one I'd grown up with.

After passing through Hanover, New Hampshire, we turned east onto Highway 112 and headed toward the White Mountains. As the road steepened, the birches gave way to firs and pines. I strained to catch a glimpse of the White Mountains. Would they be steep and dramatic like Washington's Cascades Mountains or high and eroded like the sedimentary peaks of the Rockies? As the car crested a rise, my friend Randy Meiklejohn looked over at me.

"What do you think of the White Mountains?" he asked.

"What do you mean?"

"Right there," he pointed outside the car window. "Those are the White Mountains."

When I realized that he wasn't joking, I replied, "Those aren't mountains—those are *hills*."

In the course of the trip, I came to love the rocky, windswept summits of the White Mountains, but I never considered them mountains. They were hills, bumps on the rolling, glacier-scoured landscape of northern New England. To a Northwesterner like myself, they were beautiful, but not large enough or impressive enough to qualify as mountains.

Northwestern mountains were another story. Mount Rainier, for example, towered above my native city of Seattle like a brooding colossus. Even if I was stuck in a traffic jam on the Highway 520 bridge, the presence of the mountain reminded me of a larger order, a further reference point. Mount Rainier and the rest of the local scenery impinged on human consciousness to a degree that didn't happen as much in the Northeast.

Once I completed my studies and returned to the Northwest, I began poring over the local literature, hoping to get a sense of what—beyond the dramatic scenery—made the region distinctive. It didn't take long to discover that the influence of nature on everyday Northwest life carried over to its literature and culture. The region's literature addressed a number of subjects, but the relationship between people and place proved the dominant one. Further reading convinced me that this has been the case as far back as when the first tribes settled the region thousands of years ago and began telling stories about it. This obsession with landscape pervades all of Northwest literature.

On Sacred Ground traces the history of this literature, from the rich trove of Native American myths, to the diaries and accounts of explorers and settlers, to the effusive outpourings of the Romantic writers and the sharply etched stories of Realistic writers, to the mystic visions of the Northwest School of poets, to the contemporary explosion of Northwest poetry and prose. In tracing this history, I focus on the relation between humans and the environment and explore how that relationship has evolved, from the native peoples' sense of the land's spooky, animistic qualities, to early writers' emphasis on making a living from the country, to contemporary authors' attempts to recover a sense of the landscape's spiritual qualities.

Art, like all human knowledge, begins with the particular, argues fiction writer Flannery O'Connor in her essay collection *Mystery and Manners* (O'Connor 1961, 67). O'Connor makes this claim mostly in regard to Southern literature, but her formulation also holds true for Pacific Northwest literature. "All events and experiences are local, somewhere," says the poet William Stafford, "and all human enhancements of events and experiences—which is to say, all the arts—are regional in the sense that they derive from immediate relation to felt life. It is this immediacy that distinguishes art" (Stafford 1973, 92). As Stafford points out, the immediate circumstances of this region have profoundly influenced its poetry and prose. To understand and fully appreciate this literature, it's necessary to know something of the geography, climate, and human and natural history that inspired it.

The Northwest extends from the Pacific Ocean in the west to the Rocky Mountains in the east, from Washington State in the north to the Siskiyou Mountains to the south. Some argue that the region extends beyond the forty-ninth parallel and that British Columbia and southeast Alaska should be included in the region. Others make a similar claim for northern California, citing the similarity of the climate and the presense of salmon—the region's totem animal—in the state's north coast streams.

These arguments certainly have merit, but in the present book, I felt the need to limit the discussion to what I consider the region's core. The bioregion certainly continues north of the forty-ninth parallel, but the political boundary has exerted an important influence over Northwest literature and needs to be acknowledged in any regional definition. In California, a Mediterrean climate quickly prevails as one moves south, signaling a change in everything from the flora and fauna to the quality of light. For these reasons, I have not included southeast Alaska, British Columbia, or northern California in my definition of the Northwest, and it is beyond the scope of this book to trace the rich and varied influence of Alaska, British Columbia, and northern California writers on Northwest literature. However, I have discussed authors from these areas, such as Jack London, Roderick Haig-Brown, and John Haines, who have exerted wide influence over the region as a whole.

The Northwest exhibits astonishing geographic diversity, ranging from rain forests to high deserts to alpine meadows. It is truly the *Pacific* Northwest because the Pacific Ocean exerts such a marked effect on the region's climate, as Susan Schwartz describes in *Nature in the Northwest* (Schwartz 1983, 63). Ocean winds flowing inland moderate the region's weather, making temperatures cooler in summer and warmer in winter than in other regions at similar latitudes. The Cascades and coastal mountain ranges form only a partial barrier against the ocean air, allowing it to move inland more easily than it does farther south in California. These moist ocean winds bring with them milder temperatures and greater rainfall.

Because the ocean's influence extends far inland, the region shares a similarity of climate, flora, and fauna. Interior areas such as Idaho's northern Panhandle get nearly as much rain as the Puget Sound region. Forests on the western slope of the Rocky Mountains contain many species found in coastal forests. These include trees like western hemlock, Douglas fir, and western red cedar; animals such as cougar, elk, black bear, and mule deer; and several species of trout and salmon, which run in many of the region's streams.

The overall mildness of the climate and the abundance of fish and game made the Northwest particularly attractive to early Indian peoples. The mouth of the Columbia River, for example, was one of the most densely populated areas of early North America. As Philip Drucker explains in *Indians of the Northwest Coast,* the coastal tribes and those along the Columbia and its tributaries obtained much of their annual food supply during the salmon runs and thus could devote the rest of the year to weaving, carving, painting, gambling, and storytelling (Drucker 1963, 3). Their artistic depictions of salmon, raven, wolf, otter, and other animals expressed their reverence for and dependence on the natural world. This work includes some of the finest examples of aboriginal art in North America.

Geography also played a significant role in the white exploration and settlement of the region. With the barrier of the Rocky Mountains on the east, the Siskiyous on the south, and a stormy and unpredictable maritime climate from the west, the region resisted many early attempts at exploration. By the time explorers such as George

Vancouver pierced the Northwest's natural defenses, it was relatively late in the history of European exploration, and attitudes toward nature and wild landscapes had changed. Many explorers responded to the region's aesthetic attractions as well as its utilitarian advantages, thus setting an important precedent for Northwest culture.

Explorers like George Vancouver, Meriwether Lewis, and William Clark paved the way for settlers, most of whom came from northern climes. New Englanders, Scots, English, Irish, French, Swedes, Norwegians, Danes, and Finns gravitated toward a place that reminded them of home. These immigrants usually made their living from the land, whether in timber, fishing, fur trapping, or mining. Geographic circumstances never determined the regional economy or the larger culture, but they heavily influenced it, offering the inhabitants a range of possibilities within which to live their lives.

From the beginning, the region's writers and storytellers made the landscape the dominant subject of Northwest literature. They sought to understand their relationship with the nonhuman world and express it in their work. But the land did not reveal itself easily or immediately. Writers had to wrestle to come to terms with it, raising a number of questions: What is distinctive about this place? How does the literature reflect it? What is Northwest literature? How is it unique? Is there a Northwest style? How do individual authors follow or depart from this style? In exploring these and other issues, I relate the larger story of how the region's authors struggled to see the Northwest not just as a source of material wealth but as a spiritual homeland, a place to lead a rich and fulfilling life within the context of the rest of creation.

ACKNOWLEDGMENTS

IN INTERPRETING NORTHWEST LITERATURE, I follow a long line of other critics. Over the years, the search for a regional literary identity has proved as appealing and quixotic as the search for the Northwest Passage. Like the mythical waterway, such an identity was *supposed* to exist, but the unformed nature of the region's literature defied easy analysis or sharp delineation. Lines blurred, theories foundered, and the whole enterprise collapsed in the intellectual equivalent of a patch of blackberries.

Despite these difficulties, a number of commentators gamely hacked their way through the thorny undergrowth surrounding these issues. The earliest of them mainly indulged in hand-wringing over the subject, as was the case with Edmond S. Meany in his essay "Has Puget Sound a Literature?" In the end, he concludes that no such literature existed (Meany 1889, 8–11).

John B. Horner makes great claims about the region's literature in the preface to *Oregon Literature* (Horner 1902), but of the more than seventy writers included in this anthology, only Joaquin Miller achieved any real following or distinction.

Alfred Powers's *History of Oregon Literature* includes a wealth of material—poems, stories, songs, histories, and journals—but doesn't venture an interpretation about what made this work unique (Powers 1935).

Stewart Holbrook highlights the diversity of the Northwest's climate, topography, and people in *Promised Land,* but finds nothing distinctive about its literary output, other than a tendency to focus on pioneering, a tendency common to Western writing (Holbrook 1945).

In *Northwest Harvest: A Regional Stock-Taking,* V. L. O. Chittick and other critics and writers tackle the subject of the region's cultural and literary identity, but reach no consensus. The writer Ernest Haycox even questioned whether the Northwest should be considered a distinct region at all (Chittick 1948).

Ellis Lucia observes in *This Land Around Us* that the proximity to snowcapped peaks, seas, and rivers strongly influenced the region's writers. He notes that nature as a subject figures prominently in the region's literature, but he doesn't identify it as a distinctive trait (Lucia 1969).

As the region's literary output matured, others glimpsed the emergence of a regional identity. In historian Richard Etulain's 1973 article "Novelists of the Northwest," he points out that the region had produced important novelists such as H. L. Davis (see chapter 4), James Stevens (see chapter 4), and Robert Cantwell (see chapter 3). He suggests that these authors might be the harbingers of a distinctive regional literature (Etulain 1973, 24–31).

Cantwell himself proved more skeptical about the existence of such an identity, claiming in *The Hidden Northwest* that the region's culture had no distinguishing features. He did emphasize the pervasive influence of the scenery, but didn't speculate how it might shape the region's art and culture (Cantwell 1972).

In the wake of national recognition generated by the Beat movement, the poet William Everson announced that the West Coast possessed a distinctive literary tradition. In *Archetype West: The Pacific Coast as a Literary Region,* he characterizes West Coast literature as "the symbolic configuration of archetypal force" (Everson 1976, x). Though he never defined this archetypal force, he cited examples of it in the work of John Muir, Frank Norris, Joaquin Miller (see chapter 3), and Robinson Jeffers. Everson's vagueness limits the book's usefulness, but his assertion of West Coast literature's independence emboldened others to make similar claims.

In the essay "Continuity in Northwest Literature," George Venn breaks new ground by suggesting that the landscape might serve as the focal point for a distinctive regional literature. He observes that "it may be that the environment and the human response to it will emerge as one source of continuity in the region's literature that cannot easily be dismissed" (Venn 1979, 99). Though Venn doesn't go so far as to assert this, he paved the way for a number of others who saw the environment and the human response to it as the central feature of the region's literature.

Roy Carlson's *Contemporary Northwest Writing: A Collection of Poetry and Fiction* takes a similar tack, including poems and stories that treat the landscape as a central subject. Carlson speculates that the subject of the environment could serve as the thread that unifies Northwest literature (Carlson 1979).

By the 1980s, critics began to assert the uniqueness of the region's writing and trace the pattern of its development. In "Pacific Northwest Literature—Its Coming of Age," Harold P. Simonson declares that the Northwest possesses a distinctive literature (Simonson 1980, 146–51), citing works by Ken Kesey (see chapter 4), Frederick Homer Balch (see chapter 3), and Theodore Roethke (see chapter 5) as evidence. Simonson details the process by which the region's literature matured, but he doesn't define its essential qualities.

Literature's ability to transform landscape into a sacred place served as the subject of Ron Finne's documentary *Tamanawis Illahee: Medicine Land.* The film includes readings by William Stafford (see chapter 5), Don Berry (see chapter 6), and others and offers the first extended discussion of how literature might encourage a sacred appreciation of landscape (Finne 1983).

I sought to discover what made Northwest literature distinctive in *At the Field's End: Interviews with 22 Northwest Writers.* In the course of researching that book and querying contemporary writers on the subject, I concluded that the relationship between people and place served as the unifying feature of Northwest literature (O'Connell 1998).

Other commentators reached similar conclusions. In *Beyond the*

Frontier: Writers, Western Regionalism and a Sense of Place, Harold P. Simonson saw a sense of place as a particular characteristic of Western and Northwest literature. Simonson argues that Ivan Doig (see chapter 4), James Welch (see chapter 6), Norman Maclean (see chapter 4), and other Western authors had much to teach contemporary Americans about achieving identity through commitment to place (Simonson 1989).

Glen A. Love extended these ideas in his introduction to *The World Begins Here: An Anthology of Oregon Short Fiction,* one of six volumes in the superb Oregon Literature Series *From Here We Speak: An Anthology of Oregon Poetry* (St. John and Wendt 1993), *The Stories We Tell: An Anthology of Oregon Folk Literature* (Jones and Ramsey 1994), *Many Faces: An Anthology of Oregon Autobiography* (Beckham 1993), *Talking on Paper: An Anthology of Oregon Letters and Diaries* (Applegate and O'Donnell 1994), and *Varieties of Hope: An Anthology of Oregon Prose* (Dodds 1993)—a landmark in Northwest publishing. Love argues that the state's poems and stories served an important social role by transforming what was once *space*—foreign, unfamiliar territory— into *place*—a familiar home ground. Love notes that much of the state's contemporary literature deepened the relationship between people and place (Love 1993).

Likewise, Laurie Ricou's *The Arbutus/Madrone Files: Reading the Pacific Northwest* reflects on the connection between the people and landscape of the U.S. and Canadian Northwest, demonstrating the importance of place in establishing regional identity (Ricou 2002).

In the anthology *Northwest Passages: A Literary Anthology of the Pacific Northwest from Coyote Tales to Roadside Attractions,* Bruce Barcott includes a historical sampling of Northwest literature. Barcott emphasizes "the region's role as a catchbasin for washed-up westering dreams," but doesn't venture much beyond a geographic characterization of the region's literature (Barcott 1994, xviii).

Likewise, *The Last Best Place,* an impressive anthology edited by William Kittredge and Annick Smith, doesn't attempt to define Montana's literature other than by political boundaries. This monumental work—1,158 pages—served as a great introduction to the literary tradition of the state, but shies away from describing the characteristics of that tradition (Kittredge and Smith 1988).

In the introduction to *The Portable Western Reader,* Kittredge ventures that "life in the vicinity of the great spaces does something to the mind," but doesn't define what they do to the mind or the larger literature (Kittredge 1997, xviii). Instead, the anthology gives a wonderful idea of the diversity of voices broadcast from this patch of ground.

A geographic definition is an essential starting point for defining Northwest literature, but it does not go far enough. In this volume, I have taken up what I consider the dominant issue of Northwest literature: the relationship between humans and landscape. *On Sacred Ground* argues that a distinctive Northwest literature does exist, that its primary subject is the relationship between people and place, and that its most important contribution to American literature lies in articulating a more spiritual relationship with landscape.

It can no longer be claimed that such issues are merely regional. Recent volumes such as Alfred Kazin's *A Writer's America: Landscape in Literature* (1988), Lawrence Buell's *The Environmental Imagination: Thoreau, Nature Writing and Formation of American Culture* (1995), and Simon Schama's *Landscape and Memory* (1995) illustrate the centrality of the issues not only to American culture, but to Western European and other cultures as well.

In addition to the aforementioned critics, I am also indebted to a number of others who helped make this book a reality. I would especially like to thank Giselle Smith, formerly of *Seattle Magazine,* Paul Frichtl of *Alaska Airlines Magazine,* and Paul Baumann of *Commonweal,* who serially published parts of this book. The members of my writing group—Scott Driscoll, David Downing, and Peter Blue—provided invaluable criticism and encouragement in putting together the manuscript. Professors Glen A. Love of the University of Oregon and David McCloskey of Seattle University gave generous and insightful readings of the book, encouraging me to expand and improve it. I'm especially grateful to the University of Washington Press for its dedication and professionalism in bringing the book into print, particularly to Pat Soden, director; Michael Duckworth, acquisitions editor; and Kris Fulsaas, the copy editor. Finally, I'd like to thank my wife, Lisa Sowder, for her support during a project that—like most books—took much longer than anticipated. I'm also indebted to our children—Daniel, Nicholas, and Marie—for the delight I find in rediscovering the region through their eyes.

Throughout this book, I have tried to suggest the range and scope of Northwest literature by discussing some of the best and most representative works. Inevitably I have had to exclude many wonderful poems, stories, and commentaries. Such selection is a difficult but necessary part of such a project. However, I hope that in introducing readers to Northwest literature, *On Sacred Ground* will inspire them to explore the growing list of titles in this rich, expansive field.

NICHOLAS O'CONNELL
Seattle, Washington

ON SACRED GROUND

The Spirit of Place
in Pacific Northwest Literature

1 / Early Native American Stories

*I*n January 1854, the Puget Sound region was at the brink of war. Settlers streamed into the lowlands, gobbling up land for farms, houses, and businesses. Native tribes felt pinched by the encroachments. Some welcomed the settlers. Others talked about killing them. An uneasy equilibrium threatened to erupt into open warfare.

Territorial Governor Isaac Stevens, a dapper West Point graduate, arrived in Seattle to try to end the conflict. He enlisted the help of David S. Maynard, the local Indian agent, and Chief Seattle, a leader of the Duwamish tribe, to bring together the 120 settlers and and 1,200 natives to talk peace. Stevens spoke first, encouraging the native peoples to sell the bulk of their land and retreat onto reservations.

Chief Seattle then rose to address the crowd. At six feet tall, with broad shoulders and a deep chest, he cut an impressive figure. As the crowd turned to him, he began a speech that has become the most famous document in American Indian literature. He warned the whites not to deal harshly with the local tribes in the upcoming treaty negotiations, nor to limit their ability to travel throughout the local landscape. He argued that the natives considered the shores of Puget Sound to be their homeland and a sacred space. He emphasized that wherever his people went in this country, they were walking on sacred ground.

"Every part of this country is sacred to my people. Every hillside, every valley, every plain and grove has been hallowed by some fond memory or some sad experience of my tribe.

"Even the rocks that seem to lie dumb as they swelter in the sun along the silent seashore in solemn grandeur thrill with the memories of past events connected with the fate of my people, and the very dust under your feet responds more lovingly to our footsteps than to yours, because it is the ashes of our ancestors, and our bare feet are conscious of the sympathetic touch, for the soil is rich with the life of our kindred . . . " (Grant 1891, 433–36).

Henry A. Smith, a local physician and land developer, recorded the speech and eventually published the text of it in the *Seattle Sunday Star* in 1887. The speech grew in popularity and influence, as it seemed to express the essense of the natives' attitude toward the local landscape and served as a model of ecological philosophy. University of Texas English professor William Arrowsmith read a version of it at the first Earth Day celebration in 1970. Mythologist Joseph Campbell and other well-known figures such as Prince Phillip quoted from it. Today, excerpts from Chief Seattle's speech pop up everywhere from the backs of T-shirts to exhibits at the San Diego Zoo.

There remains much controversy about the extent to which Smith embellished the chief's words, and when and even if the speech took place (Furtwangler 1997), but most contemporary Indian peoples and many experts accept it as authentic. For them, it represents the clearest and most eloquent statement of the natives' attitude toward the American landscape. It makes explicit what is implicit in many of the Northwest's tribal stories: the natives saw the land as a sacred entity, entitled to reverence and respect.

"The words [Seattle] spoke were authentic," said Vi Hilbert, an Upper Skagit elder and the author of *Haboo: Native American Stories from Puget Sound* (1985). "The man who wrote the speech didn't understand the language, but he heard the philosophy. The philosophy practiced by all of our leaders is present in that speech" (Hilbert 2000).

Seattle's speech is the most famous expression of this philosophy, but it also informs Northwest Indian myths, including those collected by Hilbert and others. These fascinating accounts of the antics of

Coyote, Raven, Mink, Pheasant, Wolf, Deer, Elk, Mouse, and other creatures provided the tribes with entertainment during the long winter months, but also served as instruction, emphasizing among other things the spiritual side of the landscape. As Ella Clark writes in the introduction to her *Indian Legends of the Pacific Northwest:* "'To the Indian in his native state,' said Martin Sampson, an Indian grandfather of the Puget Sound region, 'everything had life or spirit; the earth, the rocks, trees, ferns, as well as birds and animals, even the hail which fell from the sky, had a spirit and a language and song of its own and might be an inspiration to a warrior'" (Clark 1953, 7).

Because the native tribes believed that the earth was animate—down to every rock, tree, animal, and human being—they had to exercise caution in how they approached every aspect of their world. Many of the native stories describe the complicated rituals and taboos surrounding everyday activities such as hunting and gathering food, especially Pacific salmon, the staple of many of the tribes' diet.

The Northwest stands out from other parts of the United States for the sheer volume and range of its native stories. The region was the site of one of the richest flowerings of aboriginal culture in the entire continent. The vibrancy and complexity of this native culture drew the attention of Franz Boas, one of the founders of modern anthropology, who recorded many of the myths, arts, and customs of these amazing tribes. The myths transcribed by Boas and others became an irreplaceable record of the culture of the region's early inhabitants and one of the most valuable sources of native stories anywhere.

In addition to this wealth of transcribed myths and other materials, the Northwest also remains the home of many contemporary tribal cultures. Many Indian peoples continue the oral traditions of their ancestors, recounting stories of Raven, Mink, Coyote, Pheasant, Killer Whale, Ice, and Grizzly Bear. Wars, disease, and alcoholism ravaged many of these tribes, but enough people survived and adapted to provide living examples of native culture. Hilbert, for example, travels around the country reciting stories in Lushootseed, her native language. The vitality of contemporary Northwest native culture ensures that it will continue as a living tradition, even if it has changed considerably over the years.

NORTHWEST TRIBAL SOCIETY

Unlike most "high" and complex aboriginal cultures, the Northwest coast tribes were hunter-gatherers, not agricultural people. They subsisted primarily on the many species of salmon—king, silver, sockeye, chum, and pink—that ran in the local streams and rivers. They also caught halibut, cod, candlefish, whales, sea otters, seals, sea lions, birds, and many other kinds of marine life. Interior tribes hunted deer, elk, buffalo, and other species while supplementing their diet with salmon. Indeed, the Columbia and its tributaries provided a vast migration route for salmon into the interior of the region. Many tribes took advantage of this and set up netting and spearing sites near falls and other areas where the salmon congregated.

The abundance of salmon and other foods, as well as a temperate maritime climate in the coastal regions, allowed the tribes leisure time for telling stories, carving totem poles, performing dramas, and developing the arts to an extent virtually unknown in any other area of North America. They were perhaps the only hunter-gatherers to achieve such a high level of cultural expression, excelling at painting, sculpture, woodworking, storytelling, drama, and other arts. They were able to devote a considerable amount of time to activities such as these because the natural world around them provided all they needed to live. As author Philip Drucker observes in *Indians of the Northwest Coast:* "The bounty of nature provided that which in most other parts of the world man must supply for himself through agriculture and stock raising: a surplus of foodstuffs so great that even a dense population had an abundance of leisure to devote to the improvement and elaboration of its cultural heritage" (Drucker 1963, 3).

The close relationship to landscape common of hunter-gatherers, combined with the leisure to pursue artistic activities, led to the development of a unique culture. Northwest Coast Indian art shows a highly developed awareness of the local landscape, with many of the paintings and carvings depicting indigenous species such as killer whales, salmon, bears, frogs, otters, etc. By filling their artworks with such local creatures and emphasizing the tribes' interdependence with them, they created art that serves as an outstanding example of an ecologically inspired native art.

The quality, complexity, and sheer uniqueness of this art has impressed a number of interpreters, including Jarold Ramsey, a retired professor of English at the University of Rochester, and a leading figure in the field of Northwest Coast mythology. Ramsey, who grew up on a central Oregon ranch bordering the Warm Springs Reservation, warns that it's easy to sentimentalize American Indians' attitude toward the land, but argues that they still have a lot to teach modern American culture about ecological wisdom.

As he notes in *Reading the Fire: Essays in Traditional Indian Literatures of the Far West:* "Yet our ecological crisis is real, however we may misrepresent it, and we clearly need, as the saying goes, all the help we can get. In particular we need, beyond the political and economic incentives to clean up our land, air, and water, to find ways to cultivate an *imaginative* awareness of man's beholden place in the natural order. We should be looking closely at what they have done to inculcate in themselves the full awareness of ecological interdependence" (Ramsey 1983, 60–61).

THE HUNTER WHO HAD ELK FOR A GUARDIAN SPIRIT

Ramsey sees the story "The Hunter Who Had Elk for a Guardian Spirit" (63–64) as an example of the way Native Americans used storytelling for ecological purposes. Pioneer ethnologist Jeremiah Curtin collected the tale on the Warm Springs Reservation in 1885. The story dramatizes the conflict between a young man's obligations to his father and to his obligations to Elk, his guardian spirit. It's a story about the age-old tension between generations, showing the parent's tendency to boast about the difficulty of life in the old days and gripe about how easy the younger generation has it. But it also illustrates specifically Indian concerns, such as the practice of taking a guardian spirit, the necessity of following the advice of this spirit, the taboo against taking anything more than necessary from the land.

The story opens by describing a boy who is a very good hunter.

His father, however, claims that he was a much better hunter. He says a large elk attacked him during a hunt and scarred his forehead. In fact, the father is lying; he got the scar while gathering wood.

Then an elk visits the boy and tells him, "If you will serve me and hear what I say, I will be your master and will help you in every necessity. You must not be proud. You must not kill too many of any animal. I will be your guardian spirit."

The boy accepts the elk's offer and with its help becomes a great hunter. He kills many animals—elk, bear, deer. But he takes only what he needs—no more. His father complains that the young man is not bringing in enough game; he claims he took many more animals when he was young. So the young man kills five herds of elk. Without knowing it, he nearly kills his guardian spirit, who falls into the lake. When the young man tries to retrieve the elk, they both sink.

When they touch bottom, the young man sees thousands of bear, deer, and elk, many of which he had shot. The great Elk then asks him, "Why did you go beyond what I commanded? Your father required more of you than he himself ever did. Do you see our people on both sides? These are they whom you have killed. You have inflicted many needless wounds on our people."

The Elk reveals that the father lied about the scar. In fact, he got it from a wood chip, not from an elk. But this does not exonerate the son. He has committed a crime against the animal kingdom and he will be punished. The Elk will no longer serve as his guardian spirit.

After the Elk finishes, the young man returns home and has his wives bring his friends to his bedside. When they arrive, he tells them what happened. Shortly thereafter, the spirit leaves him and he dies.

The young man's death demonstrates the importance of obedience to the guardian spirit. The tragic tale emphasizes the primacy of the taboo against killing too much game, even if it conflicts with filial duties to parents.

"It's a story where two potential goods—the need for obedience to parents and the need to accept dictates of a spiritual guide—are in total collision," said Ramsey (2000 interview). "The problem with the boy is that he tries to have it both ways. But the deed counts. He has killed wastefully and foolishly. He has violated his understanding with his spirit guardian. This is no simple childlike story. It points a way of imagining our position in the natural world and imagining the right kinds of action toward it."

It is just such an imaginative awareness that figures so strongly in the stories, giving contemporary readers new ways of imagining the complex interdependence between human society and the natural world. The myths exhibit a depth and richness of ecological insight derived from thousands of years of residence in this corner of North America.

COYOTE MYTH

The stories include a variety of animals and mythical creatures, including trickster figures Raven and Coyote. These two characters were especially popular because they simultaneously entertained and instructed. Listeners could laugh at the antics of Coyote or Raven and still learn important lessons about tribal taboos, rituals, and history. Some of the most elaborate of these rituals dealt with catching and preparing salmon. Philip Drucker notes in *Indians of the Northwest Coast:* "All the Northwest Coast groups had long lists of regulations and prohibitions referring to the Salmon-people in order to continue to maintain good relations with these important beings" (Drucker 1963, 155).

The following Coyote myth describes some of the taboos and ritual practices associated with salmon fishing. Franz Boas collected this and many other myths in 1890 and 1891 at Bay Center in Washington State. He recorded them from Charles Cultee, one of the last remaining members of the Chinook tribe. Cultee spoke not only Chinook, but also Chehalis and the Katlamet dialect. He also provided extensive commentary on the myths and tribal languages. Boas was delighted to find so helpful a source. "My work of translating and explaining the texts was greatly facilitated by Cultee's remarkable intelligence," he said (Boas 1894, 6). "After he had once grasped what I wanted, he explained to me the grammatical structure of the sentences by means of examples, and elucidated the sense of difficult periods."

In addition to helping Boas understand these languages, Cultee proved a gifted raconteur. His versions of the stories are more detailed and complete than many found elsewhere. Cultee told Boas a wide variety of myths, including those concerning the rituals for catching and preparing salmon. The following Coyote myth describes such a ritual. As is often the case in this genre, Coyote is greedy, lustful, and lazy and suffers for these faults. His antics demonstrate a negative example, entertaining and instructing the listeners. As Ramsey observes in the essay "The Indian Literature of Oregon":

> Coyote's outrageous sexual antics, his selfishness, his general irre-
> sponsibility in the stories allowed the "good citizens" of the tribe to
> affirm the systems of norms and punishment that Coyote is forever
> comically running afoul of; at the same time they could vicariously
> delight and find release in his irresponsible freedom. My point is that
> through the "heroic" mediation of Coyote the Trickster, the people
> could have their morality both ways. They knew that his scheming but
> always reckless pursuit of women, wealth, and status would come to
> no good end, according to tribal values, but before that end arrived
> they could richly enjoy themselves, as if on holiday! *(Ramsey 1979, 15)*

Even if Coyote is not a "role model" in the contemporary sense, even if he does not represent an admirable pattern of behavior, the structure of the tale as a whole teaches that following a set of prescribed rituals will result in better catches of salmon.

At the start of the story, Coyote goes to a creek where he catches some salmon. He then brings a salmon back to his house where he cuts it open immediately, steams it, and eats it. The next day, he returns to the creek but catches nothing. He becomes angry and defecates so that he can question his excrement about his inability to bring in the salmon. The excrement responds:

"Oh, you with your bandy legs, you have no sense. When the first silver-side salmon is killed, it must not be cut. It must be split along its back and roasted. It must not be steamed. Only when they go upriver, then they may be steamed" (Boas 1894, 101).

Coyote returns to the creek the next day, follows the procedure explained by his excrement, and catches fish again. Each day that he fishes, however, he continues to violate taboos unknown to him, and so he must defecate, then consult his excrement about what he has done wrong and how he can continue catching fish. Though the story is comical and scatalogical, it reinforces the importance of following the complicated set of rituals concerning the salmon. At the end of the myth, Coyote concludes that if the tribes want to catch salmon, they must do so in the prescribed way. "The Indians shall always do in the same manner. . . . Thus shall be the taboos for all generations of people" (106).

By his antics and buffoonery, Coyote uncovers the various taboos and rituals associated with salmon fishing. Though such practices may seem arbitrary, they had as their goal the conservation and perpetuation of the salmon as a species. The tribes considered the salmon a separate people who lived in houses under the ocean. By following such rituals, the tribes hoped to encourage the return of these salmon people, upon whom they depended for their survival.

In this and many other tales, ecological themes are explicit. It is clear in the preceding myth that the storyteller wishes to communicate a certain point about how to treat a given species, in this case salmon. In other tales, however, the ecological emphasis is implicit. At the start of many tales, for example, the speaker describes a time when people and animals spoke the same language and easily understood each other. "In those days when the earth was young, trees were scarce; the land at large was open and easy to go over; there was no moon, no sun, and the people lived in a kind of perpetual twilight. They mingled with the animals; birds, beasts, and men having a common tongue" (Haeberlin 1924, 375).

This opening emphasizes the commonality between the tribes and the animals. There is not a clear separation between humans and animals as is the case in much modern American or European literature. Instead, the opening reveals that the landscape is peopled with creatures who at one time were human beings and so had to be approached in a respectful way.

COTTONTAIL BOY AND SNOWSHOE RABBIT

Nearly all of the stories exhibit this imaginative involvement with the nonhuman world. The following Nez Perce tale shows the tribe's sympathy with animals. Archie Phinney, a protégé of Boas and a Nez Perce himself, collected this story from his sixty-year-old mother during the fall and winter of 1929–30 on the Fort Lapwai Reservation. In the introduction to his book, Phinney observes that humor is characteristic of native stories. "Humor is undoubtedly the deepest and most vivid element in this mythology, the element that animates all the pathos, all the commonplace and the tragic, the element that is most wasted by transliteration" (Phinney 1934, ix).

Many of the stories in his anthology exhibit this cheerful humor and sympathy with the world of animals. Phinney cites the story "Cottontail Boy and Snowshoe Rabbit" as a particularly fine example of the subtle humor of the Indian storyteller. The tale reads like a native version of Richard Adams's *Watership Down* (1972), with the two rabbits exchanging pleasantries about the snugness and warmth of their winter burrows. After Cottontail Boy describes the comforts of his lodge, he inquires about his friend's dwelling.

> "Oh, I, too, live just comfortably from day to day," Snowshoe Rabbit told him. "I have a very comfortable living place. There is a big growth on a pine tree and my home is there at the root. Here I may just kick apart fallen chunks of wood to burn. Oh, how this now burns to coals and ashes. Then I take fatty dried meat and toast it somewhat, just to a red crispness. There I lean back and eat so heartily; eat until I feel a complete and happy gustatory contentment."

> "Yes, it seems that both of us are living very well."

> Then they said to each other, "Farewell, we will meet again sometime." (3)

This and other myths evince a great deal of sympathy with the creatures of the local landscape. The tribes viewed the world of animals with interest and understanding since they saw themselves as part of that world. They included nature and its creatures within the circle of their respect and affection. Imaginative sympathy with the non-human world is an especially valuable legacy of these stories.

THE COMING OF THE WHITES

The arrival of white explorers and fur traders in the Northwest during the late eighteenth and early nineteenth centuries profoundly changed native culture. At first these changes were mainly beneficial, for the whites traded highly sought-after nails, buttons, and other items for the plentiful beaver and otter pelts. But as more whites moved into the region, clashes over land became frequent and diseases such as smallpox and alcoholism ravaged the tribes.

Though the tribes had fought long and bitterly among themselves, the arrival of the whites posed a particularly acute threat to their survival. Both cultures had much to learn from each other, but neither seemed to be able to adjust to and reconcile itself with the other. Differing attitudes toward landscape turned out to be only one of many areas of conflict between the two peoples.

Eventually, the white settlers prevailed and the native tribes fell into a spiral of decline from which they have struggled to recover. But if they declined, they have by no means disappeared. Many have adopted customs of modern America while retaining essential elements of their ancestral culture. They have found ways to adapt to the contemporary world.

Modern American civilization, on the other hand, seems to have learned little from the native tribes. Most of the influence has amounted to window dressing—beaded leather moccasins sold at gift shops, television commercials of a tearful Indian chief, stereotypical Hollywood movies such as *Dances with Wolves.* This is unfortunate, for there is much that is admirable in the customs and cultures of the native peoples, particularly their attitude toward the American landscape, an attitude from which contemporary Americans can learn a great deal.

In drawing from natives' attitudes toward landscape, some writers have been guilty of sentimentalizing the tribes, but others have undertaken the hard work of honestly describing and trying to reconcile these two very different cultures in their poems and stories. Northwest authors D'Arcy McNickle (1936), Louis Owens (1991), James Welch (see chapter 6), Sherman Alexie (see chapter 6), Gary Snyder (see chapter 6), David Wagoner (see chapter 5), Frank Herbert (1972), Ursula K. Le Guin (see chapter 6), Craig Lesley (see chapter 6), Duane Niatum (1991), Elizabeth Moody, and those included in Andrea Lerner's *Dancing on the Rim of the World: An Anthology of Contemporary Northwest Native American Writing* (1990) have discovered ways of borrowing from the indigenous culture to create a vital, ecologically oriented body of work that contains some of the most imaginative poems and stories in contemporary American literature.

2 / Journals of Exploration and Settlement

As the fog lifted on the morning of May 18, 1792, Capt. George Vancouver sailed the sloop *Discovery* into the calm and sunny waters of Puget Sound, becoming the first explorer ever to visit this corner of the North American continent. Vancouver was midway through a voyage around the world, a voyage that took him to Africa, Asia, South America, Australia, New Zealand, and other of the world's most exotic locales. In the course of this four-year journey, the English sea captain dutifully recorded his impressions of the places he visited. For the most part, his journal entries are exact and restrained, reflecting his character as a practical, scientifically minded man, a man not easily given to flights of poetic fancy or emotional excess. But the sight of the snowcapped mountains rising above the forests and meadows of Whidbey Island moved him profoundly. While his men repaired the ship's rigging, Vancouver took time out to praise the wonders of the territory around him:

> To describe the beauties of this region, will, on some future occasion, be a very grateful task to the pen of a skillful panegyrist. The serenity of the climate, the innumerable pleasing landscapes, and the abundant fertility that unassisted nature puts forth, require only to be enriched by the industry of man with villages, mansions, cottages and other

buildings, to render it the most lovely country that can be imagined; whilst the labor of the inhabitants would be amply rewarded, in the bounties which nature seems ready to bestow on cultivation. *(Vancouver 1798, 542–43)*

As he piloted his ship farther into Puget Sound, Vancouver continued to enthuse over the appearance of the Northwest. He catalogued its flora and fauna; described its geology and weather patterns; mapped its coves, inlets, and waterways; and marveled at the customs and behavior of the native tribes. In the process he named a number of prominent geographic features—Puget Sound for Lt. Peter Puget, who did a particularly fine job of surveying; Mount Baker for Lt. Joseph Baker, who was the first of Vancouver's crew to sight the mountain; Mount Rainier for Adm. Peter Rainier, one of Vancouver's superiors in the British Navy. Many of his names and descriptions show that he was enamored with the Northwest, often mentioning its resemblance to England and speculating about possibilities for settlement.

But if Vancouver responded enthusiastically to the natural beauty of the region, he didn't see that beauty as necessarily whole and entire in itself: he believed that it required cultivation for its completion. Unlike the local tribes, who considered the region already finished after the great change from the mythical world to the present, Vancouver and other explorers saw it as a kind of raw material out of which a future civilization could be fashioned. They had some appreciation of the integrity of the land itself, but mostly of its potential for supporting a new European-style civilization.

Vancouver's voyage played an important role in preparing for such a civilization. His primary mandate was to search for the Northwest Passage, but he also was charged with exploring the area and claiming it for the British crown. His maps placed the area precisely in terms of latitude and longitude, his journals provided vivid and exact descriptions of the local landscape, and his overall survey of the Northwest Coast from California to Alaska legitimated English claims on the area.

In describing the new country, Vancouver's governing metaphor was a scientific one. He relied on mathematics to fix the place in terms of terrestrial space and depended on a scientific methodology and vocabulary to relate the region's features to those of England and elsewhere. In so doing, he adopted a Cartesian dualism with regard to the local environment. From this perspective, he considered the local landscape as essentially matter, not spirit, and therefore subject to quantification and eventual comprehension. Once understood by the human mind, the vast mechanism of the natural world then could be put to use in service of civilization.

The scientific rationalism underlying Vancouver's voyage distinguished it from earlier expeditions such as all but the last of those of his mentor, Capt. James Cook. In *New Lands, New Men,* the historian William Goetzman distinguishes between two ages of exploration: an early one epitomized by the voyages of Columbus, Cook, and others for whom trading and plundering served as primary motivations, and a later age represented by the voyage of Vancouver in which the search for scientific knowledge played an increasingly important role:

> It was the ever-growing belief in science and the idea of linear progress that made the new Age of Discovery stand off from the older age, in which Renaissance mariners sought the Indies, and Columbus, by accident, discovered a way to America. No longer did men seek marvels and fear sea monsters and anthropophagi. Instead, a new rationalism, based upon mathematics and empiricism, began to govern exploring activity, whose central focus became that of mapping terrestrial space. (*Goetzman 1986, 2*)

Of course the pursuit of science on these expeditions was not entirely disinterested. A scientific comprehension of the new country paved the way for trade, commerce, and settlement. And yet the Enlightenment ideal of a disinterested quest for knowledge gave a particular character to expeditions such as Vancouver's, leading to the beginnings of appreciation of the place for its own sake, an appreciation grounded first in a scientific apprehension, but eventually in an aesthetic one as well. It is this aesthetic sense of the region that is so striking in Vancouver's journals. Even if he sees the region as being

completed by settlement, he has at least some appreciation of the landscape in and of itself.

This nascent aesthetic appreciation of landscape gives a special character to the journals and diaries of many of the early explorers of the
Northwest. With the barrier of the Rocky Mountains on the east, the
Siskiyous and other ranges on the south, and a stormy and unpredictable maritime climate from the west, the region resisted many early
attempts at exploration. By the time explorers such as Vancouver were
able to pierce the Northwest's defenses, it was relatively late in the history of European exploration and attitudes toward nature and wild
landscapes had begun to change. In their journals, many of the
region's explorers began to voice their appreciation of the region's aesthetic attractions as well as its utilitarian advantages, thus setting an
important precedent for the region's literature. Descriptions of the
region's beauty in the early journals, combined with the sacred sense
of landscape present in many native stories, help explain why the
Northwest region eventually gave rise to such environmentally sensitive works as Barry Lopez's *Desert Notes,* Gary Snyder's *Turtle Island,*
and David Duncan's *The River Why* (see chapter 6 for all these).

By the time Vancouver had pulled up anchor and sailed for farther
shores, he and his crew had mapped the North American coast from
California to Alaska, preparing the way for later exploration and settlement. In addition, by providing the first comprehensive account
of the new country, his journal laid the textual foundation for Northwest literature.

Previous explorers Sir Francis Drake, Juan Perez, James Cook, John
Meares, and others had described bits and pieces of the Northwest,
but none had furnished as extended a narrative description as
Vancouver. Later explorers built on his foundation. Meriwether
Lewis and William Clark, David Thompson, Charles Wilkes (1852),
and others filled out the picture while settlers such as Marcus and
Narcissa Whitman, James Swan, and others continued the process of
naming and describing the Northwest in their journals.

These journals, diaries, and letters form the basis of the region's
early literature. As is the case with other periods of Northwest liter-

ature, the landscape occupies center stage in these accounts. These writers stretched and expanded the language to accommodate the new plants, animals, people, and geography they saw around them. The literature of this period is largely focused on the external circumstances of the Northwest region and devotes little time to the writers' internal or psychological response to it.

But in naming and describing the external landscape, these writers took the first tentative steps in establishing a relationship with it. Naming is the first step in coming to terms with a place. In the process of naming, that which is outward—whether a bay, river, or mountain—becomes inward, a sound, a word, a part of one's interior landscape. By naming the new land, the explorers were better able to come to terms with it.

Native Americans already had names for many of the geographic features of the place. In some instances these names were retained by the early explorers and settlers; for example, Snoqualmie, Seattle, Tacoma, Walla Walla, etc. In other instances they were supplanted, especially by early explorers such as Vancouver who had little contact with the local tribes.

In his naming, Vancouver sought similarities between the Northwest landscape and that of England. He dubbed a finger of land Dungeness Spit because it reminded him of the Dungeness lighthouse in Scotland. By naming prominent local features after British landmarks as well as colleagues and superiors, Vancouver made the new landscape seem more like home.

This tendency to look for resemblances between the Northwest and Great Britain also led him to praise certain aspects of the local landscape. Coming from a settled country where much of the wilderness had already been subdued, Vancouver preferred areas reminiscent of England. Consequently he praised the meadows and valleys of the Puget Sound region rather than the rocky, windswept coasts of northern British Columbia. When exploring Penn Cove, on Whidbey Island, Vancouver made the following observation:

The surrounding country, for several miles in most points of view, presented a delightful prospect, consisting chiefly of spacious meadows, elegantly adorned with clumps of trees; amongst which the oak bore a very considerable proportion, in size from four to six feet in circumference. In these beautiful pastures, bordering on an expansive sheet of water, the deer were seen playing about in great numbers. Nature had there provided the well-stocked park, and wanted only the assistance of art to constitute that desirable assemblage of surface, which is so much sought in other countries, and only to be acquired by an immoderate expence in manual labor. *(Vancouver 1798, 568)*

By naming and defining the Northwest in terms of science and in terms of the British Isles, Vancouver established a tentative relationship with the region, paving the way not only for explorers and settlers, but for future writers such as Jonathan Raban in *Passage to Juneau* (1999) who would build on this foundation to create a literature with a full appreciation of the aesthetic dimensions of the place.

LEWIS AND CLARK

Six years after Vancouver's voyage, an American expedition led by Meriwether Lewis and William Clark succeeded in traversing the interior of the Northwest and reaching the shores of the Pacific near the mouth of the Columbia River in November 1806. Their expedition achieved a number of objectives, including establishing American claims to this territory, preparing the way for trade and settlement, and mapping and cataloging the region in terms of science. These objectives closely reflected those of the expedition's principal sponsor, President Thomas Jefferson.

One of the most remarkable intellects of the eighteenth century, Thomas Jefferson possessed a wide variety of interests, including politics, philosophy, architecture, literature, history, geography, and science. In his *Notes on the State of Virginia* (1801), he also showed a keen understanding and appreciation of the American landscape. By sponsoring an expedition to the blank spot on the map known as the Northwest, he hoped to add to the scientific knowledge of the area and open it up to American trade and settlement.

Jefferson had long sought to organize such an expedition, but he didn't arrange official backing for it until after he became president in 1801. He then asked Meriwether Lewis, an army captain, to lead the expedition. Lewis was well qualified for the task. He was an experienced woodsman who possessed a sound practical knowledge of biology, geology, navigation, and the habits of the Indian tribes. Lewis enjoyed taking long, rambling trips through the backcountry of Virginia and generally felt more at home in the wilderness than in a town or city. He proved particularly well suited to heading an expedition that would spend two years in the wilderness.

Lewis preferred solitude to society, but he chose as his co-leader a gregarious man with an outgoing personality. William Clark, Lewis's close friend and former commanding officer, was as adept at navigating the social world of official Washington as he was at mapping stretches of uncharted wilderness. Despite the difference in their personalities, the two meshed to such a degree that in their journal entries they often seem like one person. Nearly the only thing they disagreed about was dog meat, which Lewis enjoyed and Clark hated.

The congenial relationship between the two leaders spilled over to the rest of the expedition. The morale of the forty-some members remained high throughout the trip, even though it was severely tested by unpalatable food, near starvation, physical exhaustion, and other difficulties. Despite the party's mixed racial composition—it included the Indian woman Sacagawea, who served as guide and translator; her French-Canadian husband, Toussaint Charbonneau; Clark's black slave, York; and a representative sample of white ethnicities— there seems to have been little conflict between the various members. In this mixture of races and ethnicities, the expedition represented a microcosm of American society, its journey epitomizing the westering experience of the American people. As Frank Bergon points out in his introduction to *The Journals of Lewis and Clark*, the journals served as a kind of founding epic of the American western adventure:

> Like ancient epics, they tell the story of the tribe, in this case the story of a people moving west. It is not the story of an individual frontiersman but of a pluralistic, fluctuating community of thirty-five to

forty-five people, including soldiers, woodsmen, blacksmiths, car-
penters, cooks, French engagés, a black slave, a Lemhi Shoshone
woman, and a newborn baby of mixed race, all heading west. *(Lewis
and Clark 1806, x)*

As in other works of Northwest literature, the main subject of
these journals is the American landscape, which presented such a
vast, imposing, unnerving spectacle that it absorbed the party's attention almost entirely. In seeking to come to terms with this landscape,
Lewis and Clark mapped its features mathematically, while naming
and cataloguing hundreds of new plants, animals, and geographic
features.

In describing the region, the explorers largely followed a scientific
framework, but they also celebrated the country around them. They
accurately and precisely described what they were seeing, but they also
allowed a note of wonder and awe to enter their writing. Their journals are full of descriptions of the bounty of the country, the pleni-
tude of game, the sublime aspects of the scenery. The rapturous,
songlike quality in the journals recalls the epic tradition. The explorers sing the praises of the new country and their part in discovering
it in much the same way that Virgil sang of Aeneas and the founding
of Rome in *The Aeneid* (West 1990).

After leaving Fort Mandan, North Dakota, in the spring of 1805,
the expedition's wilderness adventure began. The early part of their
journey was fraught with perils such as hostile tribes and ferocious
grizzly bears, but it also included scenes of staggering beauty. Upon
arriving at the Great Falls of the Missouri River on June 13, 1805, Lewis
hurried down a hill to gaze on what he called "this sublimely grand
specticle" (160). He was moved to write:

> Immediately at the cascade the river is about 300 yrds. wide; about
> ninety or a hundred yards of this next the Lard. bluff is a smoth even
> sheet of water falling over a precipice of at least eighty feet, the remain-
> ing part of about 200 yares on my right formes the grandest sight I
> ever beheld, the hight of the fall is the same of the other but the irreg-

ular and somewhat projecting rocks below receives the water in it's passage down and brakes it into a perfect white foam which assumes a thousand forms in a moment sometimes flying up in jets of sparkling foam to the hight of fifteen or twenty feet and are scarcely formed before large roling bodies of the same beaten and foaming water is thrown over and conceals them. *(160)*

This entry recalls similar descriptions of Niagara Falls, one of the Romantic set pieces of the sublime in the American landscape. As is evident in this passage, Lewis viewed the falls through a scientific framework, carefully estimating their height and width, but also praising their beauty and grandeur. The Romantic preference for the sublime influenced his description of the falls as much as did his understanding of mathematics and hydrology.

Further, their choice of the falls as a suitable subject for extended description distinguishes them from earlier explorers such as Vancouver who preferred the more settled, pastoral aspects of landscape. Lewis and Clark lavished their attention on objects such as waterfalls and mountain ranges, and spent considerably less time discussing the landscape's commercial or agricultural potential. Their writing reveals a fascination with the sublime in landscape, but approached through the apparatus of the scientific method.

This combination of scientific and Romantic sensibilities makes their writing particularly appealing. They delighted in the wonders of the country around them, while making careful notes of its various features. Their extensive maps placed the region in terms of latitude and longitude, while their lavish descriptions of its scenery and their sense of the importance of their journey gave epic expression to the country's western aspirations, as Stephen E. Ambrose points out in *Undaunted Courage: Meriwether Lewis, Thomas Jefferson and the Opening of the American West* (1996). For all of these reasons, the expedition played a decisive role in determining the size and shape of the United States today and in developing the region's and nation's literature. It is hard to overestimate the importance of this expedition to the country's political future or to its literary tradition.

DAVID THOMPSON

The Lewis and Clark Expedition established an American claim to the Northwest, but did not secure it. Britain in particular continued to press its interests in the area. British fur traders working for the North West Company set up a system of trading posts in the region, strengthening the British claim to the inland Northwest. One of the most energetic of these traders was David Thompson, who sought to claim the land for the English crown and exploit it for its furs. His interests were not entirely mercenary, however, as he was also a dedicated explorer who mapped and catalogued the area in the interests of science.

Born and educated in London, Thompson studied algebra, navigation, and geography—the basic tools of the explorer's trade. In 1784 he left to join the Hudson's Bay Company and promptly set out for the New World. During his early years in the company's employ, Thompson distinguished himself as a fur trader, explorer, and surveyor. He rose quickly through the ranks before joining the rival Canadian North West Company, which offered him a higher salary and more opportunity for exploration.

After joining the new company, Thompson led an expedition in 1798 to explore the forty-ninth parallel—the western border between British Canada and the United States—and in the process made the first complete survey of the upper Mississippi River. The following year, Thompson turned his attention to the Athabasca region on the eastern slopes of the Rocky Mountains. From there he made forays into the Kootenay region on the mountains' western slopes and eventually investigated the Columbia River as a possible trade route to the Pacific.

The explorer filled in many of the blank spots on the map of western North America and figures prominently in Northwest history for charting the complete course of the Columbia River, the region's principal waterway. In 1811, he was the first to navigate the river in its entirety and probably would have explored the lower river before Lewis and Clark had he not had to worry about selling furs and maintaining a series of trading posts. As Jack Nisbet points out in *Sources of the River: Tracking David Thompson across Western North America,*

Thompson was more than an explorer: "For Thompson was not just a geographer out to map a river, he was also a fur trader with the North West Company of Montreal, out to expand its domain and convert the natives to its commercial purposes. He was an agent of revolutionary change in the region: its history turns on the moment of his arrival" (Nisbet 1994, 4).

Thompson was a man with many agendas. He sought to exploit the land for its furs, claim it for Great Britain, and survey it in the interests of science. He mentions all three agendas in his journals, but spends most of his time on the third. In his journal entries he seeks to accurately describe the land around him without attempting to romanticize it. His entries are full of precise measurements of latitude and longitude, as well as careful descriptions of flora, fauna, geology, and native inhabitants.

In the course of his trip down the Columbia River in 1811, Thompson characteristically began his journal entries by providing the precise coordinates of his position before listing the names of the men in his party or invoking the protection of the Almighty. Though a religious man, Thompson saw the land primarily in scientific terms and thus showed more interest in its geographic position than its spiritual dimensions. As he floated down the river, he devoted much of his journals to describing the geology and morphology of the country along the river.

> Above and below the Spokane River the banks were often of perpendicular Rock of trap and basalt of a black gray color, in places reddish, these banks had a curious appearance to the height of about three hundred and fifty feet, from which rose another steep step, and level table to the top of the bank. *(Thompson 1916, 473)*

Thompson uses scientific terminology in his descriptions of the land and seldom indulges in extended rhapsodies over its beauty. When he does praise it, he singles out those parts that resemble an agricultural landscape. In this he demonstrates a kinship with his countryman George Vancouver, who preferred settled country to wild landscapes. As he made his way down the Columbia River through eastern Washington, Thompson observed a stretch of riverbank to his liking.

> The appearance of the country much better; the banks of moderate height with low points of good meadow land; the interior country though still bare of Woods is level without hills, the grass good and very fit for sheep. *(521)*

When Thompson and his party arrived at the settlement of Fort Astoria on July 14, they were politely received by their rivals McDougall and Stuart, whom Thompson had known when they were functionaries in the North West Company. Thompson and his party had completed a remarkable journey, proving that the entire length of the Columbia River was navigable and could provide a trade route for furs. The explorer's detailed surveys served as the basis of the first reliable maps of the interior Northwest and helped open up the land for both trade and settlement. As he concluded:

> Thus I have fully completed the survey of this part of North America from sea to sea, and by almost innumberable astronomical Observations have determined the positions of the Mountains, Lakes and Rivers, and other remarkable places on the northern part of this Continent. . . . *(502)*

As was the case with other explorers, Thompson's journals helped establish a narrative framework for the region. By naming the various features, surveying the area in terms of science, and recording his travels, he and other explorers such as Vancouver, Lewis and Clark, Alexander Mackenzie, David Douglas, Simon Fraser, and Charles Wilkes established a tentative relation with the region that later writers would build on. If these explorers largely defined the region in scientific terms, they were not entirely blind to its aesthetic aspects, even if some of them saw the land primarily as the material out of which a new civilization could be built rather than as something whole and complete in itself. The sense of wonder and awe and possibility conveyed by their writings paved the way for the settlers who soon began migrating into the region.

SETTLEMENT

On March 22, 1811, the ship *Tonquin* arrived at the mouth of the Columbia River and, after several attempts and the drowning of eight men, succeeded in crossing the river's bar and entering the tidal estuary. The ship's crew then proceeded to establish Fort Astoria on the south bank of the river, the fort being named after the expedition's sponsor, John Jacob Astor, the principal owner of the Pacific Fur Company and one of America's richest men. Given its strategic location, Astoria became one of the most important early settlements in the Northwest, serving as the base of a fur trading empire and cementing an American claim to the river and the entire region.

In *Astoria or Anecdotes of an Enterprize beyond the Rocky Mountains* (1836), distinguished America writer Washington Irving tells the story of this settlement, as well as the voyage of the *Tonquin* and of the overland journey to the fort led by William Price Hunt. The overland journey proved particularly influential in the settlement of the region, for Hunt's party discovered an easier route across the Northwest than the one taken by Lewis and Clark. This route eventually became known as the Oregon Trail.

Irving based his account on the journals of Hunt and others who participated in the expedition, as well as the correspondence between members of the Pacific Fur Company and extensive background materials, including the journals of Lewis and Clark. For this reason, *Astoria* lacks the immediacy of firsthand accounts, but adds polish, figurative language, and a concern for storytelling to the region's early literature. Irving focuses more on the relations between the expedition's participants than on the physical details of the place, but the landscape still looms large in the narrative. In describing this landscape, he often celebrates its scenic beauty and its potential for agriculture and civilization:

> About eight miles above the mouth of the Wallamot the little squadron arrived at Vancouver's point, so called in honor of that celebrated voyager by his lieutenant (Broughton) when he explored the river. This point is said to present one of the most beautiful scenes on the

Columbia: a lovely meadow, with a silver sheet of limpid water in the
centre, enlivened by wildfowl; a range of hills crowned by forests, while
the prospect is closed by Mount Hood, a magnificent mountain rising into a lofty peak and covered with snow; the ultimate landmark of
the first explorers of the river. *(Irving 1836, 68–69)*

Scenes such as this one increased American interest in the region
and spurred further settlement. Irving didn't stint in describing the
incredible hardships and sufferings of the overland party, but in giving these aspects of the journey a certain heroic treatment, he added
further appeal to the idea of migration.

Accounts such as *Astoria* piqued popular interest in the region, but
they didn't immediately send large numbers of settlers streaming west.
Would-be immigrants still faced daunting obstacles of distance, hostile native tribes, and the lack of anything resembling civilization to
look forward to at the end of their arduous journey. It wasn't until
the first missions were founded in the region that the settlement movement gained momentum.

Missionaries began arriving in the region in the 1830s. They came
primarily to evangelize the native tribes, some of which had expressed
interest in learning more about the white man's religion. In 1831 a del-
egation of Flathead and Nez Perce Indians had appeared in St. Louis
seeking further instruction in Christianity. The Methodist *Christian
Advocate and Journal* published an account of their visit that spurred
enthusiasm to proselytize the native tribes.

Marcus Whitman and Henry Spalding were two of the first to vol-
unteer as missionaries in the region. In 1836, the two men and their
wives set out from New York State and, after an overland journey of
some months, succeeded in reaching the Oregon territory. The wives,
Narcissa Whitman and Eliza Spalding, became the first white women
to cross the North American continent.

Along the way, Narcissa Whitman kept a journal and wrote a series
of letters back to her family about the trip. Her letters and journal
entries echo many of the sentiments and approaches to the land first
expressed by the early explorers. Like them, she initially approached
the westering adventure with pleasure and optimism. On June 3, 1836,

from just above the forks of the Platte River, she wrote a letter to her sister and brother:

> I wish I could discribe to you how we live so that you can realize it. Our manner of living is far prefferable to any in the States. I never was so contented and happy before. Neither have I enjoyed such health for years. In the Morn as soon as the day breaks the first that we hear is the word—arise, arise, then the mules set up such noise as you never heard which puts the whole camp in motion. *(Whitman 1836, 5)*

But as the difficulty of the journey took its toll, her enthusiasm waned. She began to miss the comforts of home and civilization. Mountain scenery still pleased her, but the long, monotonous trek through the Great Basin of southern Idaho and eastern Oregon proved trying. By the time she reached Fort Vancouver on the Columbia River, she was hungry for civilization. She took particular delight in the cultivated beauty of the fort's garden:

> After chatting a little we were invited to a walk in the garden. And what a delightful place this. What a contrast this to the barren sand plains through which we had so recently passed. Here we find fruit of every discription. Apples peaches grapes. Pear plum & Fig trees in abundance. Cucumbers melons beans peas beats cabbage, tammatoes, & every kind of vegitable, to numerous to be mentioned. Every part is very neat & tastefully arranged fine walks each side lined with strawberry vines. On the opposite end of the garden is a good Summer house covered with grape vines. *(74)*

Her appreciation of the wild, untamed landscape of the West gave way to a preference for cultivated landscapes such as this garden. As her homesickness grew more acute, her desire to fashion a home from the raw and inhospitable landscape increased. In November 1836, she and Marcus built a house at Waiilatpu, "the place of rye grass," at the confluence of Mill Creek and the Walla Walla River, an area suitable for agriculture and close to the Cayuse tribe.

Their efforts to convert the Indians and turn the house and surrounding mission into something resembling civilization demonstrated a heroism not unlike that of the early explorers of the region. Pioneer life, especially for women, could prove grim. This is evident not only in Narcissa's journal, but also in later works such as Idaho writer Mary Hallock Foote's mining saga *Coeur d'Alene* (1894) and contemporary novels of the settlement generation such as Molly Gloss's *The Jump-Off Creek* (1989) or Annie Dillard's *The Living* (1992). Still, women writers such as Frances Fuller Victor, who wrote *The River of the West* (1870); Abigail Scott Duniway, author of *Captain Gray's Company* (1859); and Shannon Applegate, who wrote *Skookum* (1988), found reasons to celebrate the arduous, exciting life.

Perhaps even harder than the work itself was the realization that the labor might be in vain. Like many early settlers and missionaries, the Whitmans' efforts came to naught. As more Indians died from diseases they believed the missionaries had deliberately spread, the Cayuse turned on the Whitmans in 1847, murdering them and burning the mission to the ground.

Despite setbacks such as the Whitman massacre, settlers continued to arrive in the territory. Like the Whitmans, many of these pioneers felt some appreciation for the landscape in itself, but most considered it as the raw material out of which a new civilization could be created. This led to an ambivalent attitude toward the local landscape: while they admired it for its intrinsic beauty, they also schemed to exploit its trees, furs, or mineral wealth.

Such ambivalence runs through the writings of James Swan, a settler who arrived on the Northwest Coast in 1852. Unlike Narcissa Whitman, Swan was fleeing the comfortable—and for him claustrophobic—society of the eastern seaboard. In 1849 he had left a wife and two children in Boston and set out for the California gold rush. After tiring of the frenzy and clamor of the boom society, he settled in Shoalwater Bay on the Washington coast. He befriended the local Indian tribes, learned their languages, and studied the intricacies of the local landscape. As much as he loved this misty, green, mysterious land, he also promoted its development. In his memoir, *The Northwest Coast or Three Years' Residence in the Washington Territory*

(1857), he takes great pains to detail the country, often mentioning the land's economic potential:

> That portion of Washington Territory lying between the Cascade Mountains and the ocean, although equaling, in richness of soil and ease of transportation, the best lands of Oregon, is heavily timbered, and time and labor are required for clearing its forests and opening the earth to the production of its fruits. . . . Either in furnishing manufacturing timber, or spars of the first description for vessels, Washington Territory is unsurpassed by any portion of the Pacific Coast. *(Swan 1857, 398)*

Swan's boosterism is evident in this and many other passages. As much as he valued the Northwest Coast for its sense of refuge, its distance from Boston, and its inherent beauty, he also praised the land for its material wealth. In his later life he even sought to bring the railroad to Port Townsend on Puget Sound and must have been gravely disappointed when the Northern Pacific Railroad chose Tacoma as its terminus instead. In his life and in his writings, Swan was an ambivalent and often contradictory figure, caught between his love of the place in its pristine, undeveloped state and his desire to see it transformed into a Euro-American-style civilization.

In their letters and journals, settlers such as Swan and Narcissa Whitman continued the process begun by the explorers of discovering, naming, and describing new corners of the territory. Where the explorers defined the land mainly in terms of science, these settlers saw it primarily in terms of its suitability for agriculture and development. Despite these utilitarian concerns, however, their writings reveal a sense of awe and wonder about the new country and a fascination with its inhabitants. In many ways, the early encounters of explorers and settlers with the region suggest narrator Nick Carraway's musings at the end of F. Scott Fitzgerald's *The Great Gatsby*:

> And as the moon rose higher the inessential houses began to melt away until gradually I became aware of the old island here that flowered once

for Dutch sailors' eyes—a fresh, green breast of the new world. Its vanished trees, the trees that had made way for Gatsby's house, had once pandered in whispers to the last and greatest of all human dreams; for a transitory enchanted moment man must have held his breath in the presence of this continent, compelled into an aesthetic contemplation he neither understood nor desired, face to face for the last time in history with something commensurate to his capacity to wonder. *(Fitzgerald 1925, 181)*

Despite their preoccupation with mapping, surveying, naming, cataloging, and settling the place, these explorers and settlers did respond to the aesthetic aspect of the country, even if they appreciated the place more for its potential for creating a new civilization than for its inherent beauty and integrity. It is this aesthetic appreciation of the landscape as much as the definition of it in terms of science that laid the groundwork for the next generation of Northwest writers.

3 / Romantic Movement

S ome sixty years after Vancouver's visit to Puget Sound, one of the first of the skillful panegyrists predicted by the English sea captain arrived in the region. Theodore Winthrop, age twenty-five, a graduate of Yale and a reserved and somewhat melancholy young man, came to the Northwest on a whim and ended up profoundly changed by the place. A descendent of the great Puritan John Winthrop, Theodore underwent a religious awakening in the course of his visit, an awakening that took place not in the confines of a church, but in the vastness of wild nature.

On April 29, 1853, Winthrop took a steamship from San Francisco north to the Oregon territory. After traveling to The Dalles, Oregon, where he suffered a mild bout of smallpox, he set out for the Puget Sound region. By August, he had reached Port Townsend, where he bribed several drunken Klallam Indians to take him by canoe down to Fort Nisqually on the southern end of Puget Sound.

The journey did not begin auspiciously. The natives soon tired of rowing and refused to go farther. In a fit of pique, Winthrop poured out their liquor. One of the natives then pulled a knife. Winthrop quickly brandished his revolver and quelled the mutiny. After this incident, the rest of the trip went well; the natives forgot about the standoff, and Winthrop managed to get a firsthand look at a region that deeply moved him. He was especially taken with the summit of Mount Rainier, which for him embodied the essence of wild nature:

> It was a giant mountain dome of snow, swelling and seeming to fill the aerial spheres as its image displaced the blue deeps of tranquil water. The smoky haze of an Oregon August hid all the length of its lesser ridges, and left this mighty summit based upon uplifting dimness. Only its splendid snows were visible, high in the unearthly regions of clear blue noonday sky. *(Winthrop 1862a, 25–26)*

Unlike Vancouver and many of the other explorers, Winthrop did not describe Mount Rainier and other aspects of the landscape in precise, scientific terms. Instead, he sought to suggest the sublime beauty of the mountain through effusive, extravagant language. This was a deliberate strategy on his part. In emphasizing the spiritual aspects of the mountain in this way, he believed he was adding something to previous characterizations of the region:

> Poet comes long after pioneer. Mountains have been waiting, even in ancient worlds, for cycles, while mankind looked upon them as high, cold dreary, crushing, as resorts for demons and homes of desolating storms. It is only lately, in the development of men's comprehension of nature, that mountains have been recognized as our noblest friends, our most exalting and inspiring comrades, our grandest emblems of divine power and peace. *(29)*

Earlier writers did not adequately appreciate the spiritual aspect of natural features such as Mount Rainier, according to Winthrop. He saw it as his responsibility to change that. His account ushers in the Romantic period in Northwest literature, with an emphasis on the sacred aspect of the local landscape, especially sublime features of it such as Mount Rainier. If Vancouver's journals epitomized a scientific, Enlightenment approach to the region, Winthrop's *The Canoe and the Saddle* signaled the shift to a Romantic appreciation of the Northwest landscape.

In many ways the Romantic movement represented a reaction

against the rationalistic ideals and methods of the Enlightenment. In works such as *Emile* (1762) and *Julie ou La Nouvelle Héloïse* (1761), the philosopher Jean Jacques Rousseau provided the outlines of the Romantic movement: reliance on the imagination rather than rational thought; the preference for subjective, poetic appreciation rather than factual delineation of an object; praise of the wilderness rather than of civilization. Instead of relying on scientific analysis, the Romantic artist sought a subjective, intuitive perception into the spiritual heart of things. Such writers and artists believed that they could more easily achieve this spiritual unity between themselves and the world around them by seeking contact with wild nature, which they considered the clearest and purest manifestation of God. For this reason, the Romantic movement valued wilderness above civilization, as Roderick Nash points out in *Wilderness and the American Mind:*

> Consequently in regard to nature Romantics preferred the wild. Rejecting the meticulously ordered gardens at Versailles, so attractive to the Enlightenment mind, they turned to the unkept forest. Wilderness appealed to those bored or disgusted with man and his works. It not only offered an escape from society but also was an ideal stage for the Romantic individual to exercise the cult he frequently made of his own soul. The solitude and total freedom of the wilderness created a perfect setting for either melancholy or exultation. *(Nash 1982, 47)*

This preference for wild nature and emphasis on personal experience distinguish the efforts of Romantic writers such as Winthrop, Joaquin Miller (1868), Frederick Homer Balch (1890), and Oregon poet Sam Simpson (1910) from those of explorers and settlers. These writers sometimes paid little attention to the external circumstances of the region while describing in great detail their own response to it, a response often filtered through the conventions of Romantic literature.

One of the first self-consciously literary treatments of the region, *The Canoe and the Saddle* describes an eleven-day period from August 21 to August 31, 1853. The canoe part of the journey covered 100 miles over two days, while the saddle portion traversed 220 miles over nine days. Winthrop's account resembles a travelogue, but differs from those of the explorers and pioneers by giving much greater weight to the pyschological and spiritual dimensions of his journey through the Northwest.

Unlike the region's earlier authors, Winthrop sought to become a professional writer. He had difficulty getting published, but after his death on June 10, 1861, in the Civil War, a number of his books were released, including the novels *Cecil Dreeme* (1861), *John Brent* (1861), and *Edwin Brothertoft* (1862) as well as his memoir *The Canoe and the Saddle* (1862). This last title proved particularly appealing. Several editions were published to keep up with the demand.

The book helped form the public impression of the region, an area little known at the time. It fueled an exaggerated, outlandish view of a Far West as a place peopled with heroic pioneers struggling to make a home for themselves against the backdrop of spectacular mountain scenery. Winthrop does nothing to discourage such a view and in fact reinforces many of the notions that influenced the tall tales and popular Western dime novels of the period. Winthrop's tendency to exaggerate seems at least partly induced by the kind of scenery he chose to highlight. Whereas Vancouver focused his attention on natural features such as meadows fit for settlement, farming, and development, Winthrop preferred the dramatic elements of the landscape, such as Mount Rainier. Throughout his journey across the Puget Sound country, the mountain looms over him, an obvious symbol for the sublime in nature.

On August 27, midway through the saddle portion of his journey, Winthrop was toiling his way up a steep path deep in the forest, concentrating on the mundane task of keeping his horse on the path. At the top of a ridge, he caught a spectacular view of Mount Rainier:

> No foot of man had ever trampled those pure snows. It was a virginal mountain, distant from the possibility of human approach and human inquisitiveness as a marble goddess is from human loves. Yet there was nothing unsympathetic in its isolation, or despotic in its distant majesty. But this serene loftiness was no home for any deity of those that men create. Only the thought of eternal peace arose from this

heaven-upbearing monument like incense, and, overflowing, filled the world with deep and holy calm. *(Winthrop 1862a, 80)*

In describing the mountain in spiritual terms, Winthrop follows a Romantic framework. While explorers and settlers had focused on the external circumstances of the region, Winthrop's account emphasizes the otherworldly qualities of nature, as exemplified by Mount Rainier. His account is valuable because it was one of the first to see the region in these terms. *The Canoe and the Saddle* glories in the natural beauty of the region and brings the spiritual side of this beauty to the fore.

Winthrop suggests this aspect of the mountain at least in part by registering the mountain's beneficial effect on him. His personal psychological journey, rather than the journey through physical space, becomes the heart of the narrative. As such, he adds a new dimension to Northwest literature, showing that inner transformation is possible through contact with wild nature:

> And, studying the light and majesty of Tacoma [Indian name for Mount Rainier], there passed from it and entered into my being, to dwell there evermore by the side of many such, a thought and an image of solemn beauty, which I could thenceforth evoke whenever in the world I must have peace or die. For such emotion years of pilgrimage were worthily spent. If mortal can gain the thoughts of immortality, is not his earthly destiny achieved? *(81)*

The spiritual nature of the mountain is revealed in the way it affects him. Contemplation of the peak brings joy and fulfillment to his soul. The sight of the mountain throughout the eleven days brings him out of his melancholy mood and makes it easier for him to endure the difficulties of his journey. By focusing on this subjective dimension of the trip and describing his personal development, from trials and tribulations of the early trip to the spiritual peace he attained by the end, Winthrop demonstrates the spiritual benefits of both of the mountain and the region as a whole. He speculates that the mountain's position above the region will positively influence future generations of Northwesterners:

Our race has never come into contact with great mountains as com-
panions of daily life, nor felt that daily development of the finer and
more comprehensive senses which these signal facts of nature com-
pel. That is an influence of the future. The Oregon people, in a climate
where being is bliss,—where every breath is a draught of vivid life,—
these Oregon people, carrying to a new and grander New England of
the West a fuller growth of the American Idea, under whose teaching
the man of lowest ambitions must still have some little indestructible
respect for himself, and the brute of most tyrannical aspirations some
little respect for others; carrying there a religion two centuries farther
on than the crude and cruel Hebraism of the Puritans; carrying the
civilization of history where it will not suffer by the example of
Europe,—with such material, that Western society, when it crystallizes,
will elaborate new systems of thought and life. *(82)*

As strained as this writing seems today, Winthrop's sentiments
strongly affected the region's literature, echoing as they did the
thoughts of Ralph Waldo Emerson, who expressed similar sentiments
about American literature in the essay "Self-Reliance":

And if the American artist will study with hope and love the precise
thing to be done by him, considering the climate, the soil, the length
of the day, the wants of the people, the habit and form of the government, he will create a house in which all these will find themselves fitted,
and taste and sentiment will be satisfied also. *(Emerson 1841, 164)*

Emerson and a long line of American writers after him believed
that the landscape and circumstances of the American continent—
not the tradition of European letters—should determine the shape
and content of the nation's literature. Winthrop adapts this approach
to the Northwest and predicts that the region will create a civilization
and literature based on wild nature. Despite his bombastic style, the
idea appealed strongly to later writers, including Robert Cantwell in
The Hidden Northwest (1972) and Timothy Egan, who used Winthop's
journey as the basis for *The Good Rain: Across Time and Terrain in the
Pacific Northwest* (1990), a narrative history of the region.

But if Winthrop succeeded in articulating an appealing goal for Northwest literature, he did not entirely succeed in achieving it in his own work. For while he introduced a Romantic preference for the spiritual in landscape and subjective consciousness to narrative accounts of the region, much of his writing remained derivative. In terms of style, for example, *The Canoe and the Saddle* owes more to American and English pastoral poetry than to the Northwest region. It would remain for the next generation of Northwest writers to create a literature that would elaborate new systems of thought and life from the circumstances of the region.

Still, Winthrop deserves credit for staking out that goal and for making progress toward it. His example inspired a generation of Romantic writers who incorporated many of his strategies in their work. At the end of *The Canoe and the Saddle,* he writes:

> And in all that period while I was so near to Nature, the great lessons of the wilderness deepened into my heart day by day, the hedges of conventionalism withered away from the horizon, and all the pedantries of scholastic thought perished out of my mind forever. *(Winthrop 1862a, 191)*

In emphasizing the spiritual nature of the Northwest landscape and giving a sense of its healing effect on himself, Winthrop charted a new course in Northwest literature. Despite his contrived style, he heavily influenced Romantic writers such as Joaquin Miller and Frederick Homer Balch, as well as later generations of Northwest authors.

JOAQUIN MILLER

The mountains of the Far West proved an irresistible subject to a generation of Northwest Romantic writers. They discovered that the bold, dramatic scenery provided a fit image for the lofty and spiritual side of nature, a side they sought to emphasize in their work. Some years after Winthrop's visit to the region, Oregon poet Joaquin Miller found the region's peaks a perfect subject for his vision of the sublime in the Northwest landscape. This scenery inspired his most celebrated work, *Songs of the Sierras,* where mountains serve as emblems of the spiritual side of nature. In a poem from that volume entitled "Sierra Grande Del Norte," he emphasizes the otherworldly aspect of the Northwest peaks: "White pyramids of Faith where man is free / White monuments of Hope that yet shall be . . ." (Miller 1871b, 188).

For Miller, the mountain scenery expressed a sense of the infinite. He compared the summits to gods and depicted them in an enraptured, rhyming verse that sought to capture their spiritual essence. He considered the Cascade Range as an extension of the Sierra Nevadas and saw mountain scenery as the unifying feature of the Northwest region and its culture.

In this way, Miller's verse fulfills Winthrop's prediction in *The Canoe and the Saddle* that the region's mountains would directly influence its culture. But contrary to Winthrop's prediction, these peaks would inspire strength and heroism, not calm and repose. Miller's poems call for a people and a civilization to match the mountains. He considered Northwest culture a direct outgrowth of this kind of scenery and emphasized its epic dimensions.

This assumption that mountain scenery provided an appropriate symbol for the rest of civilization led Miller to exaggerate many of the qualities of the region and its people. His choice of a grand, heroic voice lent dignity and importance to the lives and people of the Northwest, but also abstracted that life into a style that often owes more to English Romantic poetry than to the realities of life in the Pacific Northwest. Still, Miller proved one of the most colorful and outlandish figures in Northwest letters and brought international attention to the region and its literature.

Born on September 8, 1837, in Liberty, Indiana, Miller left Indiana with his family in 1852 and set out for Oregon. The family arrived in Oregon territory in the fall and settled near the McKenzie River. In his early years, Miller began writing poetry while attending school. He went on to work a number of jobs—pony express rider, newspaper editor, lawyer, judge—but always considered poetry his true calling.

His first volume of poems, *Specimens,* was published in Portland in 1868. A restless, ambitious writer, Miller was not satisfied with this local success. After divorcing his first wife, Theresa Dyer, whom he had married in 1862, he left for San Francisco in 1870. There, he met Bret Harte and others before moving on to New York, Scotland, and eventually England, where his career blossomed. In London, Miller found a publisher for his book *Pacific Poems* (1871). The success of this book paved the way for *Songs of the Sierras* (1871), which won Miller international fame. With his sombrero, long blond hair, and flamboyant frontier garb, the poet cut a dashing figure in London society. His autobiographical book *Unwritten History: Life Amongst the Modocs* (1873) further cemented his reputation as a kind of Byron of the Far West.

From early on, Miller considered the landscape and people of the West the dominant subject of his work. While serving as editor of the *Eugene City Review,* he wrote:

> Do you know that Oregon had ought to be the very heart of song and poetry in America? Ah, you look incredulous and think of the practical names of the Luckimute and Long Tom and Soap Creek, but never mind them, look at Mt. Hood. It is itself a Parnassus. Look at the Cascades with its dark brown of ever greens and beautiful hills. Look at the little knolls and buttes that lay stretched up and down the valley, covered with white flocks and fat herds, and listen to the foaming sea afar off that beats with eternal roar over rock bound shores, and tell me if this, our sunset home, is not a land of song and poetry. *(Frost 1967, 47)*

Though it may not seem so today, Miller was in fact revolutionary in claiming Oregon as a fit subject for poetry. Most of the region's poets wrote about their Indiana home or a relative who fought in the Revolutionary War. Though they were living in the Northwest, they didn't consider the region a fit topic for poetry.

Miller's innovation lay in bringing the form and music of English Romantic poetry to Northwest literature. He adapted these poetic techniques to emphasize the epic dimensions of life in the West. In "Exodus for Oregon," Miller illustrates the heroic aspects of this life by describing the western migration of the pioneers. This is perhaps his most fully realized poem about the Northwest, with a strong dramatic structure and carefully patterned rhythm and rhyme scheme that lend grandeur and importance to the struggles of the early settlers. Unlike most of his other work, the poem also contains vivid, particular details such as the birds following the wagon train as it crosses the Great Plains: "Strange unnamed birds, that seem'd to come and go / In circles now, and now direct and slow" (Miller 1871b, 191).

Significantly, Miller neglects to name these birds as vultures, missing an opportunity to add specificity to the poem. Although the poem succeeds in spite of this, the lack of detail weakens much of his other work. Too often Miller sacrifices fidelity to the circumstances of the Northwest to an adherence to the formulas of English Romantic poetry, giving much of his work an imitative, derivative feel. As O. W. Frost points out in *Joaquin Miller* (1967), such an approach led him to falsify his own experience of the region. This is the case with early poems such as "Oregon" and much of his subsequent work.

> His chief problem here and elsewhere is verisimilitude. He rarely achieves it for the simple reason that popular romantic traditions lead him to falsify his own experience or even to gloss over it altogether. In short, the poem ["Oregon"] is not so much about mid-nineteenth century Oregon as it is about 18th century England; it presents not so much the observations of its author as it does the deistic philosophy of a complacent, earlier generation. *(Frost 1967, 48)*

Despite his desire to make Oregon a fit subject for poetry, many of his poems filter the local Northwest landscape through the prism of the conventional pastoral verse, giving little sense of the particularity of the place. Much of his work owes more to Byron and Wordsworth than it does to the landscape of the Northwest.

This is especially the case with poems such as "The Great Emerald Land," in which Miller introduces many foreign expressions and practices, such as the sounding of the hunting horn, which had no place in nineteenth-century Oregon, though it may have been common in nineteenth-century England. "The herders drove their bands, and broke the deep repose. / I heard their shouts like sounding hunter's horn" (Miller 1871b, 202). This is not poetry "with earth adhering to its roots," in Henry David Thoreau's celebrated phrase from the essay "Walking" (1873), but derivative poetry that has more to say about a settled country like England than the wild Northwest.

Much of Miller's work and that of other Northwest Romantic poets lacked grounding in the specificity of the region's plants, animals, and people. Instead, much of this poetry simply imposed a convention-alized poetic formula and language on the life of the region.

This is particularly true in regard to Miller's and others' approach to nature. He often sought an ecstatic union between himself and the natural world, a union that he did not demonstrate in his poetry. It would take a later generation of writers to achieve a union between people and place and in their poetry.

Despite its weaknesses, Miller's poetry succeeds in bringing poetic form to bear on the Northwest region. He did not manage to make those forms new and appropriate to the place, but he helped intro-duce a poetic rhythm and music to the region's literature, demon-strating that the Northwest could serve as a rich and promising subject for poetry.

FREDERICK HOMER BALCH

Most of the early novels and stories set in the Northwest had little to do with the region itself. These stories largely followed the formula of conventional westerns, with laconic, unflappable heroes called upon to undertake Herculean tasks such as fighting Indians, leading wagon trains, directing cattle drives, rescuing damsels in distress, striking it rich in a gold mine, bringing bank robbers to justice, or battling griz-zly bears. The heroes adhered to a rigid code of manhood and found a sense of purpose in taming the wilderness and making it safe for civilization.

These "dime novels," which became wildly popular in the 1860s, ostensibly took place in the West, but aside from a few dashes of local color, they could have been set almost anywhere. The central action of these stories unfolded in deserts or mountain ranges that were never specifically named, largely because many of the authors had never vis-ited the region. The only concession they made to western geography was to sprinkle a few well-known place names such as Dodge City or Oregon City in their stories before going on to impose the same rigid western formula onto the people and place.

One of the first books to successfully depart from this approach was Oregon novelist Frederick Homer Balch's *The Bridge of the Gods: A Romance of Indian Oregon* (1890). Balch broke new ground in treating the region in a significant and interesting way. His novel concerns the evangelization of Indians by a white missionary named the Rev. Cecil Gray. Though fiction, it incorporates much historical fact and describes the local landscape with some precision.

Like Miller and Winthrop, Balch sought to make his work an outgrowth of the Northwest region: "To make Oregon as famous as Scott made Scotland; to make the Cascades as widely known as the Highlands; to make the splendid scenery of the Willamette a background for romance full of passion and grandeur, (all this) grows more and more into the one cherished ambition of my life" (Balch 1890, 294).

Unlike most other novelists of this period who wrote about the Northwest, Balch knew the region firsthand. He was born in Lebanon, Oregon, on December 14, 1861, and in 1871 moved with his family to a farm near Goldendale, Washington, on the Columbia River. He inherited literary and intellectual interests from his schoolteacher father and a strong religious sense from his pious mother. From early on, he was an avid reader of historical romances in the Romantic tradition such as Sir Walter Scott's novels and the works of Robert Burns, William C. Bryant, and other Romantic writers. In the preface of *The Bridge of the Gods,* he describes his desire to write a historical romance about Oregon:

> In attempting to present with romantic setting a truthful and realistic picture of the powerful and picturesque Indian tribes that inhabited the Oregon country two centuries ago, the author could not be indifferent to the many serious difficulties inseparable from such an enterprise. *(i)*

Balch understood the difficulty in bringing realism to historical romance, and although he doesn't always succeed in reconciling these two genres, he deserves credit for incorporating the people and place of the Northwest into his work. Balch cleverly weaves local materials into his novel, basing it on an Indian myth about a stone bridge that spanned the Columbia River. The bridge serves as a symbol for the confederation of local tribes, ruled over by the ruthless Chief Multnomah, who controls both sides of the Columbia River. When the chief rejects the Christian Gospel that protagonist Cecil preaches, the bridge collapses, foreshadowing the collapse of Multnomah's empire.

In the course of telling this story, Balch carefully depicts the lives of the native tribes along the Columbia. He includes details of the Indians' dress, customs, and demeanor. He succeeds in bringing Indian life into the novel because he knew many of the natives and was fluent in the local Chinook jargon. This allows him to render their lives with great accuracy.

But when it comes to describing the Northwest landscape, Balch proves less adept. The landscape of the Northwest looms large in his work, but its treatment is often overwhelmed by the traditions of the historical romance novel. Many descriptions seem lifted directly from these romances and have little to do with the region:

> The path that Multnomah took led through a pleasant sylvan lawn. The grass was green, and the air full of the scent of buds and flowers. Here and there a butterfly floated like a sunbeam through the woodland shadows, and a humming-bird darted in winged beauty from bloom to bloom. The lark's song came vibrating through the air, and in the more open spaces innumerable birds flew twittering in the sun. The dewy freshness, the exquisite softness of spring, was everywhere. *(78)*

This is the Northwest rendered in terms of the historical romance, a version of the place that has little to do with its actual appearance. While many of his landscape descriptions resemble this one, he occasionally depicts the region with accuracy and freshness:

> And so approaching the sea, they entered the great, wooded, rainy valley of the lower Columbia. It was like a different world from the desert

sands and prairies of the upper Columbia. It seemed as if they were
entering a land of perpetual spring. They passed through groves of
spreading oaks; they skirted lowlands purple with blooming *camas;* they
crossed prairies where the grass waved rank and high, and sunny banks
where the strawberries were ripening in scarlet masses. *(129)*

This very specific treatment of the local landscape shows how the
author is beginning to take possession of it in his prose. Although Balch
still borrows much of his language from historical romances and religious tracts, he salts this passage with names and specific descriptions
of the plants and geography of the region. This gives his work a
verisimilitude that is lacking in previous novels about the Northwest.

Throughout *The Bridge of the Gods,* Balch wrestles to bring together
the form of the historical romance and the local landscape. Though
he occasionally succeeds in this, more often than not the language
and formula of historical romance prove unsuited to describing the
region. While Balch and other Romantic writers such as Winthrop
and Miller brought literary form to Northwest literature, they had trouble reconciling these forms with a realistic depiction of the region.
Their emphasis on a personal, subjective appreciation of the place and
their appropriation of the forms of Romantic literature often got in
the way of an exact, nuanced vision of Northwest landscape and life.
If they sought a more spiritual relationship with this landscape, they
seldom realized it in their work. It would be up to the next generation of Northwest writers to find a form and language appropriate to
the raw, exuberant life of the region and its people.

4 / Realistic Writing

I t was summer in the high country of northern Montana. Ivan Doig and his family had just finished shearing a herd of 3,500 sheep, an exhausting task that should have earned them a day off. Without warning a storm blew in, panicking and scattering the vulnerable sheep. Some of the herd died of exposure. Others were trampled to death. Still others stampeded over a cliff.

In one day, most of the year's profit vanished. After this disaster, young Ivan decided that he wanted no part of a career as a farm- or ranch hand. As he wrote in *This House of Sky: Landscapes of a Western Mind*: "I looked back from the mouth of the coulee toward the dusky north ridges, still smoked with gray wisps of the storm. As much as at any one instant of my life, I can say: *here I was turned*" (Doig 1978, 222).

Though he continued to help with farm and ranch work, he had reached a decision: he would seek the schooling that would free him of the drudgery of this life and propel him toward his career as a writer. If in his early years he came to know the land through working it, later he would come to know it through writing about it.

Today Doig is an important contemporary exemplar of Western Realism, a venerable and established tradition in regional letters. He traces his literary roots back to a group of writers who came of age in the early part of the the twentieth century. The exaggeration and sentimentality of works such as Theodore Winthrop's *The Canoe and the Saddle,* F. H. Balch's *The Bridge of the Gods,* the poems of Joaquin Miller, and popular Western potboilers drew the scorn of Realistic writers who felt that this early literature bore little or no relation to the place itself. Where writers in the Romantic tradition had emphasized their individual response to the region, H. L. Davis, James Stevens, A. B. Guthrie, Vardis Fisher, Ernest Haycox, Betty MacDonald, Norman Maclean, Ken Kesey, and Ivan Doig sought to accurately depict the region and to suggest their response to it through the quality and specificity of this description. They modeled their efforts not after Romantic writers such as William Wordsworth, nor Transcendentalist authors such as Ralph Waldo Emerson and Henry David Thoreau, but on the fiction and poetry of Realistic writers such as Mark Twain, Sinclair Lewis, Theodore Dreiser, Carl Sandburg, Jack London, and Roderick Haig-Brown.

These writers often came from a working-class background and had gained an understanding of the land by struggling against it. As a result, their stories often exhibit an adversarial relationship with nature, with characters earning their identification with place not by surrendering to it but by standing up to it. These authors sought to replace the Romantic, sentimental version of the Northwest with a sharply etched portrait of the region and its people.

THE CALL OF THE WILD

The discovery of gold in the Klondike in 1879 transformed the Northwest, bringing a fresh wave of immigrants, industry, and further settlement. Like the California gold rush of 1849, this mass movement drew restless spirits from around the globe. They came to stake a claim. They came to strike it rich. They came for the sheer adventure of it, seeing it as a way to escape mundane and ordinary lives. In the end, the merchants and outfitters in Seattle and Skagway may have gained the most from the gold rush, but if few prospectors struck it rich, many returned with stories to tell and retell for the rest of their lives.

One of the most famous of these prospectors was Jack London. Born in San Francisco in 1876, London was the illegitimate son of an astrologer. He grew up in extreme poverty, supporting himself with jobs as a seaman, coal shoveler, fish patroler, laundry and mill worker, and prospector. In contrast with figures such as Joaquin Miller, London came to know the region primarily through work. Seeing the Northwest through the prism of physical labor gives a particular cast and color to his stories. A Romantic primitivism underlies the best of his work, but for London, union with nature comes not by contemplation, but by action, struggling against the landscape. His swashbuckling stories evince a gritty, hard-edged realism. There is nothing gauzy or sentimental about them.

Though London wrote about many subjects, he is best remembered for his work about Alaska and the Yukon territories, which profoundly influenced a generation of Northwest authors. His first collection of stories, *The Son of the Wolf,* was published in 1900 to great acclaim. A prolific writer who churned out 1,000 words a day, six days a week, London published two more story collections, a juvenile novel, and a Klondike novel before hitting the literary jackpot with *The Call of the Wild* in 1903. The novella quickly became one of the most popular and widely translated works of American literature.

The Call of the Wild is an adventure tale with a twist. Unlike most examples of the genre, this one is told from the point of view of a dog. Buck, a 140-pound St. Bernard and Scotch shepherd mix, lives a life of ease on his owner's ranch in the Santa Clara Valley of California. In the hands of a lesser writer, the strategy of telling a story from a dog's point of view could be limiting at best, irritating at worst, but London makes it work by demonstrating a keen knowledge of canine pyschology and an ability to relate it to human concerns.

Buck's idyllic life on the ranch ends when a worker kidnaps and sells him to a broker who ships him north. Where once Buck enjoyed free rein on his master's property, he is now confined to a packing crate and transported to Seattle. There, a man in a red sweater smashes apart the crate with a hatchet. Enraged, Buck springs at the man, releasing his pent-up fury. But the man, a breaker of dogs, catches him in midair with a club. The dog doesn't understand what hit him.

He attacks again. The man hits him harder, ruthlessly beating the dog into submission. Buck staggers around, blood leaking from his nose and mouth. The man strikes a final blow, knocking him to the ground. Bloodied but not broken, Buck learns from the drubbing. He comes to see the club as the real law of life, a law obscured by his comfortable former life on the ranch. The beating convinces him that only the strong and brutal survive:

> That club was a revelation. It was his introduction to the reign of primitive law, and he met the introduction halfway. The facts of life took on a fiercer aspect; and while he faced that aspect uncowed, he faced it with all the latent cunning of his nature aroused. *(London 1903, 20)*

The clubbing is merely the first in a series of harsh lessons he must learn. On arriving in Dyea Beach, Buck witnesses a dogfight that ends with one of the combatants being torn nearly to pieces. As London observes of the dogs, "They were savages, all of them, who knew no law but the law of club and fang" (22).

This is not the civilized world, where nobility, courage, and fair play are supposed to reign, but a world in which the law of the jungle—cunning, strength, and deception—prevail. In spite of himself, Buck learns to adapt to the new life, stealing food, defending himself, doing whatever it takes to stay alive. He gradually forgets the virtues learned in his years at the ranch. "It marked further, the decay or going to pieces of his moral nature, a vain thing and a handicap in the ruthless struggle for existence" (28).

This is a troubling conclusion for any humanitarian reader to swallow. But for London in *The Call of the Wild,* such a denigration of morality in favor of a dark, Darwinian code of survival is a precondition for reentering the primitive. The payoff for him is the regaining of an animal vitality lost amid what he considered the suffocating customs of civilized life. As Buck puts morality behind him, he grows in physical strength, his muscles hardening, his sight and scent sharpening, his whole being attaining an alertness and composure half forgotten over the generations of civilization. According to London, we all possess such instinctive knowledge, a kind of racial or tribal memory, and all it takes is the right circumstances to revive it. As Buck chases a rabbit, the primitive joy of the hunt returns:

> All that stirring of old instincts which at stated periods drives men out from the sounding cities to forest and plain to kill things by chemically propelled leaden pellets, the blood lust, the joy to kill—all this was Buck's, only it was more intimate. (39)

The forgotten instincts return, allowing Buck to survive as a member of a team of sled dogs. Spitz, the leader of the pack, recognizes Buck as a rival. At every instance, Spitz tries to provoke him, hoping to wound him and set the rest of the pack on him. Buck avoids the confrontation until he is ready for it. Spitz attacks and Buck counters by breaking two of his legs. Immobilized, Spitz has no answer for his rival's slashing jaws. Buck shows no mercy. For London, the Sermon on the Mount has no place in such an encounter. Buck moves in for the coup de grâce, wounding Spitz and allowing the rest of the pack to eviscerate him.

Rather than criticizing the cruelty of this, London celebrates the joy of the victor. "Buck stood and looked on, the successful champion, the dominant primordial beast who had made his kill and found it good" (42).

The rest of the novel treats a series of escalating conflicts, in which Buck continues to prove his mettle as a sled dog and killer. As he increases in strength and ferocity, he loses his desire to work for men and decides to return to the wild. The chance meeting with a wolf confirms his plan to leave civilization behind:

> He knew he was at last answering the call, running by the side of his wood brother toward the place from where the call surely came. Old memories were coming upon him fast, and he was stirring to them as of old he stirred to the realities of which they were in the shadows. (79)

Buck's transformation is complete when he meets a wolf pack. By defeating the strongest wolves, he is accepted into the pack. According to London, friendship, family ties, affection mean nothing to the animals. Aggressiveness, physical strength, and ruthlessness count for all. By demonstrating these qualities, Buck is accepted as the de facto leader. The book ends with Buck rejoicing in his return to the primitive life:

> When the long winter nights come on and the wolves follow their meat into the lower valleys, he may be seen running at the head of the pack through the pale moonlight or glimmering borealis, leaping gigantic among his fellows, his great throat a-bellow as he sings a song of the younger world, which is the song of the pack. *(88)*

Despite the brutal struggle for survival that underlies the story, generations of readers have reveled in the novella's celebration of primitive life. London's vivid depiction of wild nature, his mastery of the texture of working life in the Far North, and his appreciation of the strength and cunning necessary to survive in such a harsh environment also impressed the region's writers. They largely rejected his characterization of morality as the province of the weak, but they learned from his strong, realistic style and his emphasis on struggle as the means of finding identity with wild nature.

VARDIS FISHER

Few writers identify as closely with the country that formed them as Idaho's Vardis Fisher. The author of more than thirty books, many of them about the Snake River country where he grew up, Fisher made the dry, desolate landscape of southern Idaho his imaginative territory, creating memorable, if not always admirable characters from its inhabitants and giving eloquent expression to the harsh splendor and haunting loneliness of the place.

Widely considered Idaho's preeminent author, Fisher won the 1939 Harper Novel Prize in fiction for his novel *Children of God.* Though he traveled widely, including a stint teaching at New York University, he always returned to the sagebrush desert and deep river gorges of the Antelope Hills area on the western slopes of the Rocky Mountains. When novelist Thomas Wolfe came to visit, he could not find Fisher, but gained an insight into his friend from the surrounding country. On June 7, 1938, he wrote to Elizabeth Nowell:

> What I saw . . . is the abomination of desolation: an enormous desert bounded by infinitely-far-away mountains that you never get to, and little pitiful blistered towns huddled down in the most abject loneliness underneath the huge light and scale and weather and the astounding brightness and dimension of everything—all given a kind of tremendousness and terror and majesty. And this?—their pride and joy, I guess, set in a cup of utterly naked hills, a clean little town but with a sparseness, a lack of the color, open-ness, richness of Cheyenne. I've tried to find Fisher: people know him here but he's not in the phone book. Anyway, what I've seen today explains a lot about him. *(Wolfe 1956, 768)*

Wolfe's letter captures the qualities of the country and the character of those who inhabit it. Fisher embodied many of qualities—hard-headed, independent, indefatigable, and pitilessly unsentimental about the realities of making a life in the harsh surroundings. The wildness and isolation of the country strongly influenced his character. Born on March 31, 1895, in Annis, Idaho, Fisher grew up in the small farming community among hard-working Mormon families like his own. Though he later renounced the Mormon faith, he kept the habits of hard work and seriousness of purpose he'd learned from his pioneer parents.

When he was six, the family moved out of town and to a cabin on the Snake River. Fisher felt isolated and frightened in the primitive surroundings, but later in life he came to consider the river-bottom ranch his home and reference point, returning to it many times over the course of his life. Vardis and his younger brother, Vivian, were home-schooled by their mother, Temperence, who had little formal education but was determined to see that her children received it. Later, the brothers attended high school in the town of Rigby, Idaho. Fisher went on to study English at the University of Utah, where he graduated in 1920. He earned a master of arts in English from the University of Chicago in 1922 and a Ph.D. from the same institution in 1925.

After completing his doctorate, Fisher returned to the University of Utah as an assistant professor in 1925, where he taught Wallace Stegner in his freshman English class. Fisher's growing disenchantment with Mormonism soon rankled the school's conservative administration. He resigned in 1928 and took a post at New York University as an assistant professor of English. There he befriended Thomas Wolfe and met many other promising young writers. Though he reveled in the intellectual freedom of NYU, he missed the expansiveness of the West. He returned to Idaho in 1931, where he took up permanent residence, with occasional trips to Montana, Europe, and other parts of the globe.

His first novel, *Toilers of the Hills* (1928), drew from his early experiences of growing up in a Western farming community. Like many novels of the period, it is steeped in literary naturalism. As critic James H. Maguire points out:

> If literary naturalism can be said to have a formula, it might be a very general one such as "Little person fights against huge forces and loses." Central to almost all definitions of naturalism is a stress on the genre's pessimism, the result of naturalists' fascination with the view that people are subject to the iron laws of materialistic determinism. (*Maguire 2000, 57*)

Though influenced by literary naturalism, Fisher did not follow the formula very strictly. For instance, *Toilers of the Hills* is in some ways a textbook example of the genre, but in others it breaks new ground. Newly married Dock and Opal Hunter move out to the rugged Antelope Hills to homestead. They work year after year, but barely survive in the harsh land. Dock believes that they'll win out in the end, while Opal fears the landscape will crush them:

> She knew he would never yield, and she shuddered at a thought of what awaited them. Year after year of barren effort, springtimes of promise, of wild flowers and tall grass and rains, and summers of drought and locusts and hawks. And as she thought of Dock and his ways, it seemed clear to her that he was pitting himself against a vast power, an unseen and ruthless power hidden in these hills and reflected in the

passionless gray of this sky. Everywhere she looked there was something unfriendly and pitiless and hard, an unyielding force that would
slowly crush them both to its will. This was to be the dream of a lone
man's stuggle against a power that was sinister and mighty and dimly
seen. *(Fisher 1928, 27)*

Her fears are well founded. They struggle mightily to endure such
an implacable force, providing a strong element of suspense in the
story. But in the end, their exhaustive labor and shrewdness prevail:
Dock masters the intricacies of dryland wheat farming, allowing him
to profit from the increased demand for grain caused by the outbreak
of World War I.

In this way, Fisher parts company with many literary naturalists,
whose chararacters are usually annihilated by the larger forces that
imperil them. Naturalism's pessimistic and deterministic vision of life
is in some ways ideally suited for portraying the grittiness of the pioneering life, but Fisher wanted to go farther. He wanted to show how
this struggle can also strengthen character and allow people to come
to terms with a forbidding place. In this way, he demonstrates his affini-
ties with other Northwest Realistic writers, emphasizing that people
earn the right to identify with the country by demonstrating their ability to stand up to it.

His next novel, *Dark Bridwell* (1931), also borrows heavily from
literary naturalism. A stark determinism pervades the writing, with
characters hemmed in by the isolation of the country, which pushes
them to act almost against their will. The land itself assumes central
importance in the story, not as a bucolic retreat from the troubles of
the world, but as a strong and sometimes malevolent foe:

The country is as much a force in the action as is any of the characters. All of the Bridwells, except Charley hate it, and even Charley is
distressed by the Snake River, for he sees in it the insane journey of
unrest of nowhere. He prefers a calm stream. *(Flora 1965, 108)*

Dark Bridwell dramatizes the corrosive loneliness of the frontier.
While the protagonist, Charley Bridwell, revels in the isolation, his

wife, Lela, considers it a kind of prison. She stays with Charley through the births and raising of five children, but when he teaches the youngest to swear and chew tobacco, she decides to leave. The isolation of the homestead plays a part in her decision, but mostly it's the brutality and shiftlessness of her husband, who refuses to work and mercilessly beats his second son, Jed. In the end, her decision turns on Charley's character, or lack thereof, not only on the isolation of the country. In this way, the novel departs from the naturalistic formula, demonstrating that human will, not impersonal forces, makes the difference in the end.

And the landscape, while often brooding and hostile to human designs, comes alive through the quality of Fisher's description. It's not simply an indifferent wilderness, designed to diminish the characters, but a sharply etched world of sagebrush, rocks, and complicated geologic forms. He writes of the Snake River:

> The entire Antelope benchland was once its bed. But little by little, through countless centuries of toil, the river has narrowed its shores and cut downward, until to-day it lies four hundred feet below these hills, where it moved in a wide lake, and left its gravel to be buried by the wind and dust. In sinking its channel, it has eaten away the flesh of the earth and left curious skeletons of rock. It has left tablelands of stone, long since bedded again with soil, some of which now lie in long shelves, two hundred feet above its passage, and some of which are small bottomlands only a little above its present level. *(Fisher 1931, 4)*

There's nothing generic about his description of place. The novel presents a clear and definitive picture of the Antelope Hills. Though the land appears less than benign in this book, the austere beauty of the place comes to the fore in later works. It's as if Fisher needed to write out the darkness of his early life before he could come to express the land's benevolent side, which increasingly dominated his later work.

After *Dark Bridwell,* which many consider his best book, came *In Tragic Life* (1932), the first volume of his "Vridar Hunter" tetralogy, a series of autobiographical novels. Fisher next embarked on a series of long and ambitious projects: "The Testament of Man" series, depicting the evolution of man from prehistoric time to the present; numerous historical novels, including *Children of God* (1939), his best-selling work on the story of the Mormons; and many short stories, newspaper editorials, and nonfiction books.

While no one questioned Fisher's ambition, his increasing output resulted in the diminishing quality of his later work. Fisher, once mentioned in the company of Hamlin Garland, Willa Cather, and Erskine Caldwell, had trouble finding a publisher for his novels. Despite the uneven quality of some of these books, the early novels still fire the imagination, bringing to life the harsh beauty of the Antelope Hills and the spunk and determination of those who, despite formidable odds, were able to settle them.

H. L. DAVIS AND JAMES STEVENS

Two writers played an especially important role in replacing the Romantic, sentimental version of the Northwest with a sharply etched portrait of the region and its people. H. L. Davis and James Stevens became disgusted with what they considered the pathetic state of Northwest literature. Rather than working quietly to change it, the two angry young men attacked the region's literature in the 1927 pamphlet "Status Rerum: A Manifesto, Upon the Present Condition of Northwest Literature." This manifesto blasted the sentimentality of the region's poetry and fiction and blamed its literary establishment for encouraging this kind of work:

> The present condition of literature in the Northwest has been mentioned apologetically too long. Something is wrong with Northwest literature. It is time people were bestirring themselves to find out what it is. . . . Is there something about the climate, or the soil which inspires people to write tripe? is there some occult influence which catches them young, shapes them to be instruments out of which tripe, and nothing but tripe, may issue? *(Davis and Stevens 1927, 359)*

Neither Davis nor Stevens was content merely to denounce the dismal state of Northwest letters; both set out to improve the region's literature. Among other things, Davis went on to win the Pulitzer Prize in 1936 for *Honey in the Horn* (1935), a colorful comic novel about homesteading the Oregon country, while Stevens published *Big Jim Turner* (1948), a strongly realistic novel about a poet-laborer caught up in the Northwest labor struggles at the turn of the twentieth century. In these and other works, Davis and Stevens helped pave the way for a new tradition in Northwest literature, a tradition that presented a more authentic version of the region and its people.

Harold Lenoir Davis was born on October 18, 1894, at Rone's Mill near Nonpareil in Douglas County, Oregon. The eldest of four sons, Davis grew up in small Oregon towns, moving as his father sought work as a teacher. His father finally landed a permanent job as principal at the high school in The Dalles, Oregon, where Davis graduated from high school in 1912.

Davis then worked as a tax assessor and surveyor before being inducted into the army in 1918. During this stint in the military, he began his serious writing career, composing poems that were soon published in *Poetry* magazine. His work exhibited such an exact, colorful vision of the American West that his first collection, *Primapara,* won the Helen Haire Levinson Prize in 1919.

The attention accorded to his poetry eventually paved the way for his prose. In 1928 he sold two stories to *Adventure* magazine, and in 1929 H. L. Mencken's prestigious *American Mercury* accepted Davis's short story "Old Man Isabell's Wife." Mencken raved about Davis's colorful, comic style and encouraged him to write more. Davis complied by submitting a number of essays and short stories, including such important works as "Back to the Land—Oregon, 1907" (1929), "A Town in Eastern Oregon" (1930), and "Team Bells Woke Me." The acceptance of these stories by Mencken, a key arbiter of the nation's literary taste, signaled the end of the region's isolation from the national literary scene. Davis paved the way for other regional writers by showing it was possible to address local subjects and still reach a national audience, provided the writing met the highest literary standards.

In addition to soliciting shorter works, Mencken also urged Davis to write a novel. With his personal life stabilized by his marriage to Marion Lay in 1928 and his finances temporarily flush with a Guggenheim grant in 1932, Davis began work on his first novel, *Honey in the Horn*. It was published in 1935 and won both the Harper Novel Prize and the Pulitzer Prize, the first and only Oregon novel ever to do so. Although he went on to write four other novels and a number of short stories and essays, he remains best known for *Honey in the Horn,* a sharp-eyed appraisal of the Northwest and its people.

The novel concerns the coming of age of Clay Calvert, "a hard-mouthed young hellfry" (Davis 1935, 27), who bears a distinct resemblance to the central character of Mark Twain's *The Adventures of Huckleberry Finn.* Twain's celebrated novel heavily influenced the book, not only the characterization of Clay, but in the use of a vernacular narrator, the prevalence of grotesque comic characters, and the picaresque structure of the narrative. Davis's novel, however, is organized not by a journey down the Mississippi River, but by Clay's wanderings around the Oregon territory. The novel serves as a kind of regional travelogue, introducing a national audience to the diversity of the Northwest landscape and the eccentricities of its early settlers.

This is a very different Northwest from the one that appears in the early literature. Gone are the noble savages, the heroic pioneer preachers, and gentle pastoral landscapes of books such as Balch's *The Bridge of the Gods* and Winthrop's *The Canoe and the Saddle.* Here the pioneers often appear pathetic, the natives scruffy and indolent, the landscape indifferent or actively hostile to human designs. Davis scrutinizes the region much more carefully than did preceding authors. His affection for the region is tempered by an ironic, discriminating eye. In this way, the book seeks to lay claim to the *real* Northwest, not the one of popular myth.

The book's narrator follows Davis in casting a cool eye on the region and its inhabitants. In a witty and knowing way, he skewers everyone from early real estate developers to Clay's crazy uncle, Preston Shiveley, who is writing a book that resembles *The Bridge of the Gods.* The narrator accomplishes all this without assuming the role of an outsider or adopting the genteel upper-class diction of *The Bridge of the Gods.* Instead he tells the story in salty, vernacular speech that makes him seem like an insider.

He increases his authority by providing precise local names for the plants, animals, and features of the region. Unlike Joaquin Miller, Davis uses specific, local names, helping to capture the nuances of a new people and new country:

> The creek meadow in season was full of flowers—wild daisies, lamb-tongues, cat-ears, big patches of camas lilies as blue as the ocean with a cloud shadowing it, and big stands of wild iris and wild lilac and buttercups and St. John's wort. *(7)*

Honey in the Horn is full of flurries of naming and cataloguing the Northwest landscape. The narrator inventories not only the region's flora and fauna, but also its inhabitants. Davis excels at drawing quick, vivid portraits of the region's people, providing humorous and unsentimental views of settlers such as Flem Simmons, an old hermit who lives out in the woods:

> Flem Simmons was the oldest of the Peg Leg Simmons get of sons. Like the rest of them, he amounted to nothing, but in a slightly individual style. He was hard-working, good-natured, and extremely sociable, but he had lived by himself in the high mountains longer than anybody could remember, and the pressure of sociability with nobody to exercise it on had got him into the habit of talking to himself; not because he had anything to say, but for the purpose, apparently, of keeping up his practice with a monotonous formula of cusswords. *(135)*

Davis defines Flem Simmons and the book's other characters not only in terms of their personal and social or—in Simmons' case—antisocial attributes, but also in terms of their relationship to the land around them. In considering the influence of the local landscape on settlers such as Simmons, Davis comes to a remarkably different conclusion from writers such as Winthrop in *The Canoe and the Saddle* or Henry David Thoreau in *Walden.* Where Thoreau sees nature as freeing his personality of suffocating social convention, Davis sees it as reinforcing the old hermit's worst habits. The isolation of the landscape turns him into a tedious fool, so caught up in his own concerns that he has lost the ability to carry on a conversation. The landscape has not improved his character, but coarsened it:

> But living off by himself with wild animals that thought and acted all at the same clatter, and wild mountains that never thought or acted at all, had thickened the brain behind his eyes until a good half of what he saw never got through to it. The mountains did that. . . . *(136)*

Davis goes further in revising the pastoral view of the local landscape. Not only does isolation perpetuate Simmons' personality flaws, it also leads him to create a complicated set of rituals for organizing his life. Rather than living in transcendental bliss, he worries endlessly about the proper way to preserve venison, even though the deer are so plentiful on his property that he can kill one at any time:

> Simmons' life and location were such that he could have done pretty much anything he pleased. He had cut himself off from society to be independent of rules and restrictions, and the only thing he could think of to do with his freedom was to get up other rules and restrictions of his own which weren't a lick more sensible than the ones he had escaped from. *(157)*

Though Davis doesn't deny nature's positive virtues, he criticizes the Romantic and Transcendentalist notion that civilization is inherently flawed and that nature is entirely perfect. He takes a skeptical attitude toward nature; he values aspects of it, but certainly not all of it and certainly not to the exclusion of civilization.

This is apparent in his characterization of Flem Simmons. He depicts Simmons as a flawed person because he has come to terms with the natural world but not with human society; he may have found a way of surviving in the woods, but he does not know how to deal with people. As a result, Simmons is only partially developed, not whole and complete. For Davis, only characters who have resolved their relationships with both nature and society can become fully human.

In contrast to Simmons, Clay seeks to resolve both these relation-ships. He does so by facing up to conflicts with nature and with human society. He learns from the country as he learns from its people. Clay travels through the diverse geographic and climatic zones of the Oregon territory, confronting a number of difficulties as he seeks to make a life for himself. But the land does not cooperate. It is not a pleasant, benevolent pastoral landscape, but an indifferent and some-times hostile force that wreaks havoc on human civilization. When Clay and two other herders bring their sheep into the mountains, a storm and marauding coyotes threaten to decimate the herd. Clay responds with determination and tenacity and manages to bring the sheep home safely. Whether it's in saving a band of sheep, hunting elk in the Coast Range, or navigating the treacherous back roads, Clay comes of age by facing up to the challenges of the territory.

But his development does not stop there. Clay also must confront all of the difficulties of living in human society. He must learn to avoid being manipulated by adults such as his uncle, who convinces him to smuggle a pistol into a jail and gets him into trouble with the law. He must struggle to control his anger, which causes problems for him throughout the book. He must find a way to remain committed to Luce, the strong-willed daughter of an itinerant horse trader, even when the tensions in their relationship seem unbearable. Finally, he must discover a place for himself in the larger society, despite its many flaws.

The key to resolving all of these issues turns out to be Clay's meet-ing with a group of settlers. After traveling mostly by himself, he's relieved to accompany this group, with whom he has much in common:

> an entire people, a whole division of society, gathering to tackle a new country rather than live as peons in an old one, gave him a feeling of dignity and strength that, though miles beyond his own reach, was his because he belonged to these people . . . maybe they could be the ones who did the squeezing instead of the ones who got squeezed. It was not altogether a virtuously-purposed movement, but it was great one. It was happening now, and Clay felt glad he was in it. *(305)*

Clay feels drawn to the settlers, but he's not yet ready to cast his lot with them until the end of the book. He first must strike out on his own and watch his plans go to pieces. He resembles the rest of the settlers in this, for many of them tried to make a go of things on their own, only to be rebuffed by the country.

The settlers often made the mistake of believing in the apparent gentleness and tractability of the Oregon landscape. After a fairly mild winter or two, they became complacent and trusted nature to provide for them. An early winter blizzard changed all that. It killed most of their cattle and froze their artesian wells. As the narrator observes: "It was pure unfounded faith in the benevolence of nature that had led the settlers to depend on those wells to start with" (492).

When one of their party voices reluctance about moving on, an old-timer sets him straight.

> "Hell fire, feller, you're a child," he said. "Wait till you've had eight or nine different countries go to pieces on you, and you won't think any more of bunchin' the deck on one and lookin' for another than you would of changin' your shirt. We'll find us some land. That's what they country's made out of, ain't it?" *(494)*

The hardships endured by these people go a long way in explaining their attitude toward the country. They don't have the luxury of a disinterested and aesthetic contemplation of it; they simply are trying to survive it. And yet despite all their privations and disappointments, they remain doggedly optimistic about their prospects. After being starved out of one place, they simply move to another, eager to find one that will support them.

This gritty optimism is attractive to Clay. As he continues to cross paths with the settlers, he comes to feel camaraderie with them. Like him, the settlers have come of age by facing up to the country.

> Prosperity brought out everything in them that was childish and pompous and ridiculous and wasteful. But adversity brought them down to cases; it made even the simplest of them get in together and get work done. *(507)*

Finally, Clay decides to join the group. When they have trouble getting wagons down a steep slope, he volunteers to help. As he's working with the horses, he spots Luce, whom he'd traveled with for some time before having a falling out. She, too, has cast her lot with the settlers. The two agree to travel together again. They put their quarrels behind them and concentrate on getting the wagons down the hill. Like many of the others, they become reconciled to each other by joining in the common goal of settlement.

Clay's decision to commit himself to Luce and the settlers allows him to achieve a sense of resolution with human society. In deciding to love and care for her and remain with the settlers, he comes of age in a way that the hermit Flem Simmons could not. In his study *H. L. Davis,* Paul T. Bryant argues that for this reason the ending of *Honey in the Horn* is preferable to that of *The Adventures of Huckleberry Finn:*

> But *Honey in the Horn* succeeds where *Huckleberry Finn* finally fails. Both narratives begin with a boy who is fleeing the restrictions of society. Davis' novel reaches an acceptable resolution to the central problem of the boy's relationship with society, his attitude toward and acceptance of mankind. *(Bryant 1978, 73)*

Rather than "lighting out for the territory ahead" like Twain's famous character, Clay stays with Luce and the settlers, making his peace with human society in a way that Huck Finn does not. Bryant is right to point out that *Honey in the Horn* achieves a fuller resolution than *The Adventures of Huckleberry Finn,* but his interpretation doesn't go far enough. In ending the book in this way, Davis succeeds in achieving resolution not only with human society but also with landscape. Clay's decision to join the settlers puts to rest the book's two central conflicts—his relation to the landscape and his relation to human culture. As in much Northwest literature, Clay comes of age by facing up to the landscape as well as human society.

In taking part in the settlement, Clay commits himself to remaking the new country. He and the rest of the pioneers will grow and develop in relation to landscape as they will grow and develop in relation to each other. By engaging themselves with the land, they will strengthen and improve their individual character and that of their community as a whole. The rugged character of the Northwest landscape will bring out the best in them. In emphasizing the momentousness of the settlement movement, the narrator makes this clear. "Nobody could tell what they might do. Once enough of them had taken to the road all at once, and they had conquered half the continent" (Davis 1935, 508).

As the narrator points out, Clay and the others don't want to just settle the country, they want to conquer it. They see the land not as sacred, but as something to be subdued. They experience no effortless merging into place as Romantic and Transcendentalist writers described, but instead endure the long, grueling struggle of coming to understand the place through making a living from it. In its approach to landscape, *Honey in the Horn* displays a hard-edged realism, not the sentimental Romanticism of early Northwest literature.

Today, many commentators condemn such attitudes as cultural imperialism. As historian Patricia Nelson Limerick observes in *The Legacy of Conquest: The Unbroken Past and the American West:* "The history of the West is a study of a place undergoing conquest and never fully escaping from its conquest" (Limerick 1988, 26). While it's easy for Limerick and others to deplore the attitudes of the settlement generation, the historical context needs to be fully considered. As *Honey in the Horn* makes clear, the settlers often had been starved off the land. They often laid claim to areas with few and sometimes no other inhabitants. They may have sought harmony with their surroundings, but in the end they felt lucky to just survive them. Given these circumstances, it hardly seems surprising that they fantasized about conquering the country.

In later years, as settlements proliferated, such attitudes did not make much sense, as Limerick rightly points out. While the notion of conquering the land plays a prominent role in *Honey in the Horn,* Davis takes a different approach in later works, such as the novel *Winds of Morning* (1952) and the collections *Team Bells Woke Me* (1953) and *Kettle of Fire* (1959). In his later writing, Davis dramatizes the process by which people achieve unity with place and shows how that unity can be achieved without seeking to conquer the land.

In the essay "A Walk in the Woods" (1954), for example, he argues that utilitarian concerns get in the way of his appreciation of landscape. The essay's narrator takes a walk in the Oregon woods to contemplate the country, not conquer it. When practical concerns like fishing and hunting intrude, the narrator becomes annoyed; they interrupt the pleasure he takes in a leisurely examination of all the rich and varied details of the country.

In the course of the essay, he describes an abandoned settlement—all that remains of one family's dream of carving out a life for themselves in the country. He reminisces about a blackberry picking expedition on which he accidentally killed a deer. He muses about all the quirky people he's met while traveling through the backcountry. A desire to conquer the country often served as the impetus of these early experiences, but the memory of them now prepares him to view the landscape with warmth and affection, not hostility or fear. These early experiences made possible the contemplative attitude he's achieved; he wouldn't have as rich an appreciation of this landscape without the vivid memories of having worked and struggled with the land. This essay and his other late work demonstrate the unity with place he'd gained by the end of his career, a unity achieved without losing any of the sharp-eyed perspicacity that distinguishes his best work.

RODERICK HAIG-BROWN

Whistlepunks. Yarders. Skidders. Riggers. Trackmen. Loaders. The language of the logging camps and life along the rugged coast of British Columbia fills the work of Roderick Haig-Brown, a celebrated Canadian author and important figure in the Realistic tradition of Northwest letters. Haig-Brown is best known for angling stories like those in his autobiography, *A River Never Sleeps* (1946), but he also wrote extensively about the life and people of British Columbia, the place that inspired his best work, including *Timber* (1942), his first novel.

A writer who came to identify strongly with the rivers, forests, and mountains of this misty, rain-soaked coastal landscape, Haig-Brown was born in Lancing, Sussex, in England in 1908 and raised in Dorset,

Thomas Hardy country. Restless and rebellious, the young man left England in 1926 to visit the Pacific Northwest. There he found work as a scaler and timber surveyor in Mount Vernon, Washington. After his visa expired, he headed north to work on a logging operation in the remote Nimpkish River country of upper Vancouver Island, British Columbia. He kept a diary and used it as fodder for the articles he began placing in English sporting magazines.

In 1930 he returned to England, but he soon became homesick for the waters and mountains of the Northwest. Returning to Vancouver Island in 1932, he settled on the banks of the Campbell River in the house "Above Tide," where he and his wife, Ann Elmore, raised four children.

In all, Haig-Brown wrote twenty-eight books, including *Timber*. His nonfiction works served as preparation for writing fiction, one of his most cherished goals. "But now, after four books and ten years of self-training, I feel that I am ready to produce what I have always wanted to—good solid fiction about human beings" (Haig-Brown 1939, 94).

For subject matter, he turned to what he knew best: the logging trade of British Columbia. His extensive knowledge of the industry is evident throughout the novel *Timber*, deepening and enriching the plot, characterizations, and descriptions of the place. His understanding of loggers gives the story an unimpeachable authority and integrity. This is no accident. Haig-Brown devoted himself to accurately describing this subject. In "The Writer in Isolation," he recalls from his early days in the logging camps:

> My friends were realists to a man; they begged me to tell the truth, all the truth, not as writers and film directors see it, but as they themselves saw it—the daily truth of hard work and danger, of great trees falling and great machines thundering, of molly hogans and buckle guys and long-splices. *(Haig-Brown 1959, 60)*

In this he succeeded. *Timber* is shot through with vivid and specific descriptions of life in the logging camps—the noise, the bustle, the sheer delight and danger of physical work.

Men were streaming up from the long narrow bunkhouses all over camp. The fallers and buckers came slowly and for the most part singly, some of them carrying sharpened saws or axes, their wrists big from chopping and sawing and wedging, their shoulders bowed by the burden of tools. The Italian graders and trackmen came in groups, talking and laughing excitedly. The others—loaders, hooktenders, chokermen, riggers, engineers, even whistlepunks—somehow holding themselves apart, each one aggressively himself, bearing about him a pride in his own quality that showed in some small, effective way. *(Haig-Brown 1942, 35)*

His knowledge of the logging trade led him to organize the novel around the conflict between loggers and timber companies, an issue of great import in the '30s and '40s throughout the Northwest. The Great Depression of the 1930s gave rise to numerous radical social movements and the organization of unions in many industries. With the coming of the unions, the fiercely independent loggers were forced to choose sides: were they with the company or with the union? The same struggle animates Ken Kesey's landmark novel *Sometimes a Great Notion* (1964), though Haig-Brown tends to side with the unionizers while Kesey sympathizes with independent loggers.

In making a case for unionization, Haig-Brown chooses two accidents to bracket his story. The novel opens with an inquest into the death of Charlie Davies, a young logger hit in the head by a log. One of his coworkers, Johnny Holt, testifies that the death was accidental, though his testimony highlights the danger of the logging trade. In the end the jury agrees, finding no fault with the company or his coworkers.

Not all loggers are so easily convinced, however. Johnny's friend Alec (Slim) Crawford sees the death as an example of why the loggers need a union. He argues that without adequate work rules, many of the men will suffer the same fate as Charlie:

"It's just a racket," Slim said. "And you guys fall for it. You keep on falling for it and making money for the companies. If you're hellish good you get by and make wages for yourselves. If you're not you try to keep up and get killed trying or else get fired because you can't make it." *(16–17)*

Johnny angrily replies, "And we'd have a bunch of foreign bastards telling us what to do . . . " (18) but has a hard time explaining why. A strong, coordinated man who makes even the most difficult work look easy, Johnny lacks the verbal skills to debate Alec on the merits of unionization. Despite their disagreements, they remain friends. This friendship drives the rest of the story, revealing the ups and downs of the logging trade, the blacklisting of union sympathizers, and the consummate skill required to do the job well.

Both men excel at the work. Johnny is especially quick on his feet— "catty," in the terms of the logging trade. Alec is more thoughtful, adept at planning and organizing. As he pores over the map of Snake Creek timber, he mentally breaks down the land into forty-acre parcels of fir, cedar, balsam, spruce, and hemlock:

> He leaned forward and worked quickly for a few moments, then sat back to look at a cross that marked the first spar tree on the spur and a lightly shaded area of timber that would come to it. I know that one, a big fir standing between two cedars; and the next one after that can be the spruce just beyond Mosquito Creek. *(273)*

He demonstrates a detailed knowledge of the landscape, even if he uses that knowledge in the service of cutting down trees. Like other loggers, his livelihood is directly tied to the trees. He doesn't have the luxury of contemplating them for their own sake. For him, felling trees is a way to make a living.

But Alec's approach to the land is not simply an economic one. Though the novel mainly treats the disputes over unionism and the dangers of logging, it also reveals the therapeutic qualities of wild nature. To escape the pressures of his job, Alec takes an overnight hike into the woods. As he climbs to a high point above the timber, he searches for perspective on his life:

But the Gulf of Georgia was blue far over on his right, Vancouver Island hazy beyond it, and to the left of him the close peaks were hard and massive, mounting blackly into the patched snow. He sweated and worked with the single purpose of getting across the country, and while his hands gripped and his legs strained his mind was vigorously active, shutting him closely in upon himself with the ceaseless pattern of probing thought. *(353)*

By the end of his trip, he decides to leave the logging operation. He understands that the company will not improve its safety standards and that he can no longer depend on Johnny and wife Julie for company. He needs to find a wife and start a family of his own. Tragically, he never has a chance to carry out this resolution. Shortly after he returns to work, he's killed in a logging accident. His death could have been prevented had the company not stinted on equipment.

Though Alec's death is affecting, it doesn't have the full dramatic impact it might have. It reveals little about his character and says more about Haig-Brown's desire to bring the novel to a close. In this it demonstrates a persistent weakness in the novel. The book's characters lack the weight and solidity of those in Thomas Hardy's *The Mayor of Casterbridge,* for example. Haig-Brown gets the logging details right, but many of the characterizations feel flat and predictable, failing to fully engage the reader's interest and sympathy.

Despite these shortcomings, *Timber* does an excellent job of bringing to life the culture of a logging camp—the bravado of the best loggers, the tensions between labor and management, and the skillful, complicated, dangerous work needed to fell trees. It sketches a fine portrait of the working life of coastal British Columbia, bringing the landscape and the people together in story.

After *Timber,* Haig-Brown turned increasingly to writing about wildlife and the environment. As a logger, he sympathized with those who made their living from the woods, but as a fisherman and naturalist he realized that the land could not sustain the pressure of industrial civilization. His work took on a didactic tone as he emphasized the need to protect the land and its wild creatures. As Glen A. Love points out in the introduction of the 1993 edition of *Timber,*

"Haig-Brown, nevertheless, did his best, in his own civilized and reasonable way, to turn aside the industrial juggernaut, which has since felled the ancient forests of British Columbia, and the rest of the world, at a breakneck pace" (xxi).

In later works like *A River Never Sleeps* (1946), *On the Highest Hill* (1949), and *The Living Land: An Account of the Natural Resources of British Columbia* (1961), Haig-Brown continued this work, decrying the destruction of the landscape while celebrating the details of climate, geography, biology, and history that make the Northwest region unique. In this he served as an inspiration for British Columbia authors Emily Carr, Ethyl Wilson, and Jack Hogkins as well as writers thoughout the larger region.

A. B. GUTHRIE

Few novels evoke the majesty of the American West as eloquently as A. B. Guthrie's *The Big Sky* (1947). The book is a paean in praise of the region before settlement—the sweep of the prairies, the sublimity of the mountains, the unmitigated wildness of the country. The book celebrates the West's savage, untamed aspect, when native tribes and mountain men roamed its vastness, hunting, trapping, and living off the land.

Many consider it the definitive portrait of the mountain men and their impact on the American West, at least in part for its fidelity to the facts and circumstances of the era. Guthrie went to great pains to ensure the accuracy of its details and descriptions. Like many stories in the Realistic tradition of Northwest literature, *The Big Sky* was written in reaction to the Romantic stories that preceded it. "I started writing it because I thought no honest story of the mountain men had been told. The books all made a hero of the mountain men—romantic stuff. I wanted to tell an honest story" (O'Connell 1998, 150).

In addition to historical accuracy, the novel reveals Guthrie's love for the country and sympathy for its people. The book's three main characters, Boone Caudill, Dick Summers, and Jim Deakins, are some of the most memorable figures in Western literature, distinct individuals who embody the tensions of the era—Boone the quintessential misanthropic mountain man, Jim his talkative, likable companion, and Dick somewhere between the two, a man who serves as a bridge between the rugged frontiersmen and the settlers who follow. *The Big Sky* chronicles the early western migration in the 1830s, when trappers and mountain men began to filter into the country, wittingly or unwittingly paving the way for the settlement that would follow. A keen sense of nostalgia pervades the book, the author clearly lamenting the loss of the region's primitive innocence. However, the novel is anything but sentimental, graphically depicting the dirt, violence, and primitivism of frontier life.

Guthrie's ability to paint the full range of Western experience comes at least in part from his early acquaintance with the region itself. Born in Bedford, Indiana, on January 13, 1901, the author and his family soon moved to Choteau, Montana, where he spent his childhood fishing and hunting and exploring the territory. At fourteen, he got a job on the Choteau *Acantha,* a weekly newspaper where he learned to set type, compose pages, and run the press—a typical apprenticeship for a newspaper writer of his day. He obtained a degree in journalism at the University of Montana in 1923, worked a series of menial jobs, and then became a reporter at the *Lexington Leader* in 1926. He stayed at the newspaper until 1947, when the success of *The Big Sky* allowed him to quit to write full-time.

The novel tapped into a deep American myth, that of a return to the wild. In its celebration of primitive life, it echoes London's *The Call of the Wild* and a long line of other American classics. As Wallace Stegner points out in his introduction to the 1975 edition of *The Big Sky:*

> Caudill is the avatar of the oldest of all the American myths—the civilized man recreated in savagery, rebaptized into innocence on a wilderness continent. His fabulous ancestors are Daniel Boone, who gives him his name, and Cooper's Leatherstocking; and up and down the range of American fiction he has ten thousand recognizable siblings. (*Guthrie 1975, ix*)

Guthrie's ability to create unsparingly honest and compelling portraits of his characters distinguishes the book from others in the genre. Boone, the novel's protagonist, exhibits a deep streak of violence, leaving his home in Kentucky after mistakenly believing that he has killed his abusive father. But he is not simply a villain, nor a stereotypical gunslinger. He is a complicated character, showing great sensitivity to the land around him and a real capacity for friendship.

He joins up with Jim Deakins, his redheaded, extroverted alter ego, to trap beaver out West. The two quickly become apprentice hunters in a trading outfit run by Dick Summers and the Frenchman Jourdonnais, who are conducting a smuggling operation. They plan to return a young Blackfeet girl, Teal Eye, to her father, thereby earning his friendship and trade. In the course of this journey up the Missouri River, Boone climbs a bluff to get a good look at the country:

> From the top Boone could see forever and ever, nearly any way he looked. It was open country, bald and open, without an end. It spread away, flat now and then rolling, going on clear to the sky. A man wouldn't think the whole world was so much. It made the heart come up. It made a man little and still big, like a king looking out. (*Guthrie 1947, 103*)

Boone comes to loves the country as a kind of objective correlative of his own nature. It is not a passive and indifferent backdrop, but a violent and dangerous place, which calls out a similar violence in him. When Teal Eye escapes, the Blackfeet attack. The fierce, warlike tribe ends up killing all of the party save Boone, Jim, and Dick. After this baptism of fire, Boone understands that living in this country requires guile, courage, and a degree of ruthlessness, qualities that he discovers in himself. Later, when Boone finds a beaver caught in his trap, he has few qualms about killing it:

> She let out a soft whimper as he raised the stick, and then the stick fell, and the eye that had been looking at him bulged out crazily, not looking at anything, not something alive and liquid any more, not something that spoke, but only a bloody eyeball knocked from its socket. It was only a beaver's eye all the time. (*175*)

Boone's deep streak of violence allows him to survive and make a living off the country. It takes a certain savagery to carve out a life on the frontier. Boone is entirely prepared for this. He is strong and bold and cold-blooded enough to thrive in the harsh world of the early West.

His symbolic union with the place is sealed when he returns to the Blackfeet camp to marry Teal Eye, whom he had fallen in love with on their journey up the river. She and her tribe embody the primitive vigor of the West. By marrying into the Blackfeet clan, he earns the right to identify with the country.

But if his propensity for violence allows him to survive the country, it also turns out to be his tragic flaw. When Teal Eye gives birth to a baby with red hair, Boone immediately suspects Jim is the father. He shoots Jim and abandons Teal Eye and the baby, even though he later discovers that his own grandfather had red hair. In this way, he reveals himself incapable of curbing his violent side, making it impossible for him to adapt to the changes that are coming with the increase in settlements. His days are numbered. He and the mountain men who pioneered the West are now seeing their way of life disappear.

> "I don't guess we could help it," Summers answered, nodding. "There was beaver for us and free country and a big way of livin', and everything we done it looks like we done against ourselves and couldn't do different if we'd knowed. We went to get away and to enj'y ourselves free and easy, but folks was bound to foller and beaver to get scarce and Injuns to be killed or tamed, and all the time the country gettin' safer and better known." *(366)*

At the end of the novel, Boone vanishes into the darkness outside Dick Summers' farm in Missouri, still seeking the next blank spot on the map. Guthrie's ending implies that Boone and the other mountain men are finished. They brought on their own demise by mapping and exploring the territory, paving the way for the tide of settlers who will civilize the place, making it an anathema to Boone and his compatriots. Tragically, they contributed to their own demise.

But not all the mountain men have difficulty adapting to the changing West. In the succeeding volume, *The Way West* (1949), Dick Summers agrees to guide a wagon train to the Oregon territory. The group consists of Irvine Tadlock, an organizer with political ambitions in the new territory; Lije Evans, a Missouri farmer; his wife, Becky; and their son, Brownie. Through Summers' leadership, the group overcomes many hardships and privations on their journey. His combination of pluck, optimism, and sheer energy is critical to the group's success in reaching the Oregon territory. Unlike Boone, Summers is at home in both the wilderness and human civilization.

The Way West brilliantly re-creates the epic western migration, a crucial aspect of U.S. history, earning it the Pulitzer Prize in 1950. In this and his later books, Guthrie has played an instrumental role in shaping Westerners' sense of themselves and the country they live in. *These Thousand Hills* (1956), *Arfive* (1970), and *The Last Valley* (1975) further dramatize the settling of the new land. Guthrie also penned screenplays for the landmark movies *Shane* (1953) and *The Kentuckian* (1955). He is the author of *The Big It* (1960), a book of short stories; *Big Sky, Fair Land* (1988), a collection of environmental essays; and *A Field Guide to Writing Fiction* (1991). He died of lung failure in 1991, but his books live on as realistic, complex depictions of the region and its history.

BETTY MACDONALD

Despite novels like Guthrie's *The Big Sky* and Davis's *Honey in the Horn*, the general public still considered the West a place of magnificent scenery, heroic pioneers, and boundless possibility. Inspired by the work of Romantic writers and dime novelists, generations of Americans continued to move West. Many of these immigrants were particularly intrigued by the opportunity of making a living from the land, a living not dependent on the whims of bosses, but on the richness and bounty of the country itself. The U.S. government encouraged such notions by publishing pamphlets on the advantages of alfalfa, wheat, and chicken farming. People read these pamphlets with a religious fervor, believing that the West offered them an opportunity to operate their own farms and fulfill all of their dreams.

It was just such a vision of an agrarian utopia that led Betty MacDonald and her first husband, Robert Heskett, to buy a chicken farm on the Olympic Peninsula in Washington State in 1927. Though they eventually succeeded in making a living raising chickens, they certainly didn't find the circumstances idyllic. The wilderness around them appeared largely hostile, while the chickens proved more demanding than any supervisor. In spite of these hardships, and partly because of them, she managed to make a very successful book out of the whole adventure. Her autobiography, *The Egg and I* (1945), sold more than a million copies and inspired a feature film as well as the Ma and Pa Kettle series of comic movies. The book introduced a generation of Americans to the Northwest and demolished many Romantic notions about homesteading.

Born in Boulder, Colorado, in 1908, MacDonald traveled throughout the West in her early years as her father pursued a career as a mining engineer. The family eventually settled in Seattle, Washington, where they lived in the wealthy neighborhood of Laurelhurst. In addition to attending school there, MacDonald took lessons in singing, piano, French, ballet, and folk dancing, skills that did not prove an especially useful preparation for life on a chicken farm.

In 1927 she married Heskett, who was then working as an insurance salesman. Shortly after their marriage, he told her of his dream of buying a chicken farm. MacDonald dutifully supported him in this venture, but never adapted to the rugged lifestyle. The mountains behind their farm, for example, never appeared sublime or spiritual to her, but malevolent and forbidding:

> Despite its location, I never had the feeling that our small ranch was nestled on the protective lap of the Olympic Mountains. There was nothing protective about them. Each time I looked out of a window or stepped out of doors, I was confronted by great, white haughty peaks staring just above my head and doing their chilly best to make me realize that was once a very grand neighborhood and it was curdling their blood to have to accept "trade." We were there with our ugly little buildings and livestock, but, by God, they didn't have to associate with us or make us welcome. They, no doubt, would have given half their timber if they could have changed the locale to Switzerland and brushed us off with a nice big avalanche. *(MacDonald 1945, 65)*

MacDonald expended an extraordinary amount of energy on ordinary household chores such as cooking, cleaning, bathing, and trying to stay warm. The care and feeding of the chickens proved even more exhausting, as many of them seemed more inclined to suicide than survival. With its wisecracks and corrosive commentary on the virtues of the simple life, *The Egg and I* represents a kind of feminist revision of *Walden,* with a 1930s housewife responding sarcastically to the Transcendentalist philosophy of Henry David Thoreau:

> Being lonely all of the time, I used to harbor the idea, as who has not, that I was one of the few very fortunate people who was absolutely self-sufficient and that if I could just find myself a little haunt far from the clawing hands of civilization with its telephones, electric appliances, artificial amusements and people—people more than anything—I would be contented for the rest of my life. Well, someone called my bluff and I found that after nine months spent mostly in the stimulating company of the mountains, trees, the rain, Stove and the chickens, I would have swooned with anticipation at the prospect of a visit from a Mongolian idiot. *(92)*

For entertainment and companionship, she falls back on her neighbors, who are not the strong, self-reliant settlers described in Joaquin Miller's poems, but instead the earthy Ma and Pa Kettle:

> Mrs. Kettle had pretty light brown hair, only faintly streaked with gray and skinned back into a tight knot, clear blue eyes, a creamy skin which flushed exquisitely with the heat, a straight delicate nose, fine even white teeth, and a small rounded chin. From this dainty pretty head cascaded a series of busts and stomachs which made her look like a cooky jar shaped like a woman. Her whole front was dirty and spotted and she wiped her hands continually on one or the other of her stomachs. She had also a disconcerting habit of reaching up under her dress and adjusting something in the vicinity of her navel and of reaching down the front of her dress and adjusting her large breasts. These adjustments were not, I learned later, confined to either the privacy of the house or

a female gathering—they were made anywhere—any time. "I itch—so I scratch—so what!" was Mrs. Kettle's opinion. *(114)*

The couple and their many children barely make ends meet because of Pa's laziness and incompetence. He survives by borrowing from his neighbors and prevailing on them to work for free. As was the case with Flem Simmons in Davis's *Honey in the Horn*, the natural surroundings seem to influence him in a negative rather than a positive way, inclining him to strew his property with junk:

> The farm was fenced with old wagons, parts of cars, broken farm machinery, bits and scraps of rope and wire, pieces of outbuildings, a parked automobile, old bed springs. The barnyard teemed with jalopies in various stages of disintegration. *(112)*

The Kettles and other neighbors provide some companionship, but MacDonald never gets used to the rigors of frontier life. After several years of endless work and much isolation, she's ready to call it quits. She rejoices when her husband tells her about a chicken farm for sale near Seattle:

> I coasted around the house propelled by visions of linoleum floors, bathtubs, electric stoves and flushing toilets. It seemed to me that from now on life was going to be pure joy. *(287)*

Once they buy the new farm, she gladly bids good riddance to the Olympic Peninsula. MacDonald never achieves identification with the natural world, as is the case with characters in some Realistic novels. The hard work of farm life doesn't prepare her for unity with nature, but instead makes her crave further separation from it. By the end of the book, she is content to turn her back on the wilds and return to the city in search of household conveniences and stimulating conversation.

After *The Egg and I*, MacDonald went on to write a number of other autobiographical works, including *The Plague and I* (1948), *Anybody Can Do Anything* (1950), *Onions in the Stew* (1955), as well as the Mrs.

Piggle-Wiggle children's books. However, she remains best known for the *The Egg and I,* which went a long way toward undermining Romantic notions about the Northwest.

KEN KESEY

Few novels give a better sense of the circumstances of the Northwest than Ken Kesey's *Sometimes a Great Notion* (1964). Set in Wakonda, Oregon, a down-at-the-heels logging and fishing town, the book paints a vivid picture of life on the west side of the Cascade Mountains in the late 1950s and early '60s. Unlike the work of the Romantic writers, this is a novel absolutely packed with details about the region and its people. It is a rich, thick gumbo of a book, which succeeds like few others in suggesting the atmosphere of the place—the sogginess of the climate, the riotous nature of the vegetation, the toughness of those able to make a living from the land. Significantly, the novel opens by describing the landscape, a crucial actor in the story:

> Along the western slopes of the Oregon Coastal Range . . . come look: the hysterical crashing of the tributaries as they merge into the Wakonda Auga River. . . . The first little washes flashed like thick rushing winds through sheep sorrel and clover, ghost fern and nettle, sheering, cutting . . . forming branches. Then, through bearberry and salmonberry, blueberry and blackberry, the branches crashed into creeks, into streams. Finally, in the foothills, through tamarack and sugar pine, shittim bark and silver spruce—and the green and blue mosaic of Douglas Fir—the actual river falls five hundred feet . . . and look: opens out upon the fields. *(Kesey 1964, 1)*

After establishing the natural setting through the use of specific names of plants, Kesey goes on to describe the tangled wood structure of main character Hank Stamper's house. A pole projects out from the top of the house. From the end of the pole a human arm dangles and twists in the wind. Four of its fingers are tied down, leaving the erect middle finger to express Stamper's contempt for those who have pressured him to join the local lumber union. Stamper believes he can stand up to the country with no help from a union and little from a community. With his motto, "Never give an inch," Stamper is the quintessential Western hero, a rugged individualist who has succeeded in making a living from the landscape, but has made little effort to get along with the community.

Unlike many heroes in Western literature, however, Stamper is a carefully sculpted character, a specific individual, the product of a particular time and place in Oregon. He may share traits with archetypal Western heroes, but he is no stereotype. He is one of Kesey's many achievements in *Sometimes a Great Notion,* a generational saga about Oregon logging that provides the atmosphere, detail, and concreteness missing in Romantic accounts of the country.

Kesey accomplishes this in part through his knowledge of the region. He was born in 1935 in La Junta, Colorado, but grew up mainly in Oregon, where he accompanied his father on fishing and hunting trips and gained a deep understanding of and respect for the natural world and the working-class men and women who made their living from it. He attended the University of Oregon, where he obtained a bachelor of arts in 1957, and Stanford University, where he did graduate work from 1958 to 1961, studying with Wallace Stegner, among others. His was a distinguished class; his fellow grad students included Larry McMurtry.

Though *Sometimes a Great Notion* stands as his most significant contribution to Northwest literature, Kesey is best known for his first novel, *One Flew Over the Cuckoo's Nest* (1962), which was made into an Academy Award–winning movie of the same name. The novel concerns the conflict between the free-spirited Randle Patrick McMurphy, a patient in a mental hospital, and Nurse Ratched, the hospital's chief administrator, who seeks to enforce a code of fear and conformism among the patients. The book illustrates the conflicts between the individualistic McMurphy and the rigid Nurse Ratched, who in the end succeeds in having McMurphy lobotomized. The novel is an indictment of Americans' willingness to sacrifice individual freedom to social control and conformity.

One Flew Over the Cuckoo's Nest won Kesey a wide and enthusiastic audience, particularly among the counterculture movement of the 1960s. He played a prominent role in the movement though his leadership of the Merry Pranksters, a group that traveled around in a bus, staging "happenings" and experimenting with hallucinogenic drugs. Tom Wolfe's *The Electric Kool-Aid Acid Test* (1968), an account of the Merry Pranksters in particular and the Psychedelic movement in general, earned Kesey the status of a cult figure.

Thematically, *One Flew Over the Cuckoo's Nest* is a precursor to *Sometimes a Great Notion.* The second novel exhibits many of the same tensions between the individual and society, but broadens and complicates them. In *Sometimes a Great Notion,* the central character, Hank Stamper, struggles not only with society, but with the natural world as well. And unlike the view of the natural world in Romantic literature, nature in this novel is anything but a passive background. As the novel makes clear, it's wildly indifferent to human needs and desires:

> And for *another* thing, there was nothing, *not a thing,* about the country that made a man feel Big And Important. If anything it made a man feel dwarfed, and about as important as one of the fish-Indians living down on the clamflats. Important? Why, there was something about the whole blessed country that made a soul feel whipped before he got started. Back home in Kansas a man had a hand in things, the way the Lord aimed for His servants to have: if you didn't water, the crops died. If you didn't feed the stock, the stock died. As it was ordained to be. But there, in that land, it looked like our labors were for naught. The flora and fauna grew or died, flourished or failed, in complete disregard for man and his aims. A Man Can Make His mark, did they tell me? Lies, lies. Before God I tell you: a man might struggle and labor his livelong life and make no mark! None! No permanent mark at all! I say it is true. *(20–21)*

It takes a man as strong and capable as Hank Stamper to carve out a life in the midst of this green curtain. But the very qualities that allow him to prevail against the landscape make it difficult for him to get

along in his local community. When his independent logging operation comes into conflict with the union-dominated townspeople,
Stamper's unwillingness to compromise ruins his marriage, leading
his wife, Viv, to have an affair with his half-brother, Leland. Though
Hank prevails against the town, he ends up losing his wife and family in the process.

In this way, *Sometimes a Great Notion* presents a fuller and more
complex picture of the Northwest and its people than that found in
the work of Romantic writers. Hank's toughness and resolution allow
him to survive in the woods, but they ensure his isolation from family and community. His virtue in one arena turns out to be his tragic
flaw in another. The novel furnishes a much deeper insight into a pro-
totypical character such as Hank than did the work of Joaquin Miller,
for example.

Kesey achieves this complexity in part by employing a more complicated narrative strategy. He borrows freely from William Faulkner
in using multiple perspectives to tell the story, giving accounts of events
from Hank's and Leland's points of view. In this way, Kesey creates a
rich, satisfying narrative.

Though he went on to write a number of other books, including
the essay collection *Demon Box* (1986) and the novel *Sailer Song* (1992),
Kesey made his biggest contribution to Northwest literature with
Sometimes a Great Notion. The novel succeeds like few others in presenting a detailed and comprehensive view of the Northwest and its
people, expressing what it was really like to live and work along the
west slopes of the Oregon Cascades in the late twentieth century.

NORMAN MACLEAN

Many stories in the Realistic tradition emphasize the conflict between
people and place. Characters in these stories often define themselves
by standing up to the country. As writers became familiar with the
place, however, they often changed their approach to it, seeing the
landscape more as a homeland than a battleground. They continued
to create characters who struggled against the landscape, but these
characters increasingly came to appreciate the land as a worthy adver-

sary and to identify strongly with it. Such an approach informs Norman Maclean's classic novella *A River Runs Through It* (1976).

In many ways, *A River Runs Through It* covers very similar territory to that of Kesey's *Sometimes a Great Notion*. Maclean, however, emphasizes how engaging with landscape can lead to a deep identification with it, and this identification in turn can lead to an individual's reconciliation with family and community, something Hank Stamper wasn't able to accomplish. In *A River Runs Through It*, the land becomes the focal point of personal, familial, and communal identity, allowing a much more comprehensive sense of resolution than that achieved in *Sometimes a Great Notion*. This is just one of the many achievements of this masterful work.

A River Runs Through It dramatizes a merging with place not unlike that sought by the Romantic writers, but prepared for by a process as arduous as that endured by characters in Realistic stories such as Davis's *Honey in the Horn* and MacDonald's *The Egg and I*. The main characters in the novella must earn the right to identify with the country by proving themselves tough enough to stand up to it. This process of testing themselves does not become an end in itself, but a means by which characters achieve identification with the landscape. There is none of the effortless merging with place envisioned by Romantics, but a long and difficult struggle that results in seeing the country as home.

This sense of struggle as the process by which one wins identification with place takes on an explicitly Christian dimension in the novella. The narrator Norman's trials serve as a kind of purgatory through which he must pass before achieving peace and wholeness. Without his fierce struggle to come to terms with his family and the landscape, he would not experience the epiphany that occurs at the end of the book. His personal sufferings prepare the way for his final sense of grace and merging with place.

The son of a Presbyterian minister, Maclean proves especially skilled at adapting biblical stories to suit his purposes. Working out of the Old and New Testaments, Maclean uses the Judeo-Christian tradition as the basis for a deep and abiding identification with place. In his hands, Christianity becomes a kind of religion of nature, with fly-fishing serving as a kind of equivalent of the Christian liturgy. In this way, the novella uses Christian theology and the activity of fly-fishing to dramatize the process by which one earns identification with landscape.

A River Runs Through It and the other stories in the collection of the same name bring together Maclean's practical knowledge of fishing, logging, firefighting, and woodsmanship with his deep sensitivity to the language and prose rhythms of the Bible as well as Shakespeare, William Wordsworth, Robert Browning, Robert Frost, Ernest Hemingway, and the tradition of English and American literature. Born in 1902 in Clarinda, Iowa, Maclean spent much of his youth in and around Missoula, Montana. While in his teens, he began working for the U.S. Forest Service, but he eventually chose to pursue a career as a college English professor. He earned his Ph.D. from the University of Chicago in 1940 and taught there from 1930 until his retirement in 1973. After retiring, he took up writing full-time, publishing *A River Runs Through It* in 1976 and working on a nonfiction account of the 1949 Mann Gulch forest fire until his death in 1990. This account, *Young Men and Fire,* was published in 1992.

In much of his work, Maclean shows himself to be both an experienced outdoorsman and an astute literary craftsman. He packs his stories with practical details of fly-fishing, tree cutting, and fighting forest fires while relating them with an ear finely attuned to poetic rhythms. Such an approach gives his work an integrity of fact and a suggestiveness of feeling that help dramatize the sometimes mysterious connections between humans and the environment. According to Maclean in "The Hidden Art of a Good Story: Wallace Stegner Lecture," the stories in *A River Runs Through It* rest on three closely related aspirations:

1) to depict the art and grace of what men and women can do with their hands in the region of the country that I was brought up in and know best;

2) to impart with a description of these arts something of the feeling that accompanies their performance or, indeed, of intelligently watching them performed; and

3) of seeing in the parts of nature where they were performed something like the beauty, structure, rhythm and design of the arts themselves. *(Maclean 1988, 29)*

This threefold approach to narrative underlies all of the stories in the collection. They all depend on the realistic and dramatic descriptions of life in western Montana to make clear the link between the human world and the natural world. All pay scrupulous attention to physical details of people and places, demonstrating his allegiance to the Realistic and naturalistic traditions in fiction writing and a particular debt to the work of Ernest Hemingway. In *At the Field's End: Interviews with 22 Pacific Northwest Writers,* Maclean makes this clear:

> Hemingway was an idol of mine for a while, as he was for practically all of us of that generation. . . . Unlike a lot of people who thought a lot of Hemingway, I still think a great deal of him. Now Hemingway is in disrepute as a kind of fake macho guy. I realized that he put on kind of a show, but on the other hand I don't see how you could be a real American writer unless you knew Hemingway well, and had learned a great deal from him. He was a master of dialogue of a certain kind, that very tight, crisp kind. He was a master of handling action, too. . . . In a page or even a paragraph he could tell you the most complicated action. So I don't fall into the school of so-called modern critics who dislike Hemingway. *(O'Connell 1998, 229)*

Hemingway's influence is felt throughout Maclean's works, but perhaps nowhere more strongly than in *A River Runs Through It.* The parallels between the novella and Hemingway's stories such as "Big Two-Hearted River" (1924) are clear and deliberate. Maclean follows Hemingway's lead in providing the physical details that will produce in the reader the feeling of catching a fish. In meticulously rendering such details, Maclean is able to describe and dramatize actions simultaneously, and so suggest the connections between humans and landscape.

Like Hemingway, Maclean is as much interested in fishing's ability to test and perfect character as he is in its pastoral qualities of rest and repose. In Hemingway's *The Old Man and the Sea* (1952), the old fisherman Santiago proves his mettle by bringing in an immense marlin. In *A River Runs Through It,* Norman and his brother Paul go fishing to get away from the troubles of their family, but they also see in fishing a way to prove their manhood. In the novella, fishing serves as a point of struggle between men and the environment. They earn their right to identify with the landscape by proving themselves tough enough to stand up to it.

In this way Maclean shows his affinity with other Western Realistic novelists such as H. L. Davis, James Stevens, Ken Kesey, and Ivan Doig. Like them, Maclean gained his understanding and appreciation of the wilderness by working within it. As a result, the stories in his collection exhibit an adversarial relationship with nature, with characters earning their identification with place not by surrendering themselves to it but by engaging themselves with it.

This is the case with Norman and his brother Paul's attitude toward the surrounding country. They count themselves tough at least partly because they are the products of this tough country and this especially tough river. The Big Blackfoot River is no meandering brook:

> It isn't the biggest river we fished, but it is the most powerful, and pound per pound, so are its fish. It runs straight and hard—on a map or from an airplane it is almost a straight line running due west from its headwaters at Rogers Pass on the Continental Divide to Bonner, Montana, where it empties into the South Fork of the Clark Fork of the Columbia. It runs hard the whole way. *(Maclean 1976, 12)*

In contrast to some of the earlier Realistic writers, Maclean seeks a deep sense of oneness with the landscape. But he suggests that this sense of connection comes by struggling with the country. By working to outwit the wild and discriminating trout of the Big Blackfoot River, Norman and Paul earn their sense of identification with landscape.

This sense of connection with landscape is achieved through fly-fishing. More than just a sport or pastime, it is a kind of religion of nature, a ritual through which humans are reconciled to each other and the world around them. From the very first line of the novella,

Maclean makes this obvious: "In our family, there was no clear line between religion and fly fishing" (1).

Fly-fishing attempts to bridge the gap between humans and the natural world, but it does not always succeed. The relation between people and place always remains vulnerable to a principle of disarray. Maclean sees this as fundamental to the human condition. He cites his father's belief in original sin as an explanation for why it occurs. "As a Scot and a Presbyterian, my father believed that man by nature was a mess and had fallen from an original state of grace" (2).

Modern civilization is not the problem; human nature is. As a consequence, man must struggle to regain this sense of grace and perfection. This is especially the case with fly-fishing, one of the most artful and difficult ways of catching fish, but one that mirrors the metaphysical world and thereby holds out the hope of reestablishing an ideal relationship with landscape. "As for my father, I never knew whether he believed God was a mathematician but he certainly believed God could count and that only by picking up God's rhythms were we able to regain power and beauty" (2).

Norman and Paul follow their father's example in seeking to pick up these rhythms through fly-fishing, and thereby achieve a sense of unity with landscape and family. As Maclean says of himself: "Something within fishermen tries to make fishing into a world perfect and apart—I don't know what it is or where, because sometimes it is in my arms and sometimes in my throat and sometimes nowhere in particular except somewhere deep" (37).

The novella is organized around five fishing trips. On each of these trips, Norman seeks this sense of unity with place and family, but he only partly achieves it. On the first of these trips, Norman falls far short of perfection. He catches one big trout, thereby achieving some measure of harmony with the river, but he remains alienated from his brother. Paul may be a genius with a fly rod, but he is also a drinker, a fighter, and a gambler, and his behavior has landed him in jail. Norman understands that his brother needs help, but does not know how to help him.

On the second of these trips, Norman comes a bit closer to perfection, at least with regard to his brother. Norman manages to talk to Paul about his problems and even offers to help him with money. Paul doesn't respond directly, but appreciates Norman's efforts. Norman feels reconciled with his brother, though not with the river, as he does not catch many fish.

On the third trip, Norman attains a sense of unity with the river, but not with his family. His brother-in-law, Neal, invites himself and Rawhide, a woman he picked up in a bar, along with Norman and Paul, thus violating the family code against bringing women fishing. Norman and Paul simply leave the two of them to their bait fishing and go off fly-fishing. After catching several large trout, Norman takes a break from casting and sits down to watch the river and forget the difficulties of his family:

> I sat there and forgot and forgot, until what remained was the river that went by and I who watched. On the river the heat mirages danced with each other and then they danced through each other and then they joined hands and danced around each other. Eventually the watcher joined the river, and then there was only one of us. I believe it was the river. (61)

Norman achieves a sense of oneness with the river, but only by blocking out the problems with his family. This sense of harmony is shattered when he and his brother discover that Neal has not been fishing but instead has been having intercourse with Rawhide on a sandbar. Both Norman and Paul are furious at this violation of their family river, but they take their anger out not on Neal, who is protected by their mother-in-law, but on Rawhide, kicking her as she gets out of the car after the trip. Thus family problems blot out any sense of perfection Norman might have achieved.

On his fourth fishing trip, Norman finally achieves a sense of unity with family and nature that he has long sought. Norman easily outfishes his brother on the first large hole. He does so well that he receives the rock treatment: Paul tosses several rocks into the pool so that Norman cannot catch anymore fish. Rather than getting angry, Norman considers this the highest compliment, since he seldom can outfish his brother. On the following hole, Paul regains his form and hooks many more fish than Norman. He refuses to gloat, however, and comes back across the river to tell Norman what fly to use. With Paul's advice, Norman is then able to continue catching fish. Thus Norman achieves a perfect sense of unity; he feels at peace with his family and at peace with God's creation. The trickiness and difficulty of this achievement make the moment stand out. "So on this wonderful afternoon when all things came together it took me one cast, one fish, and some reluctantly accepted advice to attain perfection" (88).

He has long sought this experience of oneness with his family and creation and finally attains it in this shining moment. The rest of the novella prepares for this transcendent scene. This experience of perfection stands outside time and gives him an intimation of eternity. As he says: "Poets talk about 'spots of time' but it is really fishermen who experience eternity compressed into a moment" (44).

But in a fallen world, such moments of perfection are impossible to sustain and sometimes they are even followed by tragedy. Such is the case for the Maclean clan. Shortly after the fishing trip, the police find Paul in an alley, beaten to death with a gun butt, with no explanation as to the cause or perpetrator of the crime. Though Paul's death profoundly shocks Norman and the rest of his family, it takes nothing away from the reality of their last fishing trip together. Instead, it sets off by contrast that wonderful trip and makes it seem even more luminous.

This scene serves as a good example of the narrative method that Maclean employs throughout the novella. All of the story's major scenes operate by contrast: the climactic moment is accompanied by its opposite; tragedy closely shadows any triumph. In this, Maclean's work shows the influence of the great Shakespearean tragedies such as *King Lear* or *Hamlet*.

For both Maclean and Shakespeare, such an approach is more than simply a formal device. It also suggests a vision of life that comprehends both the tragic and the transcendent and demonstrates that these two categories can be reconciled into a deeper sense of union.

In the final scene, the narrator fishes the Big Blackfoot River as an old man and experiences an even deeper sense of perfection than he felt on his final fishing trip with his father and Paul. His vision of life at the book's end comprehends not only that final transcendent fishing trip but also Paul's tragic death, which has taken him most of his life to come to terms with. Norman now feels both a oneness with creation and oneness with the fallen nature of the human condition:

> Eventually, all things merge into one, and a river runs through it. The river was cut by the world's great flood and runs over rocks from the basement of time. On some of the rocks are timeless raindrops. Under the rocks are the words, and some of the words are theirs. *(104)*

All of the events and memories of his past life merge together in this one moment and join with the waters of the Big Blackfoot River to connect up with all of creation. The words of his brother and father are gathered with those of the Gospel to underlie this creation and also animate it, making it possible for Norman to achieve the deepest sense of perfection.

The book's final line, "I am haunted by waters" (104), reinforces this sense. This line serves notice that Norman has assimilated the outer landscape of the Big Blackfoot River into his inner landscape. He uses the term "haunted" to suggest that this experience of oneness with the river and with his family includes both a sense of transcendence and a sense of tragedy. This double vision allows him to achieve reconciliation with the river, his family, and the fallen but numinous world.

In carefully depicting the struggles between the people and landscape of the Northwest, Maclean follows the lead of other Realistic writers, but in showing how such a struggle makes possible a union with place, he points the way toward works of contemporary ecological fiction. *A River Runs Through It* suggests how a sense of the spiritual dimensions of landscape makes possible dignified relationships with the land, family, and human society.

IVAN DOIG

The landscape of western Montana occupies center stage throughout the stories of Ivan Doig. From the early memoir *This House of Sky:*

Landscapes of a Western Mind (1978) to the fictional series *English Creek* (1984), *Dancing at the Rascal Fair* (1987), *Ride with Me, Mariah Montana* (1990), and *Mountain Time* (1999), and the novel *Bucking the Sun* (1996), his characters act out their lives as much in relation to the landscape as in relation to each other:

> You can't be around that landscape without it being on your mind. The weather governed our lives on the ranch, often determined whether the entire year was a success or not. Our lives turned on the weather, in combination with the landscape. This carries over into my writing. (O'Connell 1998, 332)

Like the other authors discussed in this chapter, Doig approaches the subject of landscape through the conventions of Realistic and naturalistic fiction. His emphasis on accuracy of description differs markedly from what he calls the "Cowboy myth," the Romantic, exaggerated view of the West that prevailed in Romantic literature and dime novels and still appears in popular fiction like that of Louis L'Amour. In revising this Romantic view of the West, Doig follows in the footsteps of other Realistic Western writers.

But if Doig shares many of the attitudes and approaches of these Realistic writers, he differs from them in significant ways. Doig belongs to a succeeding generation of Realistic Western writers, a generation that includes Norman Maclean and essayists William Kittredge (*Hole in the Sky: A Memoir* 1992), Mary Clearman-Blew (*All But the Waltz: Essays on a Montana Family* 1991), and Judy Blunt (*Breaking Clean* 2002). For him and most of this generation, the story of the settlement of the land gives way to the story of the Western diaspora. Much of his best works describe not the settlement but the leaving of the land.

In this he shows himself to be a transitional figure in Western writing. His works serve as a bridge between writers in the Realistic tradition and those of the Northwest School and its contemporary exponents. Like the other authors within the Realistic tradition, Doig learned about the land by working with it and sometimes against it. He and his characters earned their right to identify with it by being tough enough to stand up to it.

But this earlier adversarial relationship with landscape gives way to one of emotional and even spiritual identification with it, a trait he shares with Norman Maclean as well as poets of the Northwest School. Doig's work combines realistic and tough-minded depictions of farming and ranching with an elegiac celebration of that life and of the Western landscape. His best works, such as *This House of Sky* and *English Creek*, contain some of the most moving evocations of Western rural life in contemporary American literature.

Doig has traveled great distances in his life. He was born in 1939 in White Sulphur Springs, Montana, and grew up in northern Montana along the Rocky Mountain Front, where many of his novels take place. In his early years, he worked as a cowboy, sheepherder, and farm- and ranch hand. Seeing the difficulty of making a living doing this, Doig became the first in his family to go to college. He attended Northwestern University in Chicago, where he obtained a bachelor of arts in journalism in 1961 and a master of science in journalism in 1962.

After graduating, Doig worked as a journalist in the Chicago area. After obtaining a Ph.D. in history at the University of Washington in 1969, he settled in Seattle and launched his career as a freelance writer. Though Doig has lived on the west side of the Cascades for almost thirty years and has set two of his books on the Northwest Coast, his imagination keeps returning to what he calls "the blue remembered hills" of northern Montana.

A low-key man not prone to exaggeration or excess in his life or his work, Doig characterizes himself as a hard-working writer who approaches his métier with the same emphasis on integrity and craftsmanship with which he approached ranching. Like other writers in the Realistic tradition, he is especially concerned with authenticity, which he sees as essential to good writing:

> It takes on a rightness in itself. I can't defend it financially. A lot of writers would not bother to defend it in terms of the time and energy it takes. But by God, you ought to do it right, it seems to me, even if it does take more time and energy. Nobody ever said this was going to be an easy business to be in. Some of this goes back to the people I

grew up around. There simply was a right way to build a haystack or fix a fence, in these people's minds— my dad among them. *(327–28)*

This combination of attention to detail combined with his pursuit of the highest standards of literary art has earned him an enthusiastic local and national audience. His stories are steeped in the soil of Western farm and ranch life, and yet are of the highest literary merit. He endured many lean years as a freelance writer before gaining national prominence with the memoir *This House of Sky*. The book was nominated for a Pulitzer Prize and allowed him to quit magazine freelancing and devote himself entirely to books.

This House of Sky follows the Doig family as they struggle to survive the forbidding landscape of the Mountain West. Though they feel great affection for the land, they also realize that it can quickly rob them of their livelihood. But if the landscape is harsh and indifferent, it also has a fragile and vulnerable side. One of the most persistent themes in the memoir is the need to treat the land with reverence and respect. Throughout the book, Doig reserves harsh criticism for those who ruin and despoil the land, especially for corporations that buy up failed farms and then exploit the land and those who work for them. As Elizabeth Simpson observes in her book *Earthlight, Wordfire: The Work of Ivan Doig:*

> Doig's disgust with the inequities of the leasing system, which favors large ranches over small homesteads, crackles through his books, appearing in *This House of Sky* as an occasional invective against Rankin, a rancher who pieced his holdings together out of failed homesteads, pastured too many animals on his land, worked his men too hard. The theme is developed more fully in the Montana Trilogy. *(Simpson 1992, 21–22)*

This theme figures prominently in his other works as well, including *Winter Brothers* (1980), a memoir of a winter spent in the Puget Sound region; *The Sea Runners* (1982), an adventure story; and his magnum opus, a fictional series about the McCaskills, a Scottish family whose lives parallel the settlement and diaspora of the American West:

The McCaskills make what a lot of America has made—a dramatic and often tragic circle to the land and from the land. They arrive with hope and take up a piece of the American earth as a homesteader. Then after a generation, two generations, sometimes three or four, they make the discovery that the land couldn't take that kind of habitation. *(Doig 1995)*

The McCaskill trilogy traces a quintessentially American story, the pattern of which lies deep in our national psyche. As Doig recounts the struggles of the McCaskill clan, he raises a number of larger questions about the American experience: How can people treat the land responsibly? What does it mean to be a good steward of the land?

Jick McCaskill, the main character in two of these novels, thinks hard about these issues and tries to find a way to address them. The first novel of the series, *English Creek,* describes his coming of age, a process that takes place as much in relation to the landscape as it does in relation to family and society. He proves his manhood by demonstrating himself competent to stand up to the country as well as by showing personal maturity and a capacity for leadership. His coming of age is guided by his mother and father, both of whom respect the land and encourage him to approach it in this way. One of the many strong female characters in Doig's fiction, Jick's mother, Beth, gives the Fourth of July speech in honor of Ben English, the settler after whom the creek was named:

There is much wrong with the world, and I suppose I am not known to be especially bashful about my list of those things. But I think it could not be more right that we honor in this valley a man who savvied the land and its livelihood, who honored the earth instead of merely coveting it. *(Doig 1984, 160)*

She contrasts Ben English's approach with that of corporate farmer Wendell Williamson, who buys up failed farms and exploits them and the men he hires to run them. These two opposing approaches to the land and its people appear throughout Doig's fiction. The conflict between them fuels much of the drama in the series, and characters are judged both by how they treat each other and by how they treat the land. Doig argues through Beth McCaskill and others that the land should be honored. One of the persistent themes in this book and in the rest of the series is the need to treat the land with care and respect, and not exploit or destroy it through greed, recklessness, or rapaciousness.

In Jick's coming of age, he undergoes the normal adolescent experiences of tasting whiskey for the first time, feeling the pleasures and sharp pangs of sexuality, and assuming adult responsibilities. But in addition, he learns to treat the land with respect and even reverence. It is not just the background for these experiences, but the foreground as well.

This attitude is carried over to *Ride with Me, Mariah Montana*, the third book of the series, where Jick appears as an older man retired from his ranch. While the intervening book, *Dancing at the Rascal Fair*, goes back in time to treat his parents' settling of Montana, *Ride with Me* moves to the contemporary scene to dramatize the leaving of the land. The book takes place in 1989, the year of Montana's centennial celebration.

After the death of his wife, Jick leases his farm, buys a Winnebago, and travels around Montana at his leisure. This pattern ends abruptly when his daughter Mariah convinces him to allow her and her former husband, Riley, to travel with him. *Ride with Me* is a picaresque novel that follows their journey. The threesome crisscross the state, with Mariah taking photographs and Riley writing stories about the centennial for the *Montanian* newspaper.

While Mariah and Riley work on their centennial series, Jick ponders what to do with his ranch. His daughter Mariah has no interest in ranching, so he sees no point in passing it down to her. He refuses to sell it to the Double W corporation that has been buying up farms and ranches all around him because he knows that they will exploit the land. He'd like to sell it to someone who would take care of it properly, but no such buyer emerges.

The reader occasionally gets glimpses of Jick's mental process as he struggles with his decision, but the nature of that decision is not disclosed until the end of the book. Doig sets up a nice parallel between this novel and *English Creek* by having Jick give the centennial speech on the Fourth of July in Gros Ventre. He follows in the footsteps of his mother by emphasizing the importance of the land and the need to treat it properly. In the course of the speech, he reveals his decision about the ranch. He will sell it to The Nature Conservancy, an organization that will protect it as a sanctuary for buffalo and wild grassland. Of this decision he says:

> I guess I see this as giving back to the earth some of the footing it has given to me and mine. . . . If we McCaskills no longer will be on that particular ground, at least the family of existence will possess it. That kind of lineage needs fostering too, I've come to think—our kinship with the land. *(Doig 1990, 314)*

With this decision, Jick manages to sell his property and ensure that it will be cared for properly. The decision reveals his love for the land and his desire to see it preserved. In this he follows the rest of his family in taking seriously the stewardship of the land, even when that stewardship involves taking leave of it.

Through Jick and other characters in his work, Doig demonstrates himself to be a principled and tough-minded conscience for the American West. Having come to know the region through working it as a farm- and ranch hand, he knows both its intractability and vulnerability. It's a big country but it still needs care and protection. Though much of Doig's work takes place in rural Montana, his stories have implications for the rest of the Northwest.

Doig's experience as a farm- and ranch hand as well as his passion for accuracy give his work a hard-edged realism similar to that of writers like H. L. Davis, Ken Kesey, and Betty MacDonald. But like Norman Maclean, he goes one step further. He sees the process of working the land as a means of creating kinship with it. The adversarial relationship with landscape gives way to one of respect and identification. In this way, his work resembles that of the poets of the Northwest School, who chose different means but similar ends to achieve kinship and identity with the region's landscape.

5 / The Northwest School

David Wagoner was walking along the Hoh River Road when it happened. The lush undergrowth, hanging moss, and immense cedars overwhelmed him. He had never seen anything like it before. The unbelievable greenness bewildered and beckoned him. He left the road and entered the forest.

He walked over moss as soft as shag carpet, logs as hollow and brittle as old bones, soil as dark and protean as something from the dawn of the world. He went deeper into the woods, examining nurse logs, bands of lichen, and bushes full of berries. When he looked up to get his bearings, he could no longer see the road. He was lost in a rain forest, with no idea of how to find his way out.

Nothing in his Midwestern upbringing had prepared him for this. "Where is the road?" he wondered. "How will I find the car?"

He tried to retrace his footsteps, searching in vain for some sign of his passage. He parted curtains of devil's club, sword fern, and vine maple. Each patch of forest looked like the last. Nature, which had seemed so gentle and docile before, now seemed dangerous and indifferent to him. Fear knotted his stomach. He plunged into another thicket, unsure of where he was heading.

When he finally stumbled onto the road a half hour later, something in him had changed. He no longer thought of nature as a passive backdrop, but a real presence, a kind of reference point that could help him stay found in other areas of his life. Wagoner wrote of the experience in the poem "Staying Found":

> He was no longer lost in the woods
> Or in cities as he had always been,
> Not knowing it. Now, he would stay found.
> *(Wagoner 1987, 125)*

This was a decisive moment for him, a true turning point. It marked the end of his life as a Midwesterner, and the beginning of his life as a Northwesterner. It strengthened his allegiance to the Northwest School, a celebrated group of poets who found their identity as much in nature as in society. Carolyn Kizer wrote of the school in the July 16, 1956, issue of *The New Republic:*

> In this same rainy, misty area, on which the sun never (or almost never) rises, with a climate tempered by the Japanese current and protecting mountains, with living traces of pioneer and Indian days, with a State University whose recent fame rests on its denial of a platform to J. Robert Oppenheimer and its football scandals, where anything resembling night-club or cafe life is almost unknown, a new Pacific school of poets is emerging. *(Kizer 1956)*

This new Pacific school of poets would come to transform not only Northwest literature, but American literature as well. For a time in the late '50s and early '60s, the center of American poetry moved West, to the University of Washington campus, where a transplanted Midwesterner named Theodore Roethke composed some of the most important poems of modern American literature and taught the craft of poetry to many of the nation's most promising young poets, including David Wagoner.

Through his writing and teaching, Roethke brought national renown to himself and the university's poetry program, but more than that, he succeeded in raising the level of the region's literature. During his tenure at the University of Washington, there occurred a creative flowering that changed and matured Northwest literature. His example profoundly influenced a number of Northwest poets including Richard Hugo, Carolyn Kizer, David Wagoner, Tess Gallagher, James Mitsui, Madeline DeFrees, and Nelson and Beth Bentley.

The ripple effect of Roethke's influence continues to the present. The reputation of the university as a center of poetry drew Linda Bierds, Richard Kenney, Heather McHugh, Colleen McElroy, and many other talented poets and writers to the program. The strength and persistence of his influence makes him one of the most important figures in the region's literature.

Roethke's influence on Northwest poetry extends beyond his students to other poets throughout the region, whether they welcomed that influence or not. Roethke's achievement put the region on the nation's literary map, ensuring consideration for poets who had often been marginalized as being merely "regional." But if they benefited from his prestige and popularity, they often bridled at the limitations of what came to be called the Northwest School. When Roy Carlson asked to include Sandra McPherson's poems in his anthology *Contemporary Northwest Writing,* she shot back: "I hope the book isn't going to be full of clams and salmon and all that" (Carlson 1979, 7). Others like Mary Barnard, Vern Rutsala, Kenneth O. Hanson, William Stafford, Judith Barrington, Earle Birney, Robert Wrigley, and John Haines had to distinguish themselves from the Northwest School so as to put their own distinctive stamp on the region's poetry. The effort required to emerge from Roethke's shadow demonstrates the strength of his influence.

THEODORE ROETHKE

In discussing Roethke, it's useful first to call attention to his intense love of the natural world and to emphasize the important part this played in his personal and poetical development. As he wrote in an essay for a class in English composition at the University of Michigan:

> I have a genuine love of nature. It is not the least bit affected, but an integral and powerful part of my life. I know that Cooper is a fraud—that he doesn't give a true sense of the sublimity of American scenery.

I know that Muir and Thoreau and Burroughs speak the truth. *(Roethke 1965d, 4)*

This love of nature became one of the hallmarks of his poetry. Throughout his work, he celebrates the natural world in all its vibrancy and diversity. Although his poetry treats many subjects, it addresses itself above all to the question of the appropriate relation between the individual and natural world.

In this thematic concern, Roethke demonstrates his affinity with many of his literary predecessors in the Northwest, including the Northwest Coast Indians, explorers, settlers, Romantic writers like Joaquin Miller, and Realistic authors such as H. L. Davis. All of these authors defined themselves in relation to the environment. Roethke shared these concerns, but approached them differently. Like the Romantic writers, he sought a spiritual relationship with the landscape, but he employed a means of achieving this as exacting as that of the Realistic writers. While he came to know the land as carefully and precisely as many naturalistic and Realistic writers, his method was not through work and physical struggle, but through a meditation that yielded a mystical connection with it.

In opposition to the attitude of struggle with the land, which characterized the approach of Realistic writers like Norman Maclean in *A River Runs Through It,* Roethke elaborated a spiritual relationship between people and place based on merging of the self with the environment, bringing man and nature together into a distinct, organic whole. He saw the environment not as something to measure himself against, but as something within which he could find himself. He believed that human nature found its fullest expression when seen as a part of nature, not as separate and alienated from it. His poetry represents a search for a unity of humans and nature, a unity that he finally achieved and gave expression to in the "North American Sequence" of *The Far Field* (1965).

Roethke's love of the natural world started early. He was born in 1908 in Saginaw, a small town in central Michigan surrounded by sugar beet farms and second-growth timber. Roethke's grandfather, William Roethke, had moved to the area in 1872 from Prussia, where he had been Bismark's chief forester. William bought twenty-two acres in West Saginaw and started a market garden, which furnished fruits and vegetables during the area's lumber boom. The business grew with the town, and eventually he was able to build a big greenhouse on the property and raise flowers. He called his business the William Roethke Greenhouses, and through his perseverance and dedication the enterprise flourished (Seager 1975, 9–12).

When he retired, his sons Charles and Otto took over the greenhouse. Charles kept track of the business side of things, while Otto, Theodore Roethke's father, devoted himself to the plants. He spent his days watering, clipping, pruning, and tending the carnations, roses, orchids, poinsettias, and other flowers that thrived in the hothouse environment.

Otto's son, Theodore, spent most of his early life around the greenhouse. Some of Roethke's earliest memories concern it and the plants and flowers within. As he says of his childhood:

It was a wonderful place for a child to grow up in and around. There were not only twenty five acres in the town, mostly under glass and intensively cultivated, but farther out in the country the last stand of virgin timber in the Saginaw Valley and, elsewhere, a wild area of cut-over second-growth timber, which my father and uncle made into a small game preserve. *(Roethke 1965a, 8)*

Given these surroundings and his family's horticultural background, it is not surprising that Roethke came to identify strongly with growing things, but he preferred the wild, uncultivated landscape to nature under glass in the greenhouse. Despite his appreciation of the wonderful flowers that grew inside the artificial environment, he never felt at ease with the effort to exploit and control nature. For Roethke, the greenhouse became a symbol of mankind's dominance of nature.

They [the greenhouses] were to me, I realize now, both heaven and hell, a kind of tropics created in the savage climate of Michigan, where austere German-Americans turned their love of order and their terrifying efficiency into something truly beautiful. *(8)*

Although Roethke loved the hothouse flowers, he felt ambivalent about the methods of cultivating them and the ends toward which they were grown. For if the greenhouse was a kind of Eden, it was one created and maintained for business, commerce, and profit. Roethke rebelled against such mercenary goals, and sought a more spiritual relation with nature. His ambivalence about greenhouses was reflected in his attitude toward his father, whom the young boy seems to have both loved and feared. Many of Roethke's poems, especially those in *The Lost Son* (1948), treat the mixture of terror and anguish and affection with which he regarded his father:

> You beat time on my head
> With a palm caked hard by dirt,
> Then waltzed me off to bed
> Still clinging to your shirt.
> *(Roethke 1975, 43)*

This ambivalence toward his father continued throughout most of his childhood; he seldom felt he could measure up to his father's expectations of him. While other boys might have shrugged this off, Roethke proved an unusually sensitive young man; slights that others might have ignored rankled him. These tensions might have been resolved in Roethke's adulthood, but his father's death in 1923— Roethke was fifteen at the time—prevented this resolution. He never had the chance to win his father's approval:

> For a while every boy's father is a god to him. Then, slowly, as the boy makes his own discoveries, he dwindles to a man. . . . Otto Roethke died when he was still the untainted source of power, love and the lightnings of his anger. *(Seager 1975, 43)*

Otto Roethke's death seemed to freeze his image in time, making it difficult for Theodore to come to terms with his father. Thereafter, Roethke grew more serious, more thoughtful, and eventually turned to poetry to help him understand his father. Throughout his poetry, he seems to be searching for Otto's acceptance, yearning for a resolution to their relationship.

Roethke's first step in coming to terms with his father was, paradoxically, rebelling against him, especially the Prussian zeal for order and efficiency that had characterized his father's approach to the greenhouse business and the objectification of nature that this implied. Theodore instead sought to treat nature as a subject rather than an object. This was a natural and inevitable move for him, as he suspected from an early age that nature was animate and that it stood for something greater than itself. Rather than seeing nature as an object and exploiting it for profit as his father had done, he wanted to appreciate it aesthetically, and above all spiritually, as the ground of our being and as the embodiment of God.

> Everything that lives is holy. . . . One could even put this theologically: St. Thomas says, "God is above all things by the excellence of his nature; nevertheless, He is in all things as causing the being of all things. (Roethke 1965e, 24)

The poet applied this view to nature, and came to see a divine presence primarily in living, growing things. After describing the uprooting of a piece of moss in the poem "Moss Gathering," Roethke laments:

> And afterwards I always felt mean, jogging back over the logging road,
> As if I had broken the natural order of things in that swampland;
> Disturbed some rhythm, old and of vast importance,
> By pulling off flesh from the living planet. . . .
> (Roethke 1975, 38)

The more closely Roethke studied nature, the more completely it came alive for him. In contrast to his father, who saw nature as something to be molded and controlled, Roethke sought not to impose his will on it, but to yield to its impositions. Its very resistance impressed and pleased him most. As he wrote in "Long Live the Weeds":

Long live the weeds that overwhelm
My narrow vegetable realm!
The bitter rock, the barren soil
That force the son of man to toil. . . . *(17)*

Here, it is the uncultivated plants, the "rough, the wicked and the wild" that keep the spirit alive. Though this poem is accomplished, it demonstrates a common problem in his early poetry; here Roethke hasn't fully apprehended and described nature in all its nuances. The above poem, though well crafted, is essentially a conventional lyric. It praises the unruliness of the weeds, but doesn't express this spirit in its language. There's no specificity here. Were these weeds dandelions or thistles? The poet doesn't tell us. The poem is based on concepts— "The rough, the wicked and the wild"—not on concrete objects. The poet goes on to say:

With these I match my little wit
And earn the right to stand or sit,
Hope, love, create, or drink and die:
These shape the creature that is I. *(17)*

In this way he ties the poem up in a clever rhymed package, but fails to express the nature of the weeds or what they have to teach him. This poem is as neat, tidy, and controlled as a French garden, not as random and unkept as a weed patch. Though wild nature is held up as the ideal, the form of the poem does not dramatize its wildness. The structure does not match the meaning. The sound does not match the sense.

Choosing a form like the sonnet for the subject of weeds handicaps his project from the start. In following this form, he is forced to strain his diction and alter his syntax so that the sentences will conform to the requirements of the sonnet. The sentence "These shape the creature that is I" may fit nicely with the rhythm and rhyme scheme, but it makes the poem appear artificial and contrived, not at all the way one would think a poet inspired by nature would express himself.

Roethke still needed more contact with wild nature before he could fully appreciate it and incorporate it into his poetry. Like Thoreau, who had to spend a year at Walden Pond before he could begin to understand the sublimity of American scenery, Roethke had to do his apprenticeship in the woods, marshes, and waterways before he could give voice to their wildness.

That apprenticeship began when Roethke moved to Seattle in 1947. After obtaining his bachelor of arts from the University of Michigan in 1929 and a master of arts from Harvard in 1931, Roethke taught at several East Coast colleges such as Bennington and University of Pennsylvania. But he had a hankering to see the West Coast, and when the University of Washington offered him a teaching job, he took it.

Although Roethke generally seemed pleased with the region, he didn't take to the city of Seattle immediately. Shortly after arriving, he wrote to some friends, "The town is the worst bore in the U.S.: not a decent restaurant, nothing but beauty parlors and 'smart' shops and toothy dames with zinc curls" (Mills 1968, 172).

If he disliked the city, he fell in love with the local landscape:

> The campus is a riot of wonderful natural life—as well as new buildings and old. There is no need to barber and pamper the landscape; everything grows green and strange—the rhododendron, holly, hawthorne, horse chestnut, pink and white dogwood, Japanese cherry, Scotch broom, and the ever-present evergreens. Even the stones and sides of trees bear a fine mossy sheen. In one corner of the University area, across from a block of apartments, is a rich thicket, dripping and dense, mossy and dark. At the other end rise the usual frightening monoliths to science; but somehow you feel that the natural—and the human—worlds are not going to be overwhelmed. *(Seager 1975, 173)*

The lushness of the region's vegetation impressed him immediately, but it took a while for its influence to affect his poetry. In the meantime, Roethke continued to explore such themes as his early life in Michigan and his relationship with his father. When he wasn't writing, he was teaching, and he proved a brilliant, if eccentric, professor.

Faculty and students at the UW in those days got used to seeing Roethke shuffling around the campus, singing tunelessly, his pockets stuffed with scraps of paper, random notes he would eventually turn into poems. His secretary Gloria Campbell describes him in the following manner:

> I never addressed him by other than Mr. Roethke although I thought of him as the lumbering bear. . . . His hulking body resembled a huge beast. He walked forward on his feet, head down, long arms dangling. He seemed to have a disrapport with his body. It always amazed me to think that he played tennis, but I was told by some who had seen him on the court that Roethke was an aggressive and skilled player. *(Broughton 1975, 77)*

Roethke stood six feet, two inches tall, and weighed 220 pounds, this bulk maintained at least partly by a diet of thick steaks and imported beer. There was simply a lot of him, in every way. As he once said of himself, "I may look like a beer salesman, but I'm a poet."

This most unlikely looking of poets turned out to be "an absolutely incandescent teacher," according to Carolyn Kizer (O'Connell 1998, 116). Students from all over the country flocked to the University of Washington to do their apprenticeship under the great man. A number of poets who studied with Roethke became renowned in their own right, including Pulitzer Prize winners Kizer and James Wright. Rather than teaching them to imitate his style, he insisted that they develop their own. As Kizer points out:

> One of the great things that Ted did was to keep any of us from imitating him. If we tried, he would mock us and tease us so mercilessly that we never tried that again. . . . But if you think of those of us who studied with Ted, like [Richard] Hugo, Jim Wright, and David Wagoner and me, we don't write anything like him, and we don't write like each other. That is the hallmark of a really great teacher: to encourage you to find your own voice. *(101–18)*

But not all his students remembered him only with fondness. Richard Hugo had several run-ins with the temperamental Roethke:

He was such an outrageous and sometimes insufferable person that I sort of got the impression that since I was outrageous and insufferable, too, that if this man with all the things that were plaguing him, all the terrible troubles he had, the agonies that he went through, that if he could like himself well enough to create something beautiful out of this, that there was hope for me. He liked me, I think, probably as much or better than I liked him. I found myself being very angry at him sometimes. But when he died and I was walking into the Boeing Company out at Renton and I read about his death in the paper, I literally fell against the fence. I realized that he had meant a lot more to me than I had ever admitted to myself. . . . *(Broughton 1975, 42)*

Roethke may have been insufferable at times, but he also made an important difference in the careers of many of his students. In his celebration of nature, he particularly influenced David Wagoner, Richard Hugo, and Nelson Bentley. And even if his students didn't share his affinity with nature, they learned from his care with punctuation, the strong rhythm of his poetry, and his dedication to craft. A number of his students became teachers, and they in turn shaped the next generation of poets, causing a ripple effect that insured that Roethke's influence would continue into future generations.

In addition to excelling as a teacher, Roethke also proved a superb reader. He electrified audiences with interpretations of his own and other poets' work. He prided himself on this talent, and worked hard to perfect it. In his emphasis on the oral dimension of poetry, he turned poetry readings into bravura performances, and helped paved the way for the many reading series that take place in Seattle today, including those at the University of Washington, the Elliott Bay Book Company, Red Sky Poetry Theater, Seattle Arts and Lectures, Richard Hugo House, and other venues.

Shortly after he arrived at the University of Washington, he began to receive what would prove to be a long string of distinguished literary awards, including the Pulitzer Prize in 1953 for *The Waking*. Carolyn Kizer remembered Roethke's reaction to the prize:

I was in the classroom when Ted got called out. He came back a few minutes later looking rather odd, and tried to pick up the thread of the talk he was giving. Then he stopped dead and said, "I've just won the Pulitzer." We all leapt to our feet, screamed and hugged each other and jumped up and down. *(O'Connell 1998, 116)*

Many other prizes followed. He won the National Book Award in 1958 for *Words for the Wind* and in 1965 for *The Far Field*. The awards fulfilled some of his need for acceptance and secured his reputation as one of the most influential poets of his age.

With his career thus established, he gave up bachelorhood for marriage. On a trip to New York City in December 1952, Roethke ran into a former student, Beatrice O'Connell. In the course of his stay there, they became reacquainted. One night Beatrice invited him over to her apartment for dinner:

She had some steaks which she thought were quite nice but Ted was not impressed—they weren't thick enough. After some drinks, Beatrice told him she had been in love with him since Bennington, thinking that Ted at forty-four was too ancient for serious consideration, but he surprised her by saying, "It's not too late now." After that they saw each other every day and it was accepted by them both that they were soon to be married. *(Seager 1975, 206)*

The wedding took place on January 3, 1953, in a chapel of St. James Episcopal Church on Madison Avenue. W. H. Auden served as best man and Louise Bogan was matron of honor. For the honeymoon, Auden offered the newlyweds his villa at Ischia. It was a gloriously romantic spot, situated on an island off the southern coast of Italy. The honeymoon didn't prove entirely idyllic, however:

It would seem to have been a pleasant time but it was only a few weeks after the wedding that Beatrice learned why he had married her—he wanted someone to take care of him. This, of course, is familiar. All the women who knew him well say that he liked someone to call him to meals, someone to have clean shirts and pajamas ready, someone to find lost articles, to buy tickets, pack, and remember train and plane times, someone to listen to poetry first, to talk to late at night, a woman to stave off loneliness. *(210)*

As Beatrice discovered, Ted was not an easy man to be married to. He demanded a lot of time and attention. The constant care took a toll on Beatrice, and in 1956 she contracted pulmonary tuberculosis. She entered Firlands Sanatorium in January 1957, and after several months of rest was discharged. To help her recuperate, she and Ted took short trips, including one to Vancouver Island where they stayed at a salmon fishing resort near Oyster River. It was here that Roethke received the mystical illumination that inspired the "North American Sequence."

Significantly, there is no mention of Beatrice, romantic love, or marriage in the poem. Instead, it treats a deepening relationship between a man and the natural world, and describes a journey out of narrow self-absorption into an imaginative and spiritual merging with nature. This merging resembles the process whereby someone loses the ego in the love of another, but the outcome is quite different. Instead of identification with another human being and the human world, the speaker instead finds his identity in relation to the whole fabric of life. As Roethke wrote in his essay "On Identity": "If the dead can come to our aid in a quest for identity, so can the living—and I mean all living things, including the subhuman" (Roethke 1965e, 24).

Throughout his life, Roethke believed that he could find a true sense of himself only by giving himself over to something larger. Roethke saw the human personality as achieving fulfillment not in isolation, but in relation to the other. He identifies himself not just with the ego, but with the imagination and spirit that allow him to transcend the ego and establish a relationship with the other. In the early poem "Open House," Roethke makes clear his view of the self: "Myself is what I wear / I keep the spirit spare" (Roethke 1975, 3). The "myself" in this poem does not stand for the ego, but encompasses many aspects of the human personality, as he notes in "On Identity":

I am not speaking of the empirical self, the fleshbound ego; it's a single word: myself, the aggregate of the several selves, if you will. The spirit

or soul—should we say the self, once perceived, becomes the soul
(Roethke 1965e, 21).

Fulfillment lies in identifying the self with the soul, not with the
fleshbound ego. Once the true nature of the self is perceived, then
the individual can see himself or herself in all the rest of the world,
because for Roethke the soul is not limited in the same way that the
ego is. It is this perception of the self as soul that allows individuals
to break out of a narrow conception of identity and see themselves
as part of the whole. "If you can effect this then you are by way of
getting somewhere: knowing you will break from self-involvement,
from I to otherwise, or maybe even to thee." (25)

This journey from "I" to otherwise can take place between husband and wife, parent and child, friend and friend, but Roethke seems
to have experienced it largely with regard to nature. It was his exploration of the relation between humans and environment that allowed
him to break through to a level of mystical illumination. This process
began with a careful examination of plant and animal life:

The ferns had their ways and the pulsing lizards,
And the new plants, still awkward in their soil,
The lovely diminutives.
I could watch! I could watch!
I saw the separateness of things.
(Roethke 1975, 60)

Rather than leading him to feel apart from things, this realization
of the distinctness of things allowed him to see himself clearly. By
focusing intently on nature, he came to understand himself as well,
as he writes in "On Identity":

It is paradoxical that a very sharp sense of the being, the identity of
some other being—and in some instances, even an inanimate thing—
brings a corresponding heightening and awareness of one's own self,
and, even more mysteriously, in some instances, of a feeling of oneness with the universe. *(Roethke 1965e, 26)*

In going out of the self to study the particularity of plants, animals, fish, and fowl, he was able to appreciate his own distinctiveness, but also his relation to them as well. In this he differed from Romantic writers who sought a quick, effortless merging of self and nature. Roethke did the hard work of learning to see the separate entities in their distinctiveness, which in turn paved the way toward achieving a mystic vision that sees that all as one.

Such intimations of the interconnectedness of life necessitated a change in the form of his poetry. Where his early work had drawn from the lyric tradition, he began to adopt a longer, looser line to communicate the all-embracing ecstasy of this vision, as he noted in "Some Remarks on Rhythm": "There are areas of experience in modern life that simply cannot be rendered by either the formal lyric or straight prose. We need the catalogue in our time" (Roethke 1965c, 82).

In developing this new style, he turned to Walt Whitman as a model. Like Adam in Genesis, Roethke reveled in naming the creatures of the new place. By learning and using their names, he established a relation with them, the first step toward merging the self with the local environment.

In the course of Roethke's journey from "I" to otherwise, the Northwest became increasingly important to him. Here was a region only slightly altered by human design, a place that still bore the stamp of original creation, an area where he could lose himself in the immensity of wild nature and achieve the transcendence he so desired. "My imagery is coming more out of the Northwest rather than the whole of America" (Seager 1975, 269).

It was in the Northwest that Roethke experienced his most complete visions of the unity and of man and nature. This was a vision for which he had worked, wept, and prayed, and that he sought to articulate in his poetry. He accomplished this in the "North American Sequence" of *The Far Field,* which the critic Kermit Vanderbilt praised as "the great achievement in Roethke's last book" (Vanderbilt 1979, 203).

The "North American Sequence" dramatizes his personal journey from "I" to otherwise in terms of a car trip Roethke made across the North American continent. In September 1950 he bought his first car on the East Coast and drove it cross-country back to Seattle. The journey impressed him deeply, for he got a chance to experience firsthand the extent of the continent. He writes in an unsent letter just afterward:

> Here I don't know just how the material will be resolved but the next or possibly a later book will be a happy journey westward—not along the Oregon Trail but on Route 2; in a word, a symbolical journey in my cheap Buick Special. *(Seager 1975, 193–4)*

The poem deepened as he worked on it, acquiring symbolic weight as it traced not only a geographic journey, but a personal and spiritual one as well. The "North American Sequence" begins in the grimy, industrial cities of the East and ends on a wilderness beach on the western edge of the continent. This geographic movement also implies a spiritual movement, from absorption in the ego and isolation from nature to transcendence of the ego and union with nature.

Whitman's poetry serves as an important influence in describing this ecstatic union of man and nature, but Roethke also drew heavily from T. S. Eliot's "The Wasteland" and the "Four Quartets." Roethke spent much of his life in Eliot's shadow, and though he resented Eliot's dominance of Anglo-American poetry (privately, he referred to Eliot as "Terrible Tom"), he also felt considerable affinity with him. Both poets came from the Midwest, both were deeply religious men, and both decried the spiritual impoverishment of the modern age. But that is where the resemblance ended. For if they agreed on the need for a surrender of the self, Eliot saw that surrender in terms of adopting a religious faith, whereas Roethke saw it in terms of a merging of the ego with nature.

Eliot found his solution to the impoverishment of the modern age by converting to the Church of England; Roethke found his by discovering a new identity within nature. If Eliot's work evinced a primarily Christian approach to salvation, Roethke's demonstrated a fundamentally animistic one, borrowing from Christian theology, Eastern philosophy, and Indian mythology to present a view of salvation as mystical union with nature, as integration within the context of all life, human and nonhuman.

Despite his disagreements with Eliot, Roethke found the form of "The Wasteland" and the "Four Quartets" helpful in mapping out his dramatic monologue. In structuring the "North American Sequence," Roethke combined features of both of Eliot's longer poems, using "The Wasteland" as the model for "The Longing," the first poem in the sequence. Like "The Wasteland," this section diagnoses the spiritual sterility of modern civilization. It opens by describing life in a large industrial city:

> The slag heaps fume at the edge of raw cities:
> The gulls wheel over their singular garbage;
> The great trees no longer shimmer;
> Not even the soot dances.
> (Roethke 1975, 181)

The degradation of the external world implies a degradation of the human spirit. Environment and the human spirit depend on each other; when the environment is poisoned, so too is human life:

> And the spirit fails to move forward,
> But shrinks into a half-life, less than itself,
> Falls back, a slug, a loose worm. . . . (181)

A view of the self that includes only the ego and leaves little or no room for the soul creates these kinds of conditions. In the face of this sterility, the speaker in the poem is moved to ask, "How to transcend this sensual emptiness?" The answer, for Roethke, is an enlarged vision of the self, a vision that includes not only the ego, but the soul as well.

In the second section of the poem, "Meditation at Oyster River," the speaker transcends the sensual emptiness by moving to the other end of the continent. This section takes place on the west coast of Vancouver Island, with the narrator employing a precise vocabulary to name the flora and fauna, much like that of naturalistic writers such as H. L. Davis who strove for accuracy in describing the region. In this close observation of the natural world, he begins to lose consciousness of his fleshbound ego:

Over the low, barnacled, elephant-colored rocks,
Come the first tide-ripples, moving, almost without sound, toward me,
Running along the narrow furrows of the shore, the rows of dead clam
 shells. . . . *(184)*

The narrator is careful to get the look, the feel, the sound of the world right. He wants to see it with clarity and distinctness, the first step in transcending the ego. He employs the catalogue to bring the particularity of the natural world into his poem. He has moved away from the vague language and tidy lyricism of early poems like "Long Live the Weeds." By inventorying the place, the speaker brings the outer world into his private world and begins to feel whole again:

In this hour,
In this first heaven of knowing,
The flesh takes on the pure poise of spirit
Acquires, for a time, the sandpiper's insouciance,
The hummingbird's surety, the kingfisher's cunning. . . . *(185)*

Seeing the distinctiveness of the world allows him to enter imaginatively into the landscape. He extends the self beyond the confines of his skin and skull and sees himself in the world around him.

In section III of the poem, "Journey to the Interior," the poem moves back into the heartland of the continent and describes the journey out of the self in terms of a car trip:

In the long journey out of the self,
There are many detours, washed-out interrupted raw places
Where the shale slides dangerously
And the back wheels hang almost over the edge
At the sudden veering, the moment of turning. *(187)*

This section reveals the narrator's vacillation, his uneasiness in giving up the illusion of the ego and accepting the unity of all life. But he doesn't turn back; he continues on the journey. In section IV, "The Long Waters," the speaker returns to the western shore, where he con-

tinues his examination of the natural world around him. The lines of
the poem lengthen in this section, suggesting an opening out of his
personality:

> These waves, in the sun, remind me of flowers:
> The lily's piercing white,
> The mottled tiger, best in the corner of a damp place,
> The heliotrope, veined like a fish, the persistent morning glory. . . . *(191)*

The lines of the poem expand and contract in accord with the attitude of the speaker. As he opens himself up to the world, the line grows
longer; as he gathers in and embraces what he has found, the line short-
ens. In the process of this expansion and contraction, the "I" grows
beyond the bounds of ego and becomes soul, and thus finds connection with the rest of creation:

> I, who came back from the depths laughing too loudly,
> Become another thing:
> My eyes extend beyond the furthest bloom of the waves;
> I am gathered together once more;
> I embrace the world. *(192)*

In section V, "The Far Field," the speaker, having experienced
identification with all of life, comes to terms with his own death, the
final extinguishing of the ego. The section opens with a dream involv-
ing a car trip on a long peninsula, ending when the automobile
becomes mired in the sand. This dream warns of his own death, which
occurred in August 1961, shortly after he composed the "North
American Sequence." In this section of the poem, Roethke accepts the
possibility of death: "I learned not to fear infinity / The far field, the
windy cliffs of forever" (194).

This acceptance is prepared for by his ability to identify himself
with all of creation, and so a return to it in death is not to be avoided,
but desired. Because he has come to terms with his own mortality,
the speaker sees the world for what it is: "All finite things reveal
infinitude" (195). Beneath the many surface colors, textures, and

movements, he sees that there is one substance, as he writes in "On Identity":

> The "oneness" is, of course, the first stage of mystical illumination, an experience many men have had, and still have: the sense that all is one and one is all. This is inevitably accompanied by a loss of the "I," the purely human ego, to another center, a sense of the absurdity, a return to a state of innocency. *(Roethke 1965e, 26)*

Having achieved this illumination, he is ready to complete the journey from "I" to otherwise in "The Rose," the final section in the "North American Sequence." In this section, the speaker no longer identifies with the ego, but with all of creation. He can look back on the ego and all that it stands for, and does not loathe it, but accepts it as beautiful, now that he is no longer confined within it. All the disappointments of his past life are eclipsed in the glory of this transcendent moment. He remembers the roses of his childhood, and the time when his father lifted him high over "the Mrs. Russells, and his own elaborate hybrids . . . " (Seager 1975, 197).

Roethke's discovery of the right relationship with nature enables him to reclaim his relationship with his father. One of his father's lasting legacies was this love of nature. Roethke recognized the strength of his father's love of plants, but he could not abide the quality of that love. He had to find his own expression of it before he could come to terms with his father's attitude toward nature. In mapping out and defining his own relationship to nature in the "North American Sequence" of *The Far Field*, he resolved his relationship with his father as well: "What need for heaven, then, / With that man, and those roses?" (Roethke 1965b, 197).

The rose is a recurring symbol in Roethke's poetry, standing for love, beauty, passion, and transcendence. It mediates between childhood and adulthood, with the roses in the greenhouse representing his childhood, and the wild rose in the sea wind representing adulthood and his appreciation of wild nature. This reconciliation of past and present paves the way for the completion of the journey, where "I" becomes otherwise, where the speaker and nature come together in mystical union and the speaker becomes whole again. "Near this rose, in this grove of sun-parched, wind-warped madronas, / Among the half-dead trees, I came upon the true ease of myself . . . " (199).

This windy headland near the mouth of the Oyster River on Vancouver Island, British Columbia, becomes important to the poet because in seeing its particularity, he has achieved a vision of the interconnectedness of all of life. This vision is made manifest in the image of the wild rose:

> And in this rose, this rose in the seawind,
> Rooted in stone, keeping the whole of light,
> Gathering to itself sound and silence—
> Mine and the seawind's. *(199)*

In much the same way that the lotus flower represents perfect enlightenment for Buddhists, the wild rose in the sea wind symbolizes perfect union with nature for Roethke, a union achieved through transcendence of the ego and identification with wild nature. Roethke gives fullest expression to this union in the "North American Sequence" of *The Far Field*, his most complete vision of what human life should be like on this continent.

RICHARD HUGO

Poets of the Northwest School often had to discover a place that personally resonated with them before they could come to identify with the natural world and use it effectively in their work. Roethke's student Richard Hugo referred to such a place as a "triggering subject," a locale that fired the poet's imagination and allowed him to unlock his own poetic voice. The outer geography of such a landscape usually mirrored in some way the inner geography of the poet's mind and heart. In writing about such a landscape, an author could free up his imagination and produce his best work. As Hugo put it: "I suspect the true or valid triggering subject is one in which physical characteristics or details correspond to attitudes the poet has toward the world and himself" (Hugo 1979b, 5).

Roethke found his triggering subject in the intertidal zone at the mouth of the Oyster River on Vancouver Island, British Columbia, but his students had to search elsewhere. Hugo discovered his early triggering subjects in the vacant lots and abandoned houses of Seattle's West Marginal Way. Many of his early poems describe this rundown neighborhood:

> West Marginal Way was a world outside the mainstream of city life, isolated and ignored. Once you left the heavily industrialized area at the Spokane Street Bridge and started upstream from Riverside toward Boeing Hill, West Marginal Way was, in those days, a curious combination of the industrial and the rural. A brickyard, a saw mill or sand and gravel company operated here and there. More often they were idle, abandoned beside the slow river. The street itself was an old worn concrete road with cracks and hunchings. Homes were mostly scattered, like remote farms, with wild thick lawns and roofs heavily mossed. I can't recall a mowed lawn or a kept yard, or even a defined one. It was as if the people had no concept of property. The natural took over, blackberry bushes, snakeweed, scotch broom. *(Hugo 1986, 14)*

For a poet obsessed by a sense of loss and defeat, West Marginal Way served as what T. S. Eliot called the "objective correlative" for Hugo's feelings about himself and the larger world. This area triggered his authentic poetic voice and resulted in some of his first published poems. Through the care of his eye and the quality of his attention, Hugo redeems the neglected neighborhood and, in the process, the wounded parts of himself as well.

Hugo was born in 1923, in White Center, a community in southwest Seattle not far from West Marginal Way. Shortly after he was born, his mother gave him to his grandparents to raise. This early separation from his parents contributed to a sense of loss and betrayal that haunted him the rest of his life. He endured a strict, emotionally frigid, and sometimes violent upbringing at the home of his grandparents, who had already raised five children of their own and didn't much appreciate the responsibility of raising another. To allay his feelings of estrangement and worthlessness, he turned first to baseball, a sport at which he excelled, and later to poetry.

From 1943 to 1945, Hugo served in the Army Air Corps in Europe. He flew thirty-five missions as a bombardier and received the Distinguished Flying Cross. After the war he returned to Seattle, where he enrolled at the University of Washington. He studied with Theodore Roethke while completing his bachelor of arts (1948) and went on to get a master of arts in English (1952) from the same institution.

After graduating, Hugo found work at the Boeing Company as a technical writer. He married Barbara Williams in 1952 and worked at Boeing until 1963, when the couple decided to move to Italy for a year. At the end of the year, Hugo got a job as a lecturer at the University of Montana, a move that eventually led to a tenure track teaching job and a literary career, but precipitated the couple's divorce. Hugo later married Ripley Schemm in 1974.

Hugo published his first book, *A Run of Jacks,* in 1961. He composed it over a ten-year period during which he gradually discovered his triggering subjects and developed his personal style. Writing about West Marginal Way and fishing proved the key to unlocking his poetic potential. In poems like "West Marginal Way," he enters imaginatively into the rundown neighborhood and assumes an identity through it:

> One tug pounds to haul an afternoon
> of logs up river. The shade
> of Pigeon Hill across the bulges
> in the concrete crawls on reeds
> in a short field, cools a pier
> and the violence of young men
> after cod. The crackpot chapel
> with a sign erased by rain, returned
> before to calm and a mossed roof.
> (Hugo 1979a, 5)

This poem not only sets a vivid scene, it also introduces a strong, distinctive narrative voice. The narrator speaks in a blunt, unsentimental, working-class manner, a manner that became his signature:

So you are after those words you can own and ways of putting them in phrases and lines that are yours by right of obsessive musical deed. You are trying to find and develop a way of writing that will be yours and will, as [William] Stafford puts it, generate things to say. Your triggering subjects are those that ignite your need for words. When you are honest to your feelings, that triggering town chooses you. *(Hugo 1979b, 15)*

Hugo found his triggering subjects not in the sunsets and mountains of the Romantic Northwest, but in the gritty details of a rundown neighborhood. In writing about this place, he developed the muscular, alliterative style that became his trademark. Though he may have felt awkward and uncertain in his personal life, he spoke authoritatively in his poetry.

Some places are forever afternoon.
Across the road and a short field
there is the river, split and yellow
and this far down affected by the tide.
(Hugo 1979a, 5)

The poem begins in a place of physical neglect but ends with the narrator overcoming the depressed mood of the place to the point that he can make confident declarations about it. The reader is left guessing about what "forever afternoon" exactly means, but emotionally the phrase rings true, allowing the poem to conclude strongly. In this and other poems such as "Duwamish," Hugo begins by describing the details of this neglected landscape and ends by transforming the landscape and himself through writing about it. As he explains it:

For me, that poem ["Duwamish"] illuminates my need to return again and again to West Marginal Way and the river for poems. I seem to relive my early personal sense of defeat out to some sort of poetic fulfillment. My assumed right to self-pity in my youth later became my license to write a poem. I could create something out of my past personal sense of futility in language hard enough to prohibit wallowing in melancholy. *(Hugo 1986, 17)*

Hugo avoids the trap of confessional poetry by airing his grievances obliquely and indirectly. Instead of addressing his personal and subjective sense of loss, he objectifies these feelings by finding the physical equivalent of them in rundown West Marginal Way, the objective correlative to his inner psychological state. This allows him to gain critical distance on such feelings, permitting him to write about them without sentimentality. Throughout his career, Hugo uses landscapes such as West Marginal Way as triggering subjects. Other Northwest locales like the Hoh and Skagit Rivers, Tahola, Duwamish Head, Port Townsend, Fort Casey, and Kapowsin serve this function in *Death of the Kapowsin Tavern* (1965). The small towns and landscapes of Italy evoke similar feelings of loss and neglect in *Good Luck in Cracked Italian* (1969), as do the ghost and mill towns of Montana in *The Lady in Kicking Horse Reservoir* (1973). As critic Donna Gerstenberger observes about Hugo's Montana poems:

> As was true of the Northwest coast poems, Hugo's preference is for the abandoned Montana scene which he can possess. The imagined scene is often cruel and harsh, whether the scene is Milltown or Silver Star, an abandoned ranch in Montana, or the graves at Elkhorn. The landscape is wider than it was in the state of Washington, the spaces between bars and towns greater; all in all, a more comfortable correlative for loneliness than the richly lush, overgrown, and forested Puget Sound Region. *(Gerstenberger 1983, 24)*

The most celebrated poem in *The Lady in Kicking Horse Reservoir,* "Degrees of Gray in Phillipsburg," follows a strategy similar to that of the early poems, but demonstrates poetic maturity:

> You might come here Sunday on a whim
> Say your life broke down. The last good kiss
> you had was years ago. You walk these streets
> laid out by the insane, past hotels

that didn't last, bars that did, the tortured try
of local drivers to accelerate their lives.
(Hugo 1979a, 109)

Having achieved a level of personal confidence and artistic control, Hugo is able to address his feelings directly in the poem and still
maintain perfect control over it. After describing the dilapidated town
of Phillipsburg, the narrator goes on to ask:

Isn't this your life? That ancient kiss
still burning out your eyes. Isn't this defeat
so accurate, the church bell simply seems
a pure announcement: ring and no one comes? *(109)*

By this time, Hugo had managed to exorcise many of the private
demons that had plagued him early in his career. Though he returns
to such rundown locales as Phillipsburg for poetic material, he has
managed to overcome the feelings of loss and neglect that they suggest. For this reason, the poem exhibits a confidence lacking in his
early work. The narrator objectifies his own sense of worthlessness
through describing the shabbiness of Phillipsburg. Through the
cathartic process of poetry, he uses the town to acknowledge and overcome his feelings of inadequacy and loss. By the end of the poem he
is able to resist the depressing hold that the town exerts over him. The
residents may be stuck there, but he is not:

The car that brought you here still runs.
The money you buy lunch with,
no matter where it's mined, is silver
and the girl who serves your food
is slender and her red hair lights the wall. *(110)*

For Hugo, Phillipsburg and West Marginal Way served as places
upon which he could project and overcome his feelings of personal
inadequacy. He chose such places for their emotional and psychological resonance rather than for his intimate familiarity with them.

In fact, he deliberately avoided knowing too much about such places, believing that this would limit his efforts to write about them:

> I'm aware of the dangers of locating poems in overly familiar territory. Too much memory remains to interfere with the imagination. I think the West Marginal Way I created was a place where I could melodramatically extend and exploit certain feelings I had about myself and ignore others that, had I tried to root my poems in White Center, would have gotten in the way. *(Hugo 1986, 17)*

Hugo's descriptions of places like West Marginal Way or Phillipsburg demonstrate a level of surface detail like that found in works of Realistic writers, but he is less interested in accurately depicting these places than in getting the emotional resonance of the place right. As he says:

> The poet's relation to the triggering subject should never be as strong as (must be weaker than) his relation to his words. The words should not serve the subject. The subject should serve the words. This may mean violating the facts. For example, if the poem needs the word "black" at some point and the grain elevator is yellow, the grain elevator may need to be black in the poem. You owe reality nothing and the truth about your feelings everything. *(Hugo 1979b, 6)*

Hugo usually got the details of a place right, but this was not his paramount concern. He sought instead emotional, intuitive possession of the place, an understanding of what the place could express in poetry. In this, he follows into the heart of Northwest landscape the Romantic writers who sought similar perception, but Hugo achieves it by means closer to that of the Realistic writers. He does not try to express the essence of a place through florid descriptions but through telling details that conjure up this spirit of place. In this, he borrows from the strengths of each tradition.

This became not just a poetic strategy, but a personal one as well. By identifying with exterior landscapes such as those of West Marginal Way, he enlarged his sense of self and brought resolution to his acute personal problems. As was the case with Roethke, the Northwest land-scape provided a place within which to heal and perfect himself. By identifying himself with landscapes that civilization had rejected, Hugo could rehabilitate and reclaim the compromised parts of himself, a crucial step in his larger quest for identity.

CAROLYN KIZER

In his introduction to the anthology *Five Poets of the Pacific Northwest,* Robin Skelton argues that the environment represents the most significant influence on Northwest poetry. While acknowledging that the region's poets speak in a range of voices, he observes that the land-scape profoundly affects all of their work:

> Although I have said that there are many different voices in the Northwest, I must also say that the poets have all been deeply affected by their physical environment. It is obvious that, in this area, the land-scape must have a powerful influence on the art created within it. Some poets have gone directly to the sea, the rivers, the forests, and the moun-tains for their imagery; others have avoided direct description; all, how-ever, appear to have had the sense of place imprinted on their sensibilities." *(Skelton 1964, xvi)*

The sense of place figures strongly in the work of all those included in the anthology—Kenneth O. Hanson, Richard Hugo, Carolyn Kizer, William Stafford, and David Wagoner—but each poet uses it distinctively. For Hugo and Wagoner, the physical environment and their relation to it became the central subject of their verse. Kizer, on the other hand, mines the landscape for imagery and metaphor that illustrate complexities of human relationships, her triggering subject. As she says of her work: "I am interested in character. That is my sub-ject" (O'Connell 1998, 124). She explores this infinitely rich topic as revealed in various stages of human development from birth, love, and marriage to old age and death, often using the Northwest envi-ronment to put the human world in perspective.

Kizer is a poet with strong regional roots. She was born in Spokane,

Washington, in 1925, and grew up in the area. She went east to Sarah Lawrence College, where she studied with Joseph Campbell and developed an interest in classical mythology. After obtaining her bachelor of arts degree in 1945, she did graduate work at Columbia University from 1945 to 1946 and the University of Washington from 1946 to 1947. She returned to graduate school at the University of Washington from 1953 to 1954 to study with Theodore Roethke.

In addition to her poetry, Kizer has exerted an important influence on the region's and nation's literature by founding and editing the journal *Poetry Northwest* (1959–1965), serving as the first director of literary programs at the National Endowment for the Arts (1966–1970). She has taught at a number of universities throughout the country, including University of North Carolina at Chapel Hill, University of Iowa, Stanford University, Princeton University, and Columbia University. She has received numerous awards for her poetry, including the Pulitzer Prize in 1985.

Although the balancing act proved difficult, Kizer managed to combine her professional career with a personal life as a wife and mother. She married Charles Stimson Bullitt in 1948 and had three children by him before the couple divorced in 1954. In 1975, she married the architect John M. Woodbridge.

The vicissitudes and conflicts of her early married life fueled much of her work and pushed her toward an overtly political poetry, for which she became known later on. Her early poems, however, draw extensively from the natural world. Her first book, *The Ungrateful Garden* (1961), bears the stamp of Roethke's influence. The poem "The Great Blue Heron" carries a strong, three-beat line, which was also typical of Roethke's work. She describes the bird literally and figuratively, choosing evocative details to paint a picture of the ungainly heron:

He wore a hunchback's coat.
Shadow without a shadow,
Hung on invisible wires
From the top of a canvas day,
What scissors cut him out? *(90)*

Where Roethke likely would continue describing the bird or relate his reaction to it, Kizer sees the heron as a harbinger of her mother's death. The natural world becomes a metaphor for the human world. Kizer treats landscape as a jumping-off point for her triggering subjects of friendship, love, and human relationships. The poem's narrator goes on to ask, "Heron, whose ghost are you?" and makes it clear that it is a reminder of her mother's death:

> Waiting upon the day
> When, like grey smoke, a vapor
> Floating into the sky,
> A handful of paper ashes,
> My mother would drift away. *(91)*

This evocative final image demonstrates Kizer's practice of mining the landscape of the Northwest for its imagery while focusing on interpersonal relations as her subject. She draws from a number of locales, especially those reminiscent of Asian poetry, to illustrate and enlarge these subjects.

Knock Upon Silence (1965), her second book, includes many poems based on Oriental models. In "A Month in Summer," for example, she borrows a Japanese model to express feelings about falling in and out of love. In this and other poems, nature figures both as analog to the vicissitudes of loves and as respite from them.

In the collections *Midnight Was My Cry: New and Selected Poems* (1971) and *Mermaids in the Basement: Poems for Women* (1984), Kizer increasingly addresses feminist topics, finding ingenious ways of bringing the nonhuman world to bear on them. For example, in part four of the long poem "Pro Femina," from *Mermaids in the Basement,* planting serves as a symbol of woman's fecundity. In this, the landscape serves not as subject, but as metaphor and illustration of character and human relationships, aiding her search for identity.

More recent work owes little to the Northwest. In the collections *Yin: New Poems* (1984), *The Nearness of You* (1986), and *Harping On* (1995), her voice often becomes abstract, overtly political, and in some cases polemical. When she does treat Northwest subjects, as in the poem "Running Away from Home," she seeks to bury the region, not to praise it. In this anti-Northwest diatribe, Kizer inventories the scars, blemishes, and illnesses of the region—"Most people from Idaho are crazed rednecks" (Kizer 1984b, 29), "Some people from Oregon are mad orphans" (30), "Some people from Washington State are great poetasters" (31). This strident attack on the region signals a deliberate separation from it. As if to put the final nail in the coffin, she says of the city where she grew up, "After Spokane, what horrors lurk in Hell?" (32).

Such attacks don't negate the importance of her early work in forming a regional aesthetic. Through her polished verse, evocative imagery, and use of Oriental poetic forms, she demonstrates how to make the Northwest a metaphor for interpersonal relationships and for the larger social world. In this, she expands the field of Northwest literature, highlighting the importance of human love and paving the way for Tess Gallagher, Sandra McPherson, Joan Swift, Jody Aliesan, Melinda Mueller, and others.

WILLIAM STAFFORD

Unlike Kizer and others associated with the Northwest School, William Stafford never studied with Theodore Roethke or fell directly under his influence. Though he shares characteristics with these poets, he always retains a distinctive, sometimes dissenting outlook from theirs. When writing about landscape, for example, Stafford resists describing it in mystical terms as was Roethke's wont. In explaining his use of the landscape in poetry, he says:

> And so my attitude is this: where you live is not crucial, but how you feel about where you live is crucial. Since I live in the Northwest, yes, I do write about the Northwest in the sense that place names get in my poems, but as for anything mystical, it hasn't registered on me. (*O'Connell 1998, 235*)

While Stafford writes in a number of genres, he is best known for his lyric poetry, a medium particularly well suited to his whimsical, skeptical temperament. In this poetry, Stafford goes back to the earth to rediscover its sights, sounds, smells, tastes, and textures. In his struggle to understand what it has to teach him, he experiences small, momentary illuminations that help him rethink the larger truths that govern our lives. Stafford does not feel compelled to link these moments together into a comprehensive philosophy, but is content with contemplating them in their individuality and specificity. He distrusts large, incandescent, mystical experiences like that Roethke described in the "North American Sequence" of *The Far Field.* Instead, he seeks smaller, more tentative truths, whether in regard to human society or the natural environment.

Stafford was born in Hutchinson, Kansas, in 1914. He married Dorothy Hope Frantz in 1944. The couple have four children, including the poet Kim Stafford. William Stafford received a bachelor of arts in English from the University of Kansas in 1937, a master of arts in 1945, and a Ph.D. from the University of Iowa in 1955. He taught at Lewis and Clark College in Portland, Oregon, from 1948 until his death in 1993.

His first book, *Down in My Heart* (1947), concerns his experiences as a conscientious objector during World War II. His decision to become a conscientious objector and the ostracism he suffered because of it affected him profoundly. It made him suspicious of grand theories and received wisdom, an attitude that shows up in his poems. He published his first collection of poetry, *West of Your City,* in 1960. He followed that up with *Traveling Through the Dark* (1962), a collection of poems that won the National Book Award in 1963. He has written books on writing, such as *The Voices of Prose* (1966) and *Writing the Australian Crawl: Views on the Writer's Vocation* (1978). Subsequent volumes of poems such as *Someday, Maybe* (1973), *Stories that Could Be True: New and Collected Poems* (1977), *A Glass Face in the Rain* (1982), *An Oregon Message* (1987), and *The Darkness Around Us Is Deep: Selected Poems of William Stafford* (1993) have only enhanced his reputation.

Though a member of the Church of the Brethren, a Christian peace church, Stafford seldom directly introduces theology or metaphysics into his poetry. Instead he relies on the process of writing as a way of coming to tentative truths. As Judith Kitchen points out in *Writing the World: Understanding William Stafford,* "Rather than beginning with an idea, Stafford advocates beginning anywhere, with anything, and letting the idea develop through a series of moves, what he terms almost a dance" (Kitchen 1999, 11).

His poem "Traveling Through the Dark" is a good example of his method. It treats an encounter with landscape in his characteristically questioning fashion. The word "dark" appears often in Stafford's poetry and suggests a general human condition; we live in darkness and receive only momentary glimpses of light. This poem provides a such a glimpse. It opens with the narrator finding a dead deer alongside the road. He speaks with a steady, insistent rhythm that gives subtle power to his words, but not so much that they call attention to themselves. He avoids the flowery poetic diction indulged in by the Romantics:

> Traveling through the dark I found a deer
> dead on the edge of the Wilson River Road.
> It is usually best to roll them into the canyon:
> that road is narrow; to swerve might make more dead.
> *(Stafford 1977, 61)*

The narrator seems to have dealt with this situation before and knows what to do. But when he discovers that the deer is carrying a live fawn in her womb, he faces a moral dilemma. Should he take the sentimental approach and try to save the fawn, a hopeless task? Or shall he roll the doe and fawn into the river, directly causing the fawn's death but preventing further loss of life? As the narrator ponders his decision, he becomes aware of his surroundings: "around our group I could hear the wilderness listen." He realizes that the land is alive and aware of him. This underlines his connection to the doe and fawn, making him weigh his decision carefully. In the end this awareness doesn't change his decision, but it changes his sense of himself:

> I thought hard for us all—my only swerving—
> then pushed her over the edge into the river. *(61)*

By "us" he now means not just the human race, but also the doe, the fawn, and the larger natural world. This encounter with the landscape has enlarged his sense of himself and extended his range of compassion without turning it into sentimentality, linking Stafford's poem to other "road kill" literature like Gary Snyder's poem "The Dead by the Side of the Road," from *Turtle Island* (see chapter 6); Molly Gloss's short story "The Doe" (1981); and Barry Lopez's "Apologia," in *About This Life* (see chapter 6). In "Traveling Through the Dark," the wilderness aids the poet's search for identity, but in a more complicated way than for other poets of the Northwest School. It presents him with dilemmas similar to the ones he faces in human society: what is the right thing to do, given the darkness around us? Stafford has no easy answers to this question, but reaches provisional ones in his poems. As he says: "I wouldn't say that my poems are guides to conduct. They are just little flares which illuminate something, but it may not be illuminating a place you want to stay, just a place that you happen to be" (O'Connell 1998, 268).

This and other encounters with landscape often result in connection with it, but they also encourage a sense of humility in the poet. This is an advantage in Stafford's eyes, as he is suspicious of human posturing and pretension. He values nature because it forces people to reevaluate who they are and their importance or lack thereof to the world. In the poem "An Address to the Vacationers at Cape Lookout," he ends with the line "What disregards people, does people good" (Skelton 1964, 86). Landscape aids our search for identity at least in part by giving us a healthy sense of doubt about our place in the larger scheme of things.

A quietly subversive poet, Stafford remains distrustful of human ambition and the martial spirit especially. In the poem "Watching the Jet Planes Dive" (Stafford 1977, 44), he recommends going back to the "forests and mountains" for answers to our most pressing questions about how to live. There, he says, "We must find something forgotten by everyone alive." This something is not a particular philosophy, but an attitude of humility. He makes this clear with the last line: "The jet planes dive; we must travel on our knees."

The landscape is important to Stafford in this and other poems because it encourages a sense of doubt about our own designs and a sense of connection with the rest of life. It provides a way of getting back to the particular that we have lost track of in the cities, towns, cultures, and philosophies we have constructed around ourselves. Throughout Stafford's poetry, the wilderness serves as a place for rediscovering our true sense of identity, but it does not accomplish this in any grand, mystical fashion; instead, it yields the small, tentative insights that are most trustworthy in guiding and lighting our lives.

JOHN HAINES

In the spring of 1947, John Haines sold his car, bought a used army surplus truck, and headed north for Alaska. He'd been living in Washington, D.C., studying art, but the prospect of free land, solitude, and sheer adventure were too much temptation. He and a buddy navigated the primitive Alaska Highway in their four-wheel-drive rig, camping out along the way. Eventually, Haines found seventy acres of land southeast of Fairbanks on the banks of the Tanana River. With the help of his friend, he built a house and storage shed. Then the friend headed south while Haines settled in for the long, cold Arctic winter. It was his introduction to the Great Land. It was also the beginning of his career as a writer:

> Many years ago I set out to know a country, to settle in it as deeply as I could, and, as it turned out, make of that living knowledge a book. As a writer, I could do nothing else. In the end, I could not separate art and nature, the country and the writing. They depended on each other, and with good fortune would make a single work. *(Haines 1996, xii)*

Haines's writing has always been inextricably linked to the harsh, elemental landscape of Alaska, as well as other landscapes of the Pacific Northwest. In this he follows William Carlos Williams, who encouraged poets to mine the American ground for material. Haines took Williams's advice; he fished, farmed, and trapped, getting to know the country intimately. He then transformed that knowledge into some of the finest poetry and prose ever written about the Great Land.

Though he considers the Far North his true home, he was born in 1924 in Norfolk, Virginia. His father was a naval officer and the family moved often. They lived for a time in the Puget Sound region, where Haines came to love the woods of the Pacific Northwest.

After serving in the U.S. Navy (1943–46), Haines attended the National Art School in Washington, D.C. (1946–47), American University (1948–49), and the Hans Hoffmann School of Fine Art in New York (1950–52).

Although he mainly studied art in school, he gravitated to poetry shortly after moving to the Alaska homestead in 1954. It took him many years to refine his style, in part because he had no immediate mentors. Like William Stafford, Haines grew up in the shadow of the Northwest School, but kept his distance from it. He shares with Roethke a feeling for the sacred side of landscape, a penchant for a three-beat poetic line, and careful attention to the sounds and rhythms of language, but in other ways his work is quite distinctive—taut, spare, meditative—with little of the exuberance and rhetorical excess that sometimes characterizes Roethke's verse.

Haines's stylistic distinctiveness is in some ways an outgrowth of his life on the homestead. He had to struggle to make a living from the landscape. He could not retreat back to a university teaching job or the corner grocery store or the dentist office when things got tight. He had to find a way to survive the barren Arctic landscape. This sense of urgency gives his work a leanness mirroring the starkness of the land itself.

"If the Owl Calls Again," the opening poem of his first book, *Winter News* (1966), exhibits many of these qualities. The poem's narrator imagines himself taking wing with an owl, flying above the alder flats of a river, and swooping down on mice. He comes to know the character of the land through imaginatively entering the consciousness of one of its creatures. This is a strategy Haines follows throughout his work, choosing a style admirably suited to the subject. The language of the poem is pruned to essentials. There is no excessive verbiage. And yet there is nothing flat or reductive about it. Haines suggests the beauty of that cold, nocturnal world through the incantatory music of his poetry. The narrator and owl feast on a mouse "while the long moon drifts / toward Asia / and the river mutters / in its icy bed" (Haines 1966, 9). Similar delights of language abound throughout his work.

Though Haines is best known as a poet, his signature work is in some ways his memoir, *The Stars, the Snow, the Fire: 25 Years in the Alaska Wilderness* (1989). The book is a collection of essays about homesteading in Alaska, organized according to a seasonal progression from winter to spring, to fall, to winter. As he makes clear in the preface, it is not a strict chronology, but a distilled essense of that life, organized around a few key moments.

> Yet, in the brief clarity and intensity of an encounter with nature, in the act of love, and (since we are concerned with a book) in the recalling and retelling of a few elemental episodes, certain key moments in that experience can be regained. On these depends the one vitality of life without which no art, no spiritual definition, no true relation to the world is possible. *(Haines 1989, 2)*

Unlike some contemporary poets who doubt that any real knowledge of the world is possible, Haines believes we can achieve a true relation to things by grounding ourselves in the particularities of American soil and experience. He sets out to do this by pursuing the life of trapping, hunting, and homesteading and seeing what he can learn from it. The book's opening essay, "Snow," compares snow to a book that can be read and interpreted: "These seemingly random ways, these paths, these beds, these footprints, these hard, round pellets in the snow: they all have meaning" (3).

The memoir is in many ways a quest for self-knowledge through understanding what it means to live in North America. The narrator searches for answers to these questions by learning to read the country. He illustrates his ability to do this by reading the signs in the snow, describing the scene of a battle between wolves and a moose. Through the tracks, broken sticks, and bits of moss, he re-creates the conflict— three wolves moving in for the kill; the moose kicking and stabbing at them with its legs; the wolves retreating and circling back; the moose finally driving them away. After showing his prowess in interpreting this scene, the narrator then says:

What might have been silence, an unwritten page, an absence, spoke
to me as clearly as if I had been there to see it. I have imagined a man
who might live as the coldest scholar on earth, who followed each clue
in the snow, writing a book as he went. It would be the history of snow,
the book of winter. *(5)*

The Stars, the Snow, the Fire may not be the definitive book of winter, but it wonderfully evokes key aspects of the season, especially as
experienced in the remote wilderness of Alaska. The life Haines pur-
sues has changed little since the last ice age, when our ancestors hunted,
trapped, gathered food along the margins of the glaciers. Haines uses
the correspondences between homesteading and this ancestral past
to give his work a deep resonance, echoing the primitive history of
mankind.

In the chapter "Of Traps and Snares," he details the intricacies of
trapping, describing how to use snares, baits, and deadfalls to catch
rabbits, beaver, marten, lynx. He expresses horror at killing animals,
and yet argues there is a knowledge to be gained from it. Trapping
gives him a sure sense of who he is and where he is in North America.
It teaches him just how closely he is connected with the earth, for better or worse. If he fails to catch something, he will have no money to
pay for food and supplies. The urgent and violent nature of trapping
provides insight into a shadowy, ancestral world obscured by the
wealth and comfort of modern civilization:

It was far, far back in time, that twilight country where men sometimes
lose their way, become as trees confused in the shapes of snow. But I
was at home there, my mind bent away from humanity, to learn to
think a little like the thing I was hunting. I entered for a time the old
life of the forest, became part fur myself. *(31)*

For Haines, trapping is about more than just making a living, it's
also about entering imaginatively into the world of animals and the
larger food chain. This intimate, bloody familiarity gives him a sense
of who he is and how he's linked with them. In making a life on the

homestead, he achieves the goal he set for himself: sinking deeply into the place, feeling at home there, and bringing back a dark and necessary wisdom, a wisdom stripped of pretense and sentimentality. He understands that he must kill animals to live, just as the wolves survive by bringing down moose.

Through this hard-won knowledge, he comes to identify with the animals that surround him and also with the pioneers and explorers who settled the place. These people live on in the names they gave the country, in the remains of their cabins and trails, and in their spirits, which have found a place in the country.

> A wandering spirit came home to the land. In the shape of a man, it cleared a space in the forest and built a shelter from the trees at hand. It came to learn the ways of this country; to sleep and and awaken, to flourish and grow old; to watch the river, the clouds moving east, the frost in the grass. *(165)*

Though Haines does not say so, this spirit may well be a portrait of himself. He came into his own on the Richardson homestead, found his literary voice, and managed to create a world unlike that of any contemporary writer. He had to scrape to make a living, but he gained a sense of the mystical order of the landscape, its deep, numinous dimension, and this knowledge enriched and informed the rest of his life. Since then, he has gone on to write about many other subjects and places in the Pacific Northwest, but the experience of homesteading in Alaska has stayed with him, allowing him to achieve a clarity of vision that shines through all his subsequent work.

DAVID WAGONER

Few poets have made use of the Northwest landscape as extensively as David Wagoner. In the course of a long and distinguished career, Wagoner has succeeded in making the region his triggering subject, creating imaginative, meticulously crafted poems from its plants, rocks, trees, and people. Working in a middle level of diction, composing in a style as moody and lustrous as a rainy afternoon, Wagoner's poems vividly evoke the spirit of the place.

David Wagoner was born in 1926 in Massillon, Ohio, and grew up in Whiting, Indiana, a city between Gary, Indiana, and Chicago, Illinois, where heavy industry had ruined the natural world. He found inspiration for his early poems not in nature, but in the works of English poets. That all began to change in his senior year at Pennsylvania State University when he enrolled in the class of Theodore Roethke. The elder poet quickly became Wagoner's model and mentor.

After moving to the Northwest to teach at the University of Washington, Roethke encouraged Wagoner to move west, and eventually helped him land a job at the same institution. Today Wagoner is a professor of creative writing at the University of Washington, former editor of the magazine *Poetry Northwest,* and one of the preeminent nature poets in the United States. Wagoner moved to Seattle for the job, but got much more in the bargain:

> When I came over the Cascades and down into the coastal rainforest for the first time in the fall of 1954, it was a big event for me, it was a real crossing of a threshold, a real change of consciousness. . . . The change had something to do with a reassurance that I belonged in the world. I recognize a lot of my own work as an attempt to discover what my place is in the natural order of things. *(O'Connell 1998, 53)*

To understand more about this rich and promising new world, Wagoner got out of Seattle to explore. At first he accompanied the poet Richard Hugo on fishing expeditions, but he didn't like killing fish. He then became an avid bird-watcher and naturalist, learning the names and habits of the region's wild creatures. In the poem "A Guide to Dungeness Spit," he assumes the role of a modern-day Adam, naming the birds, plants, and animals of this new Eden:

> Those whistling overhead are Canada geese;
> Some on the waves are loons,
> And more on the sand are pipers.
> *(Wagoner 1976, 20)*

By learning the names of these birds, he took the first step in establishing a relationship with them. Many of the poems from this period reveal his desire for a close identification with birds, rocks, trees, even algae. Indeed, writing poetry seems for him a way of joining the poet and the subject of the poem. In "The Song," he writes: "On the shore, at the feet of trees, / By a creek, by a silent house, / He changed to what he sang . . . " (Wagoner 1987, 189). Wagoner's use of proper names allows him to avoid the gushiness and imprecision of some nature poets, but he never comes to his subjects solely as a naturalist aiming to add to his knowledge of animal behavior. He seeks not just definition or analysis of things, but connection with them.

In many of these early poems, Wagoner seems more interested in the biology and ecology of birds and animals than in human society. In the poem "Neighbors," the narrator explains his reluctance to wave back at his neighbor:

> I can't tell him I see things
> Like trees instead of his face, that I hear birds
> Instead of his wife because I imagine
> Myself belonging among those strange neighbors. *(141)*

Instead of focusing his attention on his neighbors, Wagoner concerns himself with finding ways of deepening his relationship with the natural environment. The connection between himself and place is primary for him. In the poem "Chorus," he dramatizes a realization of this connection. After startling a group of tree frogs, the poem's narrator and his companion are delighted when the frogs resume croaking:

> Again, far off, and slowly the green others
> Nearby began their hesitant answers, their answers
> Louder and clearer chorused around us
> As if we belonged there, as if we belonged to them. *(39)*

In the course of researching the biology and ecology of the region, Wagoner discovered the Northwest Indian myths transcribed by anthropologist Franz Boas. He felt an immediate affinity for them, as they dramatized the complex connections between the plants, animals, and people of the region. Not only did the stories enhance his understanding and appreciation of the area, but they also provided a model for his own work:

> The more I read about Indians and the old ways, the more I recognized some of the ways I was feeling about the woods, and the earth and plants and animals. The more I read about animism, the more I recognized a kind of natural religion that I have come to believe in.
> (O'Connell 1998, 64)

Wagoner began translating some of these stories into poetry. His collection of these translations, *Who Shall Be the Sun?* (1978), manages to bring out the wonderful strangeness of these stories. In "Song After Fasting in a Tree," the speaker fasts and watches for his spirit, which appears as an owl. The speaker grows a beak, claws, feathers, before swooping out of a tree toward a mouse:

> In the Dance of the Broken Claws, I fall
> Again, deeper, and my fast is ended
> Now, with you, Mouse-brother.
> (Wagoner 1978, 119)

The speaker's long vigil ends in transformation. He enters imaginatively into the life of the owl and draws strength from its spirit. This meditation takes him outside of himself and into the life of another creature, encouraging him to identify with all of life. By encouraging a more comprehensive sense of identity, the speaker finds himself within the larger fabric of life.

Who Shall Be the Sun? includes some of the strongest poems in his entire body of work, but Wagoner eventually grew uncomfortable with retelling tribal stories. He felt he was trespassing, manipulating a tradition that was not his own. But if he refrained from translating any more legends, he had learned much from them that he applied to his work, especially strategies for dramatizing the lives of plants and animals in poetry. Wagoner proved adept at mimicking the habits of birds, a trait he shared with the Northwest painter Morris Graves. In the poem "Nuthatch," Wagoner succeeds in suggesting the small bird's movements through the rhythm and meter of the poem:

> Quick, at the feeder, pausing
> Upside down, in its beak
> A sunflower seed held tight. . . .
> *(Wagoner 1987, 24)*

The poem's swift, sudden syntax mirrors the movements of the bird, translating this aspect of the Northwest landscape into poetry. Wagoner learned from the Native American tales to imaginatively enter the lives of animals and write about them from the inside out. He riveted his attention on the creature itself, allowing the poem's form to arise out of it, rather than trying to impose formal patterns such as the sonnet, ballad, or villanelle on top of it. Many of his poems glow with a mystic, immanent light reminiscent of that made famous by painters such as Graves, Kenneth Callahan, Mark Tobey, and Guy Anderson of the Northwest School.

In much of his poetry, Wagoner seeks to discover his identity in relation to nature, not in relation to human society. But in recent years, especially after the birth of his daughters Alexandria and Adrienne, this emphasis has changed. Many of his recent poems in *Travelling Light* (1999), concern the joys and satisfactions of human love, a love not separate from the love for plants and animals, but which Wagoner believes is best understood and appreciated within the context of the rest of life. In this sense, his later poems represent a progression and signal Wagoner's further integration of the human and nonhuman worlds.

In this way, his poetry speaks not only of the beauty of the region, but also reveals what the natural world has to offer people—a place where people can rediscover their true identity. His work provides a model for all those seeking to stay found.

6 / Contemporary Northwest Literature

Taking an evening walk near his camp in the Brooks Range of Alaska, Barry Lopez watched the midnight sun fall across the tundra, making the landscape glow with an otherworldly light. He had come to Ilingnorak Ridge to study wolves, but was astonished by the profusion of other species—red fox, ground squirrel, caribou, wolverine, grizzly bear. He was particularly taken by the birds—rough-legged hawks, whimbrels, snowy owls, jaegers, golden plovers—and the extreme vulnerability of their ground nests. When he approached the nest of a horned lark, the small bird glared back at him, her fierceness a testament to the tenacity needed to survive in the harsh environment.

Without thinking, Lopez bowed slightly, hands in the pockets of his parka, unsure of what he was doing or why. But the gesture struck him as appropriate, an outward sign of an inward intention to honor and respect the land. Lopez made that bow in 1978 and he has performed it many times since, both in his life and his writing. Each of his twelve books makes a bow of acknowledgment to the spiritual side of the land.

"The bow is a technique of awareness," Lopez explains. "We often address the physical dimensions of landscape, but they are inseparable from the spiritual dimension of landscape. It is in dismissing the spiritual dimensions that we are able to behave like barbarians. If the land is incorporated into the same moral universe that you occupy, then your bow is an acknowledgment of your participation in that universe and a recognition that all you bow to is included in your moral universe. If you behave as though there was no spiritual dimension to the place, then you can treat the place like an object" (Lopez 1998b).

Throughout his career, Lopez has sought to articulate the search for a spiritual involvement with the North American landscape. His ability to illuminate this dimension of the land has helped make him one of the premier contemporary nature writers and one of the most important figures in Northwest letters. Lopez is not alone in highlighting the numinous quality of landscape. He shares this emphasis with many contemporary Northwest authors, including Ursula K. Le Guin, Gary Snyder, and Marilynne Robinson. Like them, Lopez argues for a new relationship with North America, a relationship in which the continent is valued not only for its material wealth, but also for what it offers the spirit: a sense of home, a sense of belonging within the larger fabric of life. These authors make clear that wherever we walk on this wondrous planet, we are walking on sacred ground.

Contemporary Northwest literature addresses a wide range of topics, but the physical environment remains the dominant subject. This landscape exerts considerable influence over this body of work, whether the minimalist short stories of Raymond Carver, the fantastic imaginings of *Dune* author Frank Herbert, the cosmopolitan poetry of Denise Levertov, the memoirs of Tobias Wolff, or the countercultural novels of Tom Robbins. These and other authors have sought to find new ways of articulating what has become the primary theme in the region's literature: the relation between people and this diverse and mysterious landscape.

Like the poets of the Northwest School, contemporary writers envision a more spiritual relationship with place. In seeking to articulate this relationship, many of them venture outside of the tradition of Euro-American literature for models. Where the poets of the Northwest School followed primarily a Modernist strategy of borrowing from the tradition of Euro-American literature, contemporary figures bring a wealth of new perspectives to bear on this subject of landscape, including modern biology, anthropology, and Asian literature.

But if Northwest literature has become perspectival and post-modern, it has not become solipsistic and nihilistic. The region's writers do not consider their work a complex system of signs without referents, as deconstructionists would have it, but as a means of defining and expressing their relationship with landscape. These authors see the disciplines of ecology, anthropology, and Asian and Euro-American literature not as closed systems, as ends in themselves, but as a means of coming to terms with landscape. Contemporary Northwest writers have adapted these various traditions so as to try to break down the division between self and environment and achieve a sense of union with place.

Modern ecological thought plays an important role in achieving this union. The discoveries of modern biology serve as grounding for the work of Robert Michael Pyle in *Wintergreen: Listening to the Land's Heart* (1988), Bruce Brown in *Mountain in the Clouds: A Search for the Wild Salmon* (1983), Brenda Peterson in *Living by Water: Essays on Life, Land and Spirit* (1990), Rick Bass in *The NineMile Wolves* (1992), Richard K. Nelson in *The Island Within* (1989), and David Raines Wallace in *The Klamath Knot: Explorations of Myth and Evolution* (1983). Indeed, the natural history essay has become one of the dominant forms of Northwest literature, with Oregon rancher / writer Dayton O. Hyde, Margaret Murie, and Kathleen Dean Moore all making important contributions to the field. In contrast to the predominantly materialistic approach used in modern science, these writers use modern biological thought to depict nature not as a mechanism, but as a living organism.

The region's proximity to Asia has long shaped its culture and arts. Today's ease of travel, communication, and translation only increases the appreciation of these traditions. Many writers borrow extensively from Asian poetry and prose, including James Mitsui in *After the Long Train: Poems* (1986), Robert Sund in *Ish River: Poems* (1983), Charles Johnson in *Oxherding Tale* (1982), and Sam Hamill in *Destination Zero: Poems 1970–1995* (1995). Others like John Okada in *No-No Boy* (1981) depict the dark treatment of Asian minorities in the early years of the

Northwest, a reminder that while landscape remains the dominant subject of Northwest literature, it is not the exclusive concern of the region's writers.

In recent years, the resurgence of interest in Native American lore and legend has greatly enriched the region's writing, both by Indians and non-Indians alike: James Welch reconciles the native storytelling tradition with techniques of realistic fiction in *Fools Crow: A Novel* (1986); Craig Lesley weaves Indian legends into the contemporary novels *Winterkill* (1984) and *River Song* (1989); Sherman Alexie integrates native stories with blues music in *Reservation Blues* (1995); Canadian author Margaret Craven adapts native traditions to her novella *I Heard the Owl Call My Name* (1973), as does Don Berry in his novels *Trask* (1960) and *Moontrap* (1962). Northwest authors have proved unusually successful in blending native culture with the tradition of Euro-American letters.

Many others have made important use of the region in their work. David Guterson grounds his novels *Snow Falling on Cedars* (1994) and *East of the Mountains* (1999) in the details of the local landscape. David James Duncan's novel *The River Why* (1983) explores ecological themes through fishing. Sallie Tisdale's memoir *Stepping Westward: The Long Search for Home in the Pacific Northwest* (1991) demonstrates how her family's life became intertwined with the region. William Stafford's son Kim Stafford gives a deep sense of what it means to live here in the essay collection *Having Everything Right* (1986).

These and many other authors have made important contributions to the region's literature, but Gary Snyder, Ursula K. Le Guin, Marilynne Robinson, and Barry Lopez stand out for their role in articulating a new relationship with landscape. All four have proven adept at creating works that celebrate the spiritual unity of people and place, an increasingly important subject not just to Northwesterners but to all inhabitants of this planet.

GARY SNYDER

The hybrid nature of much contemporary Northwest literature finds early expression in the poems and essays of Gary Snyder. In the course of his long and distinguished career, Snyder combines Buddhism, anthropology, and ecology in a unique and powerful aesthetic that highlights the interpenetration of people and place. All of his work, whether poetry or prose, calls for spiritual unity with the environment of the Northwest and the rest of the North American continent.

From early on, Snyder identified strongly with wild nature. He was born in San Francisco in 1930 and shortly thereafter moved with his family to the outskirts of Seattle. They lived in an area of farms and second-growth forest that had been clear-cut early in the twentieth century. His family raised cows and tended an orchard and garden. The surrounding landscape instilled in him a sense that he was part of nature, not above or outside of it:

> People who have not experienced the fabric of nature in childhood are slightly impoverished, morally and imaginatively. Growing up in that fabric gave me a powerful moral perspective of respect and regard for all sentient beings and gave me a powerful sense of membership in a real world. I imagine that maybe the ghosts of the great trees that had gone down in the clearcut of 1905 were still hovering over the land-scape, instructing me somehow. *(O'Connell 1998, 366)*

His identification with the region deepened as he explored it further. He canoed up the length of nearby Lake Washington. He rode his bike along the old logging roads. He began climbing in the Cascade Mountains. In the course of these climbs, his calling in life became clear to him: he would become a poet and make known human responsibilities to the earth:

> I started writing poetry because I couldn't find any other way to express what I was feeling about mountaineering on the great snow-peaks of the Northwest. I climbed St. Helens when I was fifteen, Mt. Hood when I was sixteen, and then Mt. Baker and Mount Rainier when I was seventeen. That was a powerful teaching for me. It was an initi-ation by all the great gods of the land here. And so I began to write poems. *(369)*

After graduating from high school, Snyder attended Reed College in Portland, Oregon, where he earned his bachelor of arts in anthropology and literature in 1951. His thesis, "He Who Hunted Birds in his Father's Village: The Dimensions of a Haida Myth," marked the beginning of a long interest in American Indian mythology. He attended Indiana University in 1951, and then quit to attend the University of California–Berkeley from 1953 to 1956, where he did graduate studies in Oriental languages.

While at Berkeley, Snyder gained national attention for his participation in the Beat movement in poetry. There, he met and befriended Allen Ginsburg, Jack Kerouac, Kenneth Rexroth, Philip Whalen, and other Beat poets. Rexroth exerted a strong influence over the younger Snyder through his translations of Asian poetry, his sensitivity to wild nature, and his insistence on direct statements, clear imagery, and objectivity of description in verse. With Rexroth's help, Snyder soon came into his own as one of the movement's leaders, staking out his own distinctive approach to writing. In a review of *The New American Poetry 1945–1960,* an anthology of Beat poetry, Snyder defines the Beat aesthetic in the following way:

> Poetry is not "beauty," not propaganda for the Bolsheviks or capitalists or whatever, not drinking sake and enjoying the moonlight, not "recollection in tranquillity" (Wordsworth), but a combination of the highest activity of trained intellect and the deepest insight of the intuitive, instinctive, or emotional mind. . . . (Snyder 1995b, 14)

Snyder makes these claims for Beat poetry, but they more accurately apply to his work. As the writing of some of the other Beats eventually fell into wine and decline, his grew stronger and sharper. His first book, *Earth Household* (1957), is a wild, chaotic free-for-all of a work, combining poetry, journals, reviews, and observations. While it exhibits some of the excesses of Beat poetry—formlessness, political posturing, and juvenile ranting and raving—it also represents Snyder's first attempt to yoke Buddhism, ecology, and anthropology into an impressive if unwieldy mix. If *Earth Household* doesn't succeed entirely as a book, it at least shows ambition and promise.

Fortunately, Snyder didn't remain in the Beat milieu for long. He won a scholarship from First Zen Institute of America and left for Japan in 1956. He lived there twelve years, studying Zen Buddhism and slowly refining his craft. An admirer of Imagist poets Ezra Pound and William Carlos Williams, Snyder preferred concrete images over abstract ideas in his verse. He found that Oriental poetry provided useful models for this approach.

After immersing himself in Chinese and Japanese poetry, he began to produce some of his best work. His second book, *Riprap* (1959), represents a quantum leap in quality over the first. These poems are the product of rigorous pruning and judicious selection. They are precise in their details and razor-sharp in their imagery. In the poem "Mid-August at Sourdough Mountain Lookout," Snyder presents vivid descriptions of the fire lookout where he worked in the summers while going to school. The weather is so hot that "Pitch glows in the fir-cones / Across rocks and meadows / Swarms of new flies." The poem ends with these lines:

> Drinking cold snow-water from a tin cup
> Looking down for miles
> Through high still air.
> (*Snyder 1959, 1*)

As a result of his intensive training in Buddhist meditation, Snyder is able to see things as if from the inside out, and then embody them with great concreteness in his poetry. In these poems, the division between the self and the environment breaks down as Snyder enters imaginatively into the landscape and then re-creates it on the page. His practice of Zen Buddhism and familiarity with Asian poetry in the original laid the groundwork for an art that achieves the interpenetration of people and place.

Other books followed, including *The Back Country* (1967) and *Regarding Wave* (1970), in which Snyder continued to weave ecology, anthropology, and Buddhism into his work. He achieved a comprehensive synthesis of these traditions in *Turtle Island* (1974), which won the Pulitzer Prize for poetry in 1975.

Turtle Island serves as the first manifesto of the bioregional movement, a movement that seeks to replace traditional political boundaries with ecological ones. Snyder takes the title from tribal myths and applies it to all of North America: "Turtle Island—the old / new name for the continent, based on many creation myths of the people who have been living here for millennia, and reapplied by some of them to 'North America' in recent years" (Snyder 1974, 1).

The primary organizational basis of bioregionalism is ecological, but its end is political; Snyder believes that ecological boundaries offer a sounder basis for social organization than traditional political ones. He uses the name "Turtle Island" so that "we may see ourselves more accurately on this continent of watersheds and life-communities— plant zones, physiographic provinces, culture areas; following natural boundaries. The 'U.S.A.' and its states and counties are arbitrary and inaccurate impositions on what is really here" (1).

Though Snyder draws from ecological thought to create a new sense of the continent, he emphasizes the spiritual dimensions of landscape rather the materialistic aspects favored by modern science. For him, the discoveries of biology and ecology suggest a view of the land as something sacred, not mechanistic.

> The biological-ecological sciences have been laying out (implicitly) a spiritual dimension. We must find our way to seeing the mineral cycles, the water cycles, air cycles, nutrient cycles as sacramental—and we must incorporate that insight into our own personal spiritual quest and integrate it with all the wisdom teachings we have received from the nearer past. The expression of it is simple: feeling gratitude to it all; taking responsibility for your own acts; keeping contact with the sources of the energy that flow into your own life (namely dirt, water, flesh). (*Snyder 1995a, 188*)

His use of ecology in *Turtle Island* dovetails neatly with his approach to anthropology and Buddhism. He combines all of these traditions in the interest of seeing the North American continent as a sacred entity, possessing spiritual dimensions as well as physical and material ones. He highlights these spiritual dimensions because they provide a sure basis for unity and identification with the North American continent.

Snyder organizes the poems in *Turtle Island* around aspects of ecology, anthropology, or Buddhism that highlight the numinous side of the land. "Prayer for the Great Family," for example, is based on a Mohawk prayer. "Gratitude to Mother Earth, sailing through night and day— / and to her soil: rich, rare, and sweet / *in our minds so be it*" (Snyder 1974, 24). The poem adapts the Native American lore to return his work to the primitive roots of poetry, where it had a religious as well as aesthetic role in society.

In "What Happened Here Before," Snyder borrows a historical context from geology and natural history to put modern American civilization in perspective. He relates a history of the North American continent beginning three hundred million years ago. The poem describes how the sea deposited sediment, the sediment consolidated, plant and animal life arrived, and then eventually human beings appeared. Rather than putting American human history at center stage, he tries to integrate it within the larger scheme of life on this planet.

The collection also contains lyric poems based on Oriental models. In "For Nothing," Snyder achieves a concision and directness equal to some of Ezra Pound's best work. He "zeroes in" on the thing itself, in this case a flower and what sustains it, which he describes as "Snow-trickle, feldspar, dirt" (34). The poem is a heap of bright fragments, all of which serve as entry points into the landscape. Each fragment represents an instance of connection between the poet and the land. This feeling of union with the landscape becomes concrete through his concentration on specific moments and particular parts of it. His sympathy with even inanimate aspects of the environment allows him to breath life into the North American continent, a project that he believes will help put our civilization back on the right course. As he observes in "The Wilderness," near the end of *Turtle Island:*

> But the voice that speaks to me as a poet, what Westerners have called the Muse, is the voice of nature herself, whom the ancient poets called

the great goddess, the Magna Mater. I regard that voice as a very real entity. At the root of the problem where our civilization goes wrong is the mistaken belief that nature is something less than authentic, that nature is not as alive as man is, or as intelligent, that in a sense it is dead, and that animals are of so low an order of intelligence and feeling, we need not take their feelings into account. *(107)*

Throughout the collection, Snyder seeks to reanimate the landscape of North America. All of the strategies he employs here—ecological, anthropological, and Oriental—are designed to convey a sense of the landscape as a living entity, entitled to respect and reverence. Snyder suggests that the best way to appreciate this continent as a living entity is by approaching it region by region, watershed by watershed, ecosystem by ecosystem, plant by plant, boulder by boulder, seeing it as a vast and complex organism, and not as a mechanism or a patchwork of political entities. Snyder believes that in so doing, we will not only come to know the land, but to better understand ourselves and our society as well.

His next book, *Axe Handles* (1983), builds on many of the ideas and strategies developed in *Turtle Island,* but is more whimsical and less confrontational. His points are just as trenchant, but he delivers them with a humor and lightness of touch missing from earlier volumes. The last poem of the collection, "For All," describes a morning hike in the northern Rockies through such evocative details as the "Rustle and shimmer of icy creek waters," "cold nose dripping" and "smell of the sun on gravel." The beauty of the morning moves him to praise it, which he does in a parody of the U.S. Pledge of Allegiance:

> I pledge allegiance to the soil
> of Turtle Island
> and to the beings that thereon dwell
> one ecosystem
> in diversity
> under the sun
> With joyful interpenetration for all.
> *(Snyder 1992, 308)*

It's impossible to miss the playful note he strikes here, but it's important to keep in mind the seriousness of his pledge. His sense of identification and interpenetration with place leads him to joyful connection with it, but it also requires him to work to protect it. The poet has political responsibilities in regard to North America because he is inextricably bound up with it.

His collection *No Nature: New and Selected Poems* (1992) makes this explicit. The title has the enigmatic, paradoxical nature of a Zen koan. Snyder considers the term "nature" a vestige of the mentality that sees human society as separate from the rest of life. There is no nature because the term itself seeks to divide the human from the non-human, whereas Snyder sees both nature and human society as part of a larger whole. In the last poem of that volume, "Ripples on the Surface," he compares the earth to a vast household:

> The vast wild
> the house, alone.
> The little house in the wild,
> the wild in the house.
> Both forgotten.
> No nature
> Both together, one big empty house. *(381)*

This is the poetical expression of the inner transformation achieved through Zen Buddhism, Native American stories, and ecological science. These disciplines have allowed Snyder to go beyond the split between self and nature and accept the two as one, both in *No Nature* and in his collection *Mountains and Rivers Without End* (1996). In adapting these traditions to his poetry, Snyder achieves union with the North American continent and a heightened awareness of himself as well.

URSULA K. LE GUIN

Though many of Ursula K. Le Guin's stories take place on Hain, Gethen, Urras, Anarres, and other imaginary planets, they address issues of concern to contemporary earthbound readers. As she notes in the introduction to her collection *A Fisherman of the Inland Sea: Science Fiction Stories* (1994), science fiction serves as a way of indirectly discussing many of the most important issues of the day:

> Those images and metaphors used by a serious writer are images and metaphors of our lives, legitimately novelistic, symbolic ways of saying what cannot otherwise be said about us, our being and choices, here and now. What science fiction does is enlarge the here and now. *(Le Guin 1994, 5)*

In Le Guin's hands, the genre of science fiction becomes especially appropriate to discussing issues of nature and culture. In her novel *Always Coming Home* (1985), Le Guin seeks to establish a new relationship between people and place. She does this by animating the natural world and enlarging the sense of home to include more than a house, neighborhood, or city, but instead an entire ecosystem, in this case the Napa Valley of northern California in the distant future.

Though ecological themes are common throughout Le Guin's work, *Always Coming Home* is the first of her novels in which ecology takes center stage. The theme of people living in harmony with the land appears in other of her novels, such as *The Word for World Is Forest* (1972), *The Dispossessed* (1974), and the Earthsea series, and in the story collections *Searoad: Chronicles of Klatsand* (1991) and *Unlocking the Air* (1996), but it becomes the dominant subject in *Always Coming Home*. She takes it up directly to create an ecologically exemplary society, which fits seamlessly within its environment.

To invent this society, she borrows heavily on anthropological reconstructions of American Indian life. This is by no means a new strategy, as many of her other novels show a similar approach. She has long been fascinated with anthropology, an interest inherited from both her father, Alfred L. Kroeber, a renowned anthropologist who did much of his work on Californian and Northwest Coast tribes, and her mother, Theodora Kroeber, who wrote the best-selling *Ishi in Two Worlds: A Biography of the Last Wild Indian in North America* (1961).

Le Guin was born in Berkeley, California, in 1929. She received a bachelor of arts degree in French from Radcliffe College in 1951 and a master of arts degree in Romance languages from Columbia University in 1952. She first made her mark as a writer of science fiction, winning the Hugo Award three times, but eventually she branched out to write realistic fiction and nonfiction. Her interest in anthropology has always proved useful in creating imaginary societies, whether in distant galaxies or here on earth.

Always Coming Home resembles an anthropological reconstruction of a society, but in this case it is an entirely fictional one. Much of the book consists of description of the daily life of the Kesh, a predominantly agricultural people who are one of many small, distinct, local cultures that have followed the breakdown of industrial civilization as we know it. Although Kesh society is clearly based on Native American models, it also contains elements of contemporary American civilization. It's an unusual hybrid, a remarkable mix of high and low tech, and provides a glimpse into what life might be like in the twenty-second century or beyond.

If this society is ecologically exemplary, it is by no means perfect in other ways. Le Guin goes out of her way to emphasize that this society does not meet standard utopian guidelines, even if it does fall within this genre. It is not a sterile, perfect, unbelievable society, as is often the case with those in B. F. Skinner's *Walden II* (1948) or Ernest Callenbach's novel *Ecotopia* (1975), in which everything is hopelessly ideal. The character Pandora seems to speak for the author when she remarks, "I never did like smartass utopians. Always so much healthier and saner and sounder and fitter and kinder and tougher and wiser and righter than me and my family and friends. People who have the answers are boring, niece. Boring, boring, boring" (Le Guin 1985, 335).

In contrast, the Kesh society fits within its place without destroying it, but there are still wars, disappointments, petty behavior—the usual stock-in-trade of human experience. Indeed, Le Guin realizes the impossibility of permanently removing evil and suffering from the world. As one of the Kesh warriors observes: "I have come to think that the sickness of Man is like the mutating viruses and the toxins: there will always be some form of it about, or brought in from elsewhere by people moving and traveling, and there will always be the risk of infection" (411).

But even if it will not perfect human behavior, Kesh society at least achieves harmony with its environment. Le Guin devotes much of the novel to describing how the Kesh accomplish this. In this extensive use of exposition, *Always Coming Home* resembles nineteenth-century novels such as Melville's *Moby Dick* (1851), which allow ample room for digression. *Always Coming Home* is a novel that Henry James would hate; it's baggy and loose, a collection of fragments, not a unified work of art. It is constructed not as a series of scenes but as a collection of narratives and descriptions of the daily life of the Kesh.

There is little progress in the novel, at least in a temporal sense, since the novel's structure mimics Kesh culture, which doesn't see time as a progress, but as a continuum. The novel contains passages of narrative, but these passages are not consecutive; they are separated by exposition on everything from Kesh poetry to Kesh pottery. The book achieves some narrative coherence by incorporating passages from the life of Stonetelling, a young Kesh girl whose struggle to come to terms with her family and her place in Kesh society links the parts of the book together.

Stonetelling's struggle fuels the only substantial conflict in the book. Unlike characters in novels in the Realistic tradition, the Kesh have no real struggle with their environment; they fit within it so well that no real disjunction occurs between them and it. Instead, the story's main drama conflict revolves around Stonetelling and her need to reconcile the influences of her two very different parents and find her place in Kesh society. Her father is a military officer for the Condor people, a warlike, imperialistic nation that seeks domination over the Kesh and other peoples. Her mother is Kesh and eventually divorces her husband when he returns to the city of the Condor.

The narrative concerns Stonetelling's struggle to come to terms with these very different parents. It opens with her early life in the valley, describes her journey away from the valley to visit her father and the Condor people, and finishes with her return to the valley. This cycle of departure and return provides the basis for the story and yokes together the disparate parts of the book.

The descriptions of her early life in the valley demonstrate how completely the Kesh have immersed themselves in the local environment. They are a postapocalyptic people who have learned from mistakes of their ancestors, whom they call the Backward-Head people, at least partly because they had no vision for the future, and did not see how their actions would contribute to the destruction of the planet.

In contrast to their ancestors, the Kesh see no sharp distinction between themselves and the surrounding environment. They differ in quality but not in kind from the rest of the valley. They are part of a common family that includes rocks, trees, birds, and animals:

> I think it is one another whom we greet, and bless, and help. It is one another whom we eat. We are gatherer and gathered. Building and unbuilding, we make and are unmade; giving birth and killing, we take hands and let go. Thinking human people and other animals, the plants, the rocks and stars, all the beings that think or are thought, that are seen or see, that hold or are held, all of us are beings of the Nine Houses of Being, dancing the same dance. *(325)*

The Kesh worldview owes much to American Indian culture, including its pervasive animistic element. In adapting this culture to her fiction, Le Guin shows her kinship with many other contemporary writers such as Gary Snyder, Barry Lopez, James Welch, Craig Lesley, and Leslie Marmon Silko. But Le Guin distinguishes herself from these writers by mixing Native American materials with elements of high technology. As a science fiction writer, Le Guin lacks the Romantic contempt of technology common to many contemporary nature writers. Though she clearly holds a tempered view of technology, she does not reject it out of hand. She sees it as an extension of our ability to make tools and understands that it becomes dangerous only when it is emphasized to such a degree that it puts the rest of our life out of balance:

> In leaving progress to the machines, in letting technology go forward on its own terms and selecting from it, with what seems to us excessive caution, modesty, or restraint, the limited though completely ade-

quate implements of their cultures, is it possible that in thus opting not to move "forward" or not only "forward," these people did in fact succeed in living in human history, with energy, liberty, and grace? *(406)*

By drawing from her background in science fiction, she creates an ecologically harmonious society without getting bogged down in the primitivism that marginalizes some American nature writing. Witness her attitude toward the Exchange, a vast computer network linking all of the towns and cities of the world. Information is shared through the Exchange, but only one person per city is generally initiated into its use. The Exchange is not despised in the valley, but it holds no particular fascination, either. It is merely a tool, not a religion.

The Exchange plays a crucial role in the defeat of the Condor people, an imperialistic people who seek to conquer all of the surrounding societies, as they seek to tame and control their environment. The smaller towns and villages repel the advance of the Condors by passing information and organizing resistance through the Exchange. It becomes a vast command and control center that allows the smaller cultures to harass, weaken, and finally defeat the larger Condor army.

Le Guin provides an in-depth view of the Condor people during Stonetelling's visit with her father. The Condor people's cold northern capital contrasts sharply with the warm, sunny valley of the Kesh. Stonetelling soon becomes homesick. She eventually escapes from the city of the Condor and makes her way back to the valley.

Although she rejoices on returning to the valley, she has difficulty fitting back into Kesh society. To ease this transition, she performs the Kesh songs and dances to strengthen her sense of membership in Kesh society and to celebrate the Kesh's place in the valley and the surrounding natural world. These ceremonies emphasize the union between Kesh society and the other creatures of the valley. The "Initiation Song from the Finders Lodge" applies especially to Stonetelling:

Walk carefully, well loved one,
walk mindfully, well loved one,

walk fearlessly, well loved one.
Return with us, return to us,
be always coming home. *(428)*

The song suggests that living in one place can be a process of continuous discovery. If the Kesh treat the valley with respect and attentiveness, they will always be discovering new things about it. For the valley is always changing, always revealing new things, always providing them with new ways to come home to it.

This and other songs help Stonetelling reintegrate herself into Kesh society, a society caught up in the rhythms of the larger valley life. Gradually, she prepares herself to join the World Dance, the Kesh's celebration of "human participation in the making and unmaking, the renewal and continuity, of the world" (484). Once human society assumes its proper relation to the environment, it can participate in the evolution of the world without destroying or polluting the planet in the process. Since the Kesh see human society as a part of nature rather than as separate from it, they see human beings as playing a necessary role in the creation and re-creation of the world. There is a careful reciprocity in the Kesh's relationship with nature; human culture and nature are mutually interdependent, with neither overwhelming the other since both are needed to fully complete the world.

In this way, the novel envisions human society as achieving a harmonious relationship with place. Instead of seeing culture as separate and distinct from nature, *Always Coming Home* emphasizes that human culture should be integrated within nature, so that human beings can play their proper role with regard to the rest of creation. By combining Native American materials with those of modern American culture, the novel creates a remarkably realistic and hopeful vision of what human life might become in the future.

MARILYNNE ROBINSON

Few novels of any era capture the mysterious character of the inland Northwest as completely as Marilynne Robinson's 1981 novel *Housekeeping*. Robinson's haunting prose conveys the purity of the region's water, the slant of its light, and the brooding quality of its immense forests. The natural world, powerful and beautiful, assumes a central role in the story, with characters struggling to come to terms with this magnificent but sometimes malevolent landscape.

Like much contemporary Northwest literature, the novel calls for a reorientation of the relationship between people and place, but unlike Snyder and Le Guin, Robinson seeks to do this by adopting elements of the European-American literary tradition to spiritualize landscape and so break down the division between humans and environment. The novel accomplishes this by illustrating the change in consciousness of the book's narrator, Ruth, who first sees a sharp distinction between human society and the natural world and later comes to believe that such boundaries are illusory. This change in consciousness is dramatized through the change in her approach to housekeeping, an activity through which she and the book's other characters express their attitudes toward human society and the natural world.

The activity of housekeeping in this novel serves a similar purpose to that of fishing in Maclean's *A River Runs Through It:* it makes concrete the characters' attitudes toward society and the surrounding environment. Housekeeping assumes particular significance in the novel since Robinson has chosen the genre of the foundling's tale as the basis for her story. The home figures prominently in this genre, representing stability and security, as is the case with the mansion in Charles Dickens's nineteenth-century classic, *Bleak House* (1853). In this and other examples of the foundling's tale, the home serves as a place of refuge and remains sharply distinct and separate from the hostile world outside of it.

Robinson accepts no such distinction. If she appropriates key elements from this genre, she refuses to accept the ideology that usually accompanies them. Rather than emphasizing the division between home and world, her version of the foundling's tale dramatizes the breakdown of this division and its replacement with a sense of the continuity between home and larger world. Thus she adapts the form of the foundling's tale to demonstrate the essential unity of human life and the natural environment.

Like many foundlings' tales, *Housekeeping* begins with the story of an ancestor, in this case a grandfather. As was the case with many of those who moved west, he was a dreamer. He had grown up in the Midwest and came to Fingerbone, the fictional town in the novel, to see mountains. In this and some other respects, the novel reflects the experience of Robinson's own family; her maternal grandfather came west because he wanted to see mountains. He settled there and raised a family, including a daughter, Robinson's mother. Robinson's father worked in the timber industry, and in the course of his career the family moved to various places around the inland Northwest.

Robinson was born in Sandpoint, Idaho, in 1943. After graduating from high school, she went east to attend Brown University and later returned to the Northwest to complete a Ph.D. in English at the University of Washington in Seattle. Since finishing *Housekeeping,* she has published *Mother Country* (1989), a booklength exposé of the Sellafield Nuclear Plant in Britain, and *The Death of Adam: Essays on Modern Thought* (1998).

Her own family's story and that of the family in *Housekeeping* intersect at several points, but she warns that it is unwise to interpret the novel too literally in terms of her own life: "There's no point really in thinking about experience as if it would translate straightforwardly into artistic behavior, because it simply never does" (O'Connell 1998, 252). As the biographical gets translated into the fictional, it changes.

After arriving in Fingerbone, the grandfather in *Housekeeping* gets a job with the railroad, marries, and eventually sires three daughters. Shortly thereafter, he dies in a spectacular train wreck, where a locomotive jumps the track and the entire train plunges into the icy waters of Fingerbone's lake, thus leaving all of the daughters fatherless.

In this way, the story follows the conventional formula of the foundling's tale. There is the death of a parent, bereavement, upheaval, and eventual readjustment. His death necessitates a change in housekeeping, one which the grandmother selflessly undertakes:

> She had always known a thousand ways to circle them all around with what must have seemed like grace. She knew a thousand songs. Her bread was tender and her jelly was tart, and on rainy days she made cookies and applesauce. In the summer she kept roses in a vase on the

piano, huge, pungent roses, and when the blooms ripened and the petals fell, she put them in a tall Chinese jar, with cloves and thyme and sticks of cinnamon. . . . *(Robinson 1981, 12)*

The grandmother's housekeeping emphasizes the division between the home and the outside world. She is steadfast in maintaining this distinction, and when Helen, the narrator's mother, commits suicide, the grandmother devotes herself equally to raising the two grand-daughters left behind:

For five years my grandmother cared for us very well. She cared for us like someone reliving a long day in a dream. . . . She whited shoes and braided hair and fried chicken and turned back bedclothes, and then suddenly feared and remembered that the children had somehow dis-appeared, every one. How had it happened? *(25)*

The physical structure of the house is the centerpiece of this kind of housekeeping. In Fingerbone, this structure is constantly under siege from the elements, especially that of water. The town is subject to heavy snowstorms, power outages, and floods, which recall those in the Old Testament. In many ways the environment around Fingerbone not only belittles human constructions and human society, but also seems to actively destroy them. It frequently intrudes on the story, and not as a passive, submissive, docile pastoral landscape, but as an active, strange, and sometimes malevolent one that disregards the order that human beings construct for themselves.

For the grandmother, life is a constant struggle against such forces of ruin and decay. She works diligently to keep the physical structure of the house intact, and thus keep the elements at bay. She sees the world in dualistic terms, with the home representing the inner world and the environment the outer. For her there is a real separation between the two worlds and she does her best to keep the distinction clear.

Eventually the grandmother dies and the girls' Aunt Sylvie arrives to take over their care. Sylvie's approach to housekeeping contrasts greatly with that of her mother. Her housekeeping recognizes and acknowledges the continuity between the home and the world, allowing the wind, the leaves, and the crickets inside the house:

> Thus finely did our house become attuned to the orchard and to the particularities of the weather, even in the first days of Sylvie's housekeeping. Thus did she begin by littles and perhaps unawares to ready it for wasps and bats and barn swallows. *(85)*

For Sylvie the division between self and environment, between inner and outer, is false and illusory. Her sense of housekeeping would include all the world, not simply the part contained within the shell of the house. She seeks to erase the distinctions between inner and outer, letting the house deteriorate and breaking down the division between self and environment.

Sylvie's housekeeping encourages Ruth's growing awareness of the continuity between nature and human life. Ruth's dreamy personality makes her amenable to her aunt's eccentricities:

> It was a source of both terror and comfort to me then that I often seemed invisible—incompletely and minimally existent, in fact. It seemed to me that I made no impact on the world, and that in exchange I was privileged to watch it unawares. *(106)*

By contrast, her sister Lucille has little compunction about rejecting what she considers her aunt's incompetence. When the three are eating dinner in the dark, Lucille abruptly switches on the light:

> The window went black and the cluttered kitchen leaped, so it seemed, into being, as remote from what had gone before as this world from the primal darkness. We saw that we ate from plates that came in detergent boxes, and we drank from jelly glasses. *(100)*

This is the beginning of Lucille's disaffection with her family. Eventually it leads to open revolt, but in the early stages of Sylvie's housekeeping, she remains loyal, and she and Ruth are inseparable.

It is during this time that they spend a night out in the woods, a night that becomes a turning point for both of them.

In a scene reminiscent of Mark Twain's *The Adventures of Huckle-berry Finn* (1884), the two go fishing, intending to return home before dark. But they lose track of time and have to build a makeshift shelter in which to spend the night. The girls react very differently to this experience. Lucille defiantly tries to maintain the integrity of their driftwood hut, insuring the distinction between inner and outer: "For a while she sang 'Mockingbird Hill,' and then she sat down beside me in our ruined stronghold, never still, never accepting that all our human boundaries were overrun" (115). By contrast, Ruth comes to understand that the division between self and environment is an illusion, that at base, the two are one entity, an entity symbolized by the darkness:

> I simply let the darkness in the sky become coextensive with the darkness in my skull and bowels and bones. Everything that falls upon the eye is an apparition, a sheet dropped over the world's true workings. The nerves and brain are tricked, and one is left with dreams that these specters loose their hands from ours and walk away, the curve of the back and the swing of the coat so familiar as to imply that they should be permanent fixtures of the world, when in fact nothing is more perishable. *(116)*

As soon as the sky lightens, Lucille insists on leaving. She refuses to speak to Ruth on the way back. After this night out, Lucille goes her own way. She begins reading fashion magazines, seeking to adopt the look and attitudes shared by the other girls in the town, for whom human culture and society, not the immense landscape surrounding them, are the norms. Ruth seems incapable of "improving" herself in this way, and adopts Sylvie as her model, mentor, and eventually surrogate mother. This new relationship is sealed during the trip Ruth takes with her across the lake in a stolen boat: "She stood up and turned around and stooped to hold the gunwales, and I crawled under her body and out between her legs" (146).

After this trip out to an abandoned homestead, which provides an example of a house open to the elements, Ruth gives herself over to a view of the world like Sylvie's. She recognizes the continuity between self and nature, and undertakes to structure her life accordingly. The boat trip comes to symbolize the way she will lead her life. She and Sylvie will travel through the world lightly, with only minimal separation between themselves and the environment around them. They will not be encumbered by a house or possessions; the lack of such encumbrances will allow them to live close to nature and will in fact protect them:

> The immense water thunked and thudded beneath my head, and I felt that our survival was owed to our slightness, that we danced through ruinous currents as dry leaves do, and were not capsized because the ruin we rode upon was meant for greater things. *(162)*

Here, as elsewhere in the book, the lake comes to symbolize infinity, the ground of being, the well from which all things come and to which they return. Here and elsewhere in the novel, Robinson expresses an implicitly Christian, almost Calvinistic view of the world, maintaining a distinction between the world of the senses and spiritual world beyond them. But even if the sensual world is illusory, it serves as the way we experience the universal and so must be treated with care and respect.

It is only by acknowledging the existence of the spiritual substance underneath all of the superficial distinctions created by the visual world that allows one to reorder one's life so as to live lightly in the world. Sylvie helps Ruth take a step in this direction by suggesting that they ride the freight train back into town from the lake, thus taking the first step toward a life of transience, Sylvie's former lifestyle, and the one they both will now follow.

When the townspeople find out about this trip, they immediately take action. In a town as shallow-rooted as Fingerbone, evidence of such transience combined with Sylvie's lackadaisical attitude toward housekeeping are seen as a threat to the community. They begin legal proceedings to strip Sylvie of guardianship.

But they act too late; by this time Ruth has decided never to return to the town. When the sheriff tries to lure her away from Sylvie with the promise of apple pie and a good home environment—what he considers the attractions of conventional housekeeping—Ruth turns him down. Shortly thereafter, Sylvie's housekeeping gives way to house-losing. To preserve the privacy of the house from prying neighbors, she and Ruth set it afire.

In ending the book in this way, Robinson also destroys the conventional structure of the foundling's tale. Though *Housekeeping* treats the usual material of such a story—parental deaths, wills, probate courts, and a kind of ancestral mansion—it doesn't follow the classic pattern of such a tale. The novel could never be mistaken for a book like Dickens's *Bleak House*, which ends with the ancestral mansion, a symbol of stability and permanence, intact.

By changing the ending of the foundling's tale, Robinson profoundly changes its meaning. No longer does the form assume that there is a clear distinction between the home and outer world. Her version of the foundling's tale dramatizes the breakdown of this distinction and its replacement with a sense of the continuity between home and larger world. Thus she adapts the form of the foundling's tale to demonstrate the essential indivisibility of human life and environment.

Ruth achieves equilibrium with the natural world by adjusting her life so as to live lightly on the land. This necessitates a rejection of the conventional approach to home and community life and its replacement by a life of transience with Sylvie. The book ends with the two of them traveling around the West working as itinerant waitresses.

In this way Ruth achieves only partial reconciliation with family and only the most minimal reconciliation with human society. Like many other Western American heroes, Ruth and Sylvie find it nearly impossible to experience unity with both society and nature. Though Ruth and Sylvie yearn for a full reconciliation with family and at least a partial reconciliation with human society, the attitude toward nature prevailing in Fingerbone makes this difficult for them to achieve. For Ruth and Sylvie, any reconciliation between family, society, and nature must begin with a rejection of the division between nature and society, and an acknowledgement of the continuity between the two spheres. *Housekeeping* is a darker book than the others discussed here because it suggests that a complete reconciliation with society and nature will not be possible without a radical revision of American society.

BARRY LOPEZ

They never saw it coming. Barry Lopez and three scientists were making bottom trawls in a twenty-foot boat several miles out from Pingok Island on the North Slope of Alaska, one of the most desolate and remote regions of the planet. Skirting the edges of the pack ice in the Beaufort Sea, they concentrated on their work and ignored a storm moving in from the southwest. Before they realized what was happening, the wind pushed a large ice floe toward them, sealing them off from open water and pinning the craft on four sides.

Lopez and the others had prepared for such an emergency. In addition to scientific equipment, they carried flares, extra food, extra clothing, a tent, sleeping bags, and other survival equipment, including a radio. But they knew that even if someone heard their distress signal, they had no way of describing their present location, and with the storm moving in, they had no idea of how far the pack ice might drift to the east. Lest they become yet another footnote in the long record of Arctic disasters, they had to find a way to get free.

Taking advantage of a momentary shift in the ice, they managed to force the boat through a narrow passage. They widened it with ice chisels and gunned the boat's twin ninety-horsepower engines, trying desperately to reach open water. When thirty feet of ice stood in their way, they used ice anchors, lines, and a block and tackle to pull the 3,000-pound craft out of the water, across the ice, and into the next channel.

But this channel, too, was closing. Lopez went to look for another. Several hundred yards ahead, he raised his ice chisel to signal he had found one. By the time the boat reached him, however, this channel had narrowed. One of the men positioned the prow of the boat against the seaward ice, revved the engines, and widened the gap to six feet. Then he reversed course and sped up the channel. The others chopped madly at the ice, trying to keep it away from the props. Finally, they heaved and lifted and shoved the boat into the open water. They were home free—or so they thought.

They fell into the boat, exhausted from the effort. The seas were now running at six feet. Waves burst over the top of the boat. The men erected a canvas shelter to shield them from the water and hunkered down to endure the ride back to Pingok. Like the others, Lopez was dressed in heavy clothes and foul-weather gear, but unbeknownst to him, he had torn the seams in the shoulder of his parka while freeing the boat. The right side of his body was soaked.

He shivered and drifted in and out of consciousness, unaware of what was happening and why he was so cold. Fortunately, the others recognized his predicament. They peeled off his wet garments, dressed him in dry wool clothing, and pushed him underneath the tarp to protect him from the elements. He sat in a stupor and simply tried to brace himself against the boat. When the others shouted that they had reached Pingok, he realized he was safe. He dragged himself out of the boat and into the camp, where he ate dinner and fell asleep.

After the storm passed, Lopez walked the beach and reflected on the incident. A fit, strong, barrel-chested man used to living and working outdoors, he felt embarrassed at being reduced to a dead weight, but the close call made him marvel at the early Arctic explorers who had endured much more serious hardships, traversing the forbidding landscape in flimsy crafts without adequate clothing or survival equipment. In the sixth century, St. Brendan set off from the west coast of Ireland in a small curragh made of wicker and oxhide to search for the Isles of the Blessed. What drove him to cross the Arctic landscape in such an exposed boat? After pondering the example of Brendan and other Arctic explorers, Lopez later concluded in his National Book Award–winning *Arctic Dreams: Imagination and Desire in a Northern Landscape*:

> Arctic history became for me, then, a legacy of desire—the desire of individual men to achieve their goals. But it was also the legacy of a kind of desire that transcends heroics and which was privately known to many—the desire for a safe and honorable passage through the world. *(Lopez 1986, 309)*

This desire for a safe and honorable passage through the world animates not only Arctic history, but also Lopez's work. Each of his dozen books of fiction and nonfiction represents a search for such a passage, a way of leading an honorable and dignified life with regard for the rest of creation. In works such as *Desert Notes: Reflections in the Eye of a Raven* (1976), *Of Wolves and Men* (1978), *River Notes: The Dance of the Herons* (1979), *Winter Count* (1981), *Arctic Dreams* (1986), *Field Notes: The Grace Note of the Canyon Wren* (1994), *About This Life* (1998), and *Light Action in the Caribbean* (2000), he provides the outlines of such a passage, drawing particular attention to the spiritual nature of the land, an aspect of landscape he sees our larger culture as having slighted or ignored. Lopez sees the land as mysterious, animate, and sacred, not as predictable and mechanical as a windup clock, as a Cartesian formulation would have it. He believes that Western civilization's attitude toward the land has encouraged it to get off to a bad start on this continent, exploiting North America for its material resources while ignoring its potential spiritual wealth:

> What does it mean to be rich? Is it to possess the material, tangible wealth of North America—the gold and the silver, the timber, the fish and the furs? Or is real wealth, lasting wealth, something else? Most of us, I think, believe that it is something else. We have taken the most obvious kind of wealth from this continent and overlooked the more lasting, the more valuable and sustaining experience of intimacy with it, the spiritual dimension of a responsible involvement with this place. (O'Connell 1998, 29)

Throughout his career as a writer, Lopez has sought to change this materialistic attitude toward the American continent. He sees much of American culture as cut off from the continent and spiritually impoverished as a result. He believes that nature writing can change that by putting people back in touch with the mystery inherent in the land. Many of the characters in his stories manage to get back in touch with themselves and with the larger spiritual dimension in theirs lives by encountering wild, uncultivated landscapes.

In treating such issues of spirituality through nature writing,

Lopez follows a long tradition in American literature. Many classic American works, such as Herman Melville's novel *Moby Dick* (1851) and Stephen Crane's story "The Open Boat" (1898), address questions of metaphysics in terms of landscape. As Lopez says of Melville's novel, "The open sea in *Moby Dick* makes mystery apparent. What you're dealing with is a fundamental mystery" (Lopez 1994b). Like Melville, Henry Thoreau, Ralph Waldo Emerson, and others in the Transcendentalist tradition, Lopez seeks to "reinfuse life with mystery by raising the specter of the mysterious in the land" (Lopez 1994b). But where Thoreau and Transcendentalists like Emerson considered nature divine, Lopez sees it simply as one manifestation of God's presence, although he admits to recognizing that presence more easily in nature than in human society. His sense of the sacramental quality of nature, its ability to mediate between the human and the divine, accounts for his work's resemblance to the poet and priest Gerard Manley Hopkins and other Roman Catholic writers.

In emphasizing the spiritual nature of landscape, Lopez feels a close affinity with the work of many Northwest writers and with the region itself. He has lived on the McKenzie River in western Oregon since 1968, and the region and its people have served as the raw material for much of his fiction and nonfiction. In commenting on the short-story collection *Field Notes,* he points out the spiritual dimension that the Northwest and other landscapes can bring to people's lives:

> What nature may do for the characters in some of these stories is awaken them to their own possibilities. I believe in the power of nature to heal or to impel us to more spiritually balanced lives . . . certainly today we have developed a culture so strongly consumer based that it threatens what little remains of those wild landscapes. But perhaps the larger problem is something else. We live so much of our lives inside our own heads (of which the many rooms of our fiction are so symbolic) we have lost the tonic, the imaginative stimulus, the counterpoint of those wild places. *(Lopez 1994b)*

Lopez sees his own work and that of other nature writers as counteracting this trend. He seeks to reconnect readers with this fundamental mystery by describing journeys into wild landscapes and detailing the lives of people and animals native to the place. Drawing on his own experience of these landscapes, as well as perspectives from biology and anthropology, Lopez presents a vision of a new relationship with North America, a relationship in which the continent is valued not only for its material wealth, but also for what it offers the spirit: a sense of belonging within the larger fabric of life. In articulating the search for an honorable, respectful involvement with North America, Lopez has become one of the most important American nature writers of his generation.

Born in 1945 in Port Chester, New York, Lopez grew up mostly in Southern California; his early experiences of the Mojave Desert, the Santa Monica Mountains, Zuma Beach, Big Bear Lake, Hoover Dam, the Grand Canyon, and the Los Angeles River made him especially sensitive to what he calls "classical landscapes" such as deserts, the Arctic, and the Antarctic. Though he tells stories about other kinds of landscapes, such as the semitropical western slope of the Cascade Mountains in *River Notes,* there is something about spare, elemental landscapes that particularly sparks his imagination.

In approaching a landscape, whether desert or tropical, Lopez always seeks to understand the mystery inherent within it and then to articulate that in his work. All of his narratives attempt to put the reader back in touch with the mystery of the land through storytelling, a strategy he discusses in the important essay "Landscape and Narrative." In this essay, Lopez distinguishes between two kinds of landscapes, an exterior and an interior one. Lopez defines the exterior landscape as including everything outside the self—climate, geology, plants, animals, etc. The interior landscape, by contrast, serves as "a kind of projection within the person of the exterior landscape" (Lopez 1989, 65). The character of the surrounding exterior landscape strongly influences a person's thoughts and feelings—their interior landscape—as much as do upbringing and heredity. If cut off from this exterior landscape, a person's interior landscape will atrophy and become vulnerable to a principle of disarray. Storytelling serves as a way of bringing the two landscapes back together and healing this sense of confusion:

A story draws on relationships in the exterior landscape and projects them onto the interior landscape. The purpose of storytelling is to achieve harmony between the two landscapes, to use all the elements of story—syntax, mood, figures of speech—in a harmonious way to reproduce the harmony of the land in the individual's interior. *(68)*

Stories bring an individual's interior landscape back into harmony with the mysterious order inherent in the land. They accomplish this not in a programmatic way, but by suggesting this mysterious order through storytelling.

The narrative strategy described in "Landscape and Narrative" provides a key to understanding all of Lopez's books, whether fiction or nonfiction. By carefully depicting the exterior landscape, which includes geology, biology, botany, meteorology, etc.—and the relationships between these elements—Lopez tries to reproduce the harmony of the land on the page. His stories function as distilled landscapes, communicating the mysterious truth of the land through the written word.

Many of these stories are organized in terms of a quest, with the central character journeying out into a wild landscape to gain wisdom from experiencing the land firsthand. The prototype for these characters is the narrator of Lopez's first book, *Desert Notes: Reflections in the Eye of a Raven.* This spare, sensual, paradoxical work serves as the blueprint for the rest of his works, both in its use of the narrator and in its multiperspectival approach to the subject. The book begins with the unnamed narrator's desire to discover the secrets of the desert:

The land goes not give easily. The desert is like a boulder. You expect to wait. You expect night to come. Morning. Winter to set in. But you expect sometime it will loosen into pieces to be examined.

When it doesn't, you weary. *(Lopez 1976, xi)*

The narrator senses that this landscape contains hidden, mysterious dimensions and seeks to unlock these secrets quickly. The landscape frustrates his attempts to understand it in a strictly rational, scientific way. Only when the narrator approaches it in a humble, oblique, and respectful manner does it reveal itself to him: "One morning as I stood watching the sun rise, washing out the blue black, watching the white crystalline stars fade, my bare legs quivering in the cool air, I noticed my hands had begun to crack and turn to dust" (xiii).

The narrator is rewarded for his patience as his hands are transformed into the stuff of the desert landscape, symbolizing his communion with it. After this transformation, the narrator purifies himself further by visiting a hot spring. This cleansing ritual signals the break the narrator has made with his former attitude toward the desert. Through the discipline and self-mortification of rituals such as this, he comes to know the secrets of the desert and so can come to life again:

> When he got back to the truck he poured a cup of water and placed a handful of cereal into an earthen bowl. He ate and looked out across the desert and imagined that he had come to life again. *(12)*

By stripping away the materialistic distractions of modern life, the narrator sees clearly into the heart of the desert experience and so can proceed with his quest. He sets out to learn the secrets of the desert by approaching it from a number of perspectives—personal, biological, anthropological, mystical. He does not believe that a single point of view is sufficient for understanding the complexity of a given phenomenon. Each element of the landscape must be examined from a number of angles.

In *Desert Notes,* as in many of Lopez's other books, the narrator seeks to understand a particular subject, in this case the desert, from multiple perspectives. He begins with personal experience and what his senses tell him of the line, color, texture, movement, smell, taste, and touch of the place. He then examines the creatures that live in the harsh environment, especially the raven, a patient, resourceful bird from whom much can be learned about the landscape. He also recounts stories about previous human inhabitants of the land, such as a contemplative Native American tribe and the former occupants of an abandoned elementary school. These points of view are not supported by the kind of detailed research that informs his later books, but they still offer distinct frameworks from which to view the desert experience. The essence of the desert will always remain a mystery, but it can be approached by means of these perspectives.

Viewing the desert from these perspectives allows him to glean him an essential nugget of wisdom that he can apply to his own life. The exterior and interior landscapes come together in this final insight: the desert experience teaches him to prune away the materialistic encumbrances of modern life so as to return to an original, more spiritual self. By recognizing this spiritual dimension in the land, he has rediscovered it in himself. At the end of the book, the narrator recommends a man named Leon as a guide to those seeking a way into the desert. Among Leon's qualities is an ability "to avoid what is unnecessary," the book's final line and the distilled wisdom of the desert experience.

Just as the Jewish people in the Old Testament and Jesus and John the Baptist in the New Testament strengthened and purified themselves in the desert, so too the narrator of *Desert Notes* comes to life through the discipline of the desert experience and returns to civilization with a renewed sense of purpose. This is a common theme in Lopez's books, articles, and stories: journeys into the wilderness provide us with a chance to return to an original, uncompromised spiritual self, a self often buried beneath the conventions and distractions of modern urban life.

Desert Notes is an excellent introduction to the rest of his work. Though Lopez later enlarges upon this early model, many of his narrative strategies find their first expression here: the narrator as a seeker after the spiritual secrets of the landscape; the narrator's application of biology, anthropology, and other perspectives to get closer to the heart of this mystery; and finally the change in attitude of the narrator as he comes into contact with this original mystery. These strategies occur in Lopez's other books, including his first best-seller, *Of Wolves and Men*.

In addition to introducing his work to a broad new audience, *Of Wolves and Men* received enthusiastic critical acclaim, winning the prestigious John Burroughs Medal for nature writing and earning Lopez a reputation as one of the most promising young figures in the field. While the book clearly falls within the category of nature writing, it also signals a new direction in this genre, taking a complex, searching, and multifaceted approach to its subject. Like most works in this tradition, it is organized around a natural feature, *Canis lupus,* but saying that the book is about wolves is like saying that *Moby Dick* is about whales. The book goes further than previous treatments of the subject, using wolf biology, Native American beliefs, and a story from the life of St. Francis of Assisi to examine the attitude of humans toward nature, of which the treatment of wolves serves as an especially notorious example. *Of Wolves and Men* has as much to say about human civilization as it does about natural history, and uses the natural history of the wolf to critique the materialistic assumptions of modern culture.

Lopez's reappraisal of the wolf follows in the footsteps of scientific works like Adolph Murie's *The Wolves of Mount McKinley* (1966) and L. David Mech's *The Wolf: The Ecology and Behavior of an Endangered Species* (1970) as well as popular books such as Farley Mowat's *Never Cry Wolf* (1963), a personal account of living near wolves in the Far North. These books paint a fascinating picture of the animal and highlight its most distinctive feature: its complicated social organization, an organization that resembles that of human society.

These works produce a sympathetic portrait of an animal long demonized, paving the way for *Of Wolves and Men,* which depends on the research of field biologists like Mech and Murie, but goes further in following out the sociobiological implications of their work. Lopez compares and contrasts wolf behavior with that of human beings, so as to probe the origins of humans as social animals. He believes that wolves have much to teach us in this regard:

> In a paper presented at a conference on wolves held in Maryland in 1966, it was suggested that more could be learned about the origins of man as a social animal by studying the social structure of wolf packs than could be learned by studying about primates. The suggestion was prophetic. I write now in a country and at a time when man's own brutal nature is cause for concern and when the wolf, whom man has historically accused of craven savagery, has begun to emerge as a benign creature. *(Lopez 1978, 73)*

Like *Desert Notes, Of Wolves and Men* is organized as a quest, with
the narrator seeking to discover more about wolves and what they
can teach him about human behavior. As in the previous book, Lopez
proceeds by approaching the wolf from a number of perspectives—
biological science, views of farmers and ranchers, Native American
accounts and legends, as well as personal observation:

> When I was working on the wolf book, I was attracted to the animal
> itself. When I began that book I realized that part of what I wanted to
> do was to look at the animal from the point of view of different people,
> because the notion that one kind of thinking could make the animal
> clear seemed completely ridiculous to me. Every animal is a mysteri-
> ous entity. There is a certain amount of information that you can gather,
> but there is a great deal that you never will know. *(9)*

Lopez believes that the application of these various points of view
will add to our understanding of the wolf, even if they cannot completely explain the animal. This approach is especially evident in his
attitude toward science. He devotes the first quarter of the book to
defining the wolf in terms of modern biology, describing the animal
in terms of its physiology, hunting prowess, and social behavior. But
as much as he values biology's contribution to understanding wolf
behavior, he also recognizes its limits:

> It occurred to me early on in my association with wolves that I was
> distrustful of science. Not because it was unimaginative, though I think
> that is a charge that can be made against wildlife biology, but because
> it was narrow. I encountered what seemed to me eminently rational
> explanations for why wolves did some of the things they did, only to
> find wildlife biologists ignoring those ideas. *(77)*

Science alone cannot give him a true and accurate picture of wolves;
it is merely one in a complex overlay of strategies he uses to get closer
to the truth of the species. Though Lopez does not reject the contributions of wildlife biology, he goes beyond them to consider other rel-
evant perspectives, especially those of Eskimos, who admire the

animal's hunting prowess. As he says, "But clearly there was a body of evidence which seemed both rational and pertinent and which was being ignored: what people who lived in the Arctic among wolves, who had observed them for years in the wild, thought about them" (77–78).

The perspectives of these native people vary considerably from that of Western science. In particular, the Eskimos never claim to completely understand wolves or their ways:

> When the Nunamiut speaks, he speaks of exceptions to the rules, of the likelihood of something happening in a particular situation. He speaks more often of individual wolves than of the collective wolf, of "the white wolf that lives over near Chandler Lake" or "that three-legged female who had pups last year." *(82–83)*

Since the Eskimos are hunters themselves, they identify strongly with the animal and try to emulate its ways. They admire the wolf for being a good hunter and providing for its family. Western civilization, by contrast, demonized the wolf because the animal exemplified traits it wanted to leave behind as it moved from a hunting culture to an agricultural one.

To explain Western civilization's animus toward the wolf, Lopez next moves from the field to the library. He traces the evolution of attitudes toward the wolf in European and American history and concludes that people killed wolves indiscriminately because they equated them with the wilderness, which they associated with the unholy and bestial nature in men and women. To illustrate this point, Lopez tells the story of St. Francis of Assisi and his success in preventing a wolf from attacking the city of Gubbio. St. Francis made a deal with the wolf: the residents would feed the wolf and permit it to roam freely in exchange for the wolf's promise not to harm man or beast. Lopez reads the story as an allegory for how bestial nature as symbolized by the wolf was transformed by the sanctity of St. Francis, who represented the Roman Catholic Church:

> Medieval men believed that they saw in wolves a reflection of their own bestial nature; man's longing to make peace with the beast in himself

is what makes this tale of the Wolf of Gubbio one of the more poignant stories of the Middle Ages. To have compassion for the wolf, whom man saw as enslaved by the same base drives as himself, was to yearn for self-forgiveness. *(213)*

But the wolf rarely was treated with the compassion accorded to it by St. Francis. The identification of the wolf with the bestial part in man served as the excuse for wiping out the species in many parts of the world. By projecting onto the wolf our hatred of our bestial nature, humans made the wolf a scapegoat:

> Throughout history man has externalized his bestial nature, finding a scapegoat upon which he could heap his sins and whose sacrificial death would be his atonement. He has put his sins of greed, lust, and deception on the wolf and put the wolf to death—in literature, in folklore, and in real life. *(226)*

The wolf was trapped and killed because it epitomized the wilderness which settlers sought to tame and replace with farms and ranches. Lopez observes that in the *Trapper's Guide* (1869), Sewell Newhouse put this bluntly in saying that "the trap goes before the ax and the plow, forming 'the prow with which iron-clad civilization is pushing back barbaric solitude' and causing the wolf to give way 'to the wheat field, the library, the piano'" (190–91).

This final section of the book documents human perceptions of the wolf and the wilderness it symbolizes. Lopez argues that for most of our history, perceptions about the wolf were imposed on the animal and reveal more about human beings than wolves. In the process of documenting these changing perceptions about wolves, Lopez tries to free the animal from these historical associations and return to a fresh consideration of the species. He believes that humankind has much to learn from wolves:

> When, from the prisons of our cities, we look out to wilderness, when we reach intellectually for such abstractions as the privilege of leading a life free from nonsensical conventions, or one without guilt or

subterfuge—in short, a life of integrity—I think we can turn to wolves.
We do sense in them courage, stamina, and a straightforwardness of
living; we do sense that they are somehow correct in the universe and
we are somehow still at odds with it. *(249)*

Though Lopez is interested in the wolf itself, he is especially keen
to learn what it has to teach about how to live well on the land. He
sees the wolf as a model of ecological behavior. He believes that by
studying the wolf, we can bring human society more closely into con-
gruence with wild nature. We have separated ourselves from the wilderness in the course of building modern industrial civilization; Lopez
uses the wolf as an example of how we can reorient ourselves to that
fundamental mystery and return to a life of integrity.

Of Wolves and Men brings order to the mind of the narrator through
the encounter with this one element of the external landscape. The
internal landscape of the narrator becomes whole again through contact with the original integrity of the land as epitomized by the life of
the wolf. For this reason, we should appreciate wolves in particular
and the wilderness in general for the spiritual richness they afford us,
and not eliminate them for utilitarian reasons.

His next book, *Arctic Dreams: Imagination and Desire in a Northern
Landscape,* builds on the themes and structure of the wolf book. In
his largest and most ambitious work to date, Lopez directly addresses
issues about the spiritual nature of landscape that he has raised in previous works. His quest for the spiritual side of the land seems particularly well suited to the Arctic, a mysterious, otherworldly landscape
that has long inspired wonder and awe:

This is a land where airplanes track icebergs the size of Cleveland and
polar bears fly down out of the stars. It is a region, like the desert, rich
with metaphor, with adumbration. *(Lopez 1986, xxix)*

As is his previous works, Lopez organizes this book in terms of a
quest. The narrator seeks to discover the secrets of this austere landscape, with the goal of eventually finding a place for himself within

it. His search for a way of living wisely on the land becomes the organizing feature of this and his other books:

> We have been telling ourselves the story of what we represent in the land for 40,000 years. At the heart of this story, I think, is a simple, abiding belief: it is possible to live wisely on the land, and to live well. And in behaving respectfully toward all that the land contains, it is possible to imagine a stifling ignorance falling away from us. *(xxviii)*

As Lopez makes clear throughout the book, the stakes are high in this endeavor. Unless our civilization finds some way of coming to terms with the land, we will continue to destroy the landscape and impoverish ourselves as a result. As in *Of Wolves and Men,* Lopez sounds a note of alarm here about the direction of modern civilization. He sees the exploitation of the Arctic as a microcosm for the exploitation of the entire North American continent. This ambitious approach helps explain why it won the National Book Award for nonfiction in 1986 and why it has become the most influential of all of his works.

In its scope, *Arctic Dreams* represents a progression, but it builds on all of his previous work. The narrator begins his quest to understand the Arctic by applying the perspectives of biological science. He defines the region in terms of its light and seasonal fluctuations, which are entirely different from those of temperate zones. He then moves to detail the lives of animals that have adapted to this harsh environment. He takes up muskox first, describing how the animal has made some remarkable adaptations to survive in the harsh climate, developing a thick, coarse fur that insulates it from the subzero temperatures of the Arctic winter. After presenting a scientific portrait of this animal, Lopez admits that science cannot serve as the final or complete authority on this or any other element of the landscape:

> The physical landscape is baffling in its ability to transcend whatever we would make of it. It is as subtle in its expression as turns of the mind, and larger than our grasp; and yet it is still knowable. The mind,

full of curiosity and analysis, disassembles a landscape and then reassembles the pieces—the nod of a flower, the colors of the night sky, the murmur of an animal—trying to fathom its geography. At the same time the mind is trying to find its place within the land, to discover a way to dispel its own sense of estrangement. *(xxiii)*

As this passage makes clear, Lopez does not deny the possibility of science adding to our knowledge of a place. It can bring us closer to understanding it, thus healing the division between ourselves and the landscape. The narrator brings order and calm to his own life though experiencing the beauty and harmony of the Arctic landscape. In this way he serves as a surrogate for the reader and as an example for the culture as a whole. Lopez is often intensely critical of our culture's thoughtlessness and indifference to the land, but he is quick to point out that individuals need not partake of this attitude. He believes that they can find satisfaction through touching the land, and in this way change the larger culture's orientation toward it. In *Arctic Dreams* and elsewhere, he sees such a change as essential if we are to reverse the destruction of the North American landscape and the resulting spiritual impoverishment of our culture and ourselves.

In his later works, Lopez continues to expand upon themes central to *Arctic Dreams* and his earlier works. In the book-length essay *The Rediscovery of North America* (1990), he asserts that we must go beyond an obsession with the material wealth of the continent that began with Columbus and begin to appreciate North America for its psychological and spiritual wealth if we are ever to feel at home here. He argues that the continent's most valuable resources are not its timber, fur, fish, and mineral wealth but a sense of belonging on the North American continent.

But it is one thing to assert these things, and another to provide examples of how such ideals can be realized. In recent years, Lopez has turned to fiction to accomplish this further task. In the story collection *Field Notes: The Grace Note of the Canyon Wren*, he manages to create characters who exemplify many of the traits he extols in previous books. Many of these characters are transformed by their encounters with wild landscapes. As a result of such experiences, they achieve a sense of what it means to live a dignified life both in relation to it and to their fellow human beings.

Though Lopez can be overly explicit, some might say preachy, about such themes in his work, his stories still resonate with the mystery of wild landscapes and people's remarkable experiences of them. By bringing together the exterior landscape of North America with the interior landscape of those who inhabit it, he manages to deepen and enrich our culture's sense of itself and the continent on which we live.

As he writes in the essay "Landscape and Narrative," "Truth . . . is something alive and unpronounceable. Story creates an atmosphere in which it becomes discernible as a pattern" (Lopez 1989, 69). In his recent collections *Field Notes* and *Light Action in the Caribbean,* as in his previous work, Lopez lives up to his own definition, creating stories where character and landscape come to life on the page.

All of the contemporary Northwest writers discussed here—Snyder, Le Guin, Robinson, Lopez, and others—seek to reconnect human culture with the environment. They consider the split between the human and the nonhuman as a dangerous illusion, which encourages the destruction of the environment and the spiritual impoverishment of human beings. They seek to repair this split by emphasizing the animate and spiritual nature of the land. All of them see nature as a living organism, entitled to reverence and respect, not simply as matter upon which human beings can impose their wills.

This vision of landscape as an animate and spiritual entity is crucial to connecting it not just with individuals, but with human society as a whole. If the poets of the Northwest School articulate a sense of unity between themselves as individuals and landscape, contemporary writers take this one step further in arguing for unity between nature and human culture. They draw from the traditions of Buddhism, Native American lore, modern biological science, and European-American literature to present a vision of human culture integrated within nature. In this way, they contribute something important to American and world literature: in this time of environmental crisis, they give examples of how people can find unity with landscape, not just as individuals but as a society as a whole.

These authors accomplish this in part by standing on the shoulders of their predecessors. Indian storytellers, explorers, settlers, Romantic and Realistic writers, and poets of the Northwest School all paved the way for the current flowering in Northwest literature, providing an intellectual and artistic foundation that others could build on. As *On Sacred Ground* demonstrates, the search to express the spirit of this place began with the region's early writers and continues to this day.

This search is by no means finished. As much as contemporary Northwest literature deserves praise and celebration, it suggests a direction more than a destination. There are still many questions to be resolved: How will this literature influence the larger society? Will the vision of unity between people and place ever become a reality? Will the region's literature change as people deepen their knowledge and appreciation of this place? Who among the next generation of Northwest writers will embrace and extend this vision of regional culture? These are just a few of the issues that commentators on Northwest literature will confront in the future.

This volume attempts to sketch the broad outlines of the region's poetry and prose. In arguing for a particular interpretation of Northwest literature, I hope *On Sacred Ground* will provoke an extended discussion about the relationship between literature and regional identity, encouraging readers to reflect on the important questions raised by these poems and stories.

Northwest literature grows out of a particular place, but its achievements merit national and international attention. By definition, landscape literature must begin with the local. The idea of connecting up with "the land" as a whole is too abstract to mean much. And yet the lessons learned in seeking unity with a particular landscape have direct relevance for those seeking connection with other landscapes. Through its careful description of this specific locale, rich exploration of ecological themes, and outstanding literary qualities, Northwest literature provides a promising vision of the unity of nature and culture, encouraging people to realize that wherever they go on this miraculous planet, they are walking on sacred ground.

REFERENCES

PREFACE

Drucker, Philip. 1963. *Indians of the Northwest Coast.* New York: American Museum Science Books.

O'Connor, Flannery. 1961. *Mystery and Manners: Occasional Prose, Selected and Edited by Sally and Robert Fitzgerald.* New York: Farrar, Straus & Giroux.

Schwartz, Susan. 1983. *Nature in the Northwest: An Introduction to the Natural History and Ecology of the Northwestern United States from the Rockies to the Pacific.* Englewood Cliffs, N.J.: Prentice-Hall, Inc.

Stafford, William. 1973. "On Being Local." *Northwest Review* 13, no. 3: 92.

ACKNOWLEDGMENTS

Applegate, Shannon, and Terence O'Donnell, eds. 1994. *Talking on Paper: An Anthology of Oregon Letters and Diaries.* Corvallis: Oregon State University Press.

Barcott, Bruce. 1994. *Northwest Passages: A Literary Anthology of the Pacific Northwest from Coyote Tales to Roadside Attractions.* Seattle: Sasquatch.

Beckham, Steven Dow, ed. 1993. *Many Faces: An Anthology of Oregon Autobiography.* Corvallis: Oregon State University Press.

Buell, Lawrence. 1995. *The Environmental Imagination: Thoreau, Nature Writing and Formation of American Culture.* Cambridge: Belknap Press of Harvard University Press.

Cantwell, Robert. 1972. *The Hidden Northwest.* Philadelphia and New York: J. B. Lippincott Company.

Carlson, Roy. 1979. *Contemporary Northwest Writing: A Collection of Poetry and Fiction.* Corvallis: Oregon State University Press.

Chittick, V. L. O. 1948. *Northwest Harvest: A Regional Stock-Taking.* New York: MacMillan.

Dodds, Gordon B., ed. 1993. *Varieties of Hope: An Anthology of Oregon Prose.* Corvallis: Oregon State University Press.

Etulain, Richard. 1973. "Novelists of the Northwest." *Idaho Yesterday* (summer):24–31.

Everson, William. 1976. *Archetype West: The Pacific Coast as a Literary Region.* Berkeley, Calif.: Oyez.

Finne, Ron. 1983. *Tamanawis Illahee: Medicine Land.* Portland: Oregon Council for the Humanities. Documentary film.

Holbrook, Stewart. 1945. *Promised Land.* New York: McGraw-Hill Book Company; London: Whittlesey House.

Horner, John B. 1902. Preface. *Oregon Literature.* Portland: J. K. Gill.

Jones, Suzi, and Jarold Ramsey, eds. 1994. *The Stories We Tell: An Anthology of Oregon Folk Literature.* Corvallis: Oregon State University Press.

Kazin, Alfred. 1988. *A Writer's America: Landscape in Literature.* New York: Alfred A. Knopf.

Kittredge, William. 1997. *The Portable Western Reader.* New York: Penguin Books.

Kittredge, William, and Annick Smith, eds. 1988. *The Last Best Place.* Helena: Montana Historical Society Press.

Love, Glen A. 1993. *The World Begins Here: An Anthology of Oregon Short Fiction.* Corvallis: Oregon State University Press.

Lucia, Ellis. 1969. *This Land Around Us.* Garden City, N.Y.: Doubleday & Company.

Meany, Edmond S. 1889. "Has Puget Sound a Literature?" *Washington Magazine* 1 (September):8–11.

O'Connell, Nicholas. 1998. *At the Field's End: Interviews with 22 Northwest Writers.* Seattle: University of Washington Press.

Powers, Alfred. 1935. *History of Oregon Literature.* Portland, Ore.: Metropolitan Press Publishers.

Ricou, Laurie. 2002. *The Arbutus / Madrone Files: Reading the Pacific Northwest*. Corvallis: Oregon State University Press.

Schama, Simon. 1995. *Landscape and Memory*. New York: Alfred A. Knopf.

Simonson, Harold P. 1980. "Pacific Northwest Literature—Its Coming of Age." *Pacific Northwest Quarterly* (October):146–51.

———. 1989. *Beyond the Frontier: Writers, Western Regionalism and a Sense of Place*. Fort Worth: Texas Christian University Press.

St. John, Primus, and Ingrid Wendt, eds. 1993. *From Here We Speak: An Anthology of Oregon Poetry*. Corvallis: Oregon State University Press.

Venn, George. 1979. "Continuity in Northwest Literature." *Northwest Perspectives: Essays on the Culture of the Pacific Northwest*. Edited by Edwin R. Bingham and Glen A Love. Seattle and London: University of Washington Press.

1 / EARLY NATIVE AMERICAN STORIES

Adams, Richard. 1972. *Watership Down*. London: Rex Collings, Ltd.

Boas, Franz. 1894. *Chinook Texts*. Washington, D.C.: Government Printing Office.

Clark, Ella. 1953. *Indian Legends of the Pacific Northwest*. Berkeley: University of California Press.

Drucker, Philip. 1963. *Indians of the Northwest Coast*. Garden City, N.Y.: Natural History Press.

Furtwangler, Albert. 1997. *Answering Chief Seattle*. Seattle and London: University of Washington Press. (This work discusses the problems with interpreting and dating Chief Seattle's speech. I have chosen to follow historian David Buerge's opinion that the speech mostly likely took place on January 12, 1854, but the precise date may never be known, as Furtwangler points out.)

Grant, Frederick James. 1891. *History of Seattle, Washington*. New York: American Publishing and Engraving Company.

Haeberlin, Hermann. 1924. "Star Husband (Second Version) in the Mythology of Puget Sound." *Journal of American Folklore* 37: 371–78.

Hilbert, Vi. 1985. *Haboo: Native American Stories from Puget Sound*. Seattle and London: University of Washington Press.

———. 2000. Interview. January 4.

Lerner, Andrea. 1990. *Dancing on the Rim of the World: An Anthology of Contemporary Northwest Native American Writing.* Tucson: University of Arizona Press.

Phinney, Archie. 1934. *Nez Perce Texts.* New York: Columbia University Press.

Ramsey, Jarold. 1979. "The Indian Literature of Oregon." *Northwest Perspectives: Essays on the Culture of the Pacific Northwest.* Edited by Edwin R. Bingham and Glen A. Love. Seattle: University of Washington Press.

———. 1983. *Reading the Fire: Essays in the Traditional Indian Literatures of the Far West.* Lincoln: University of Nebraska Press.

———. 2000. Interview. January.

2 / JOURNALS OF EXPLORATION AND SETTLEMENT

Ambrose, Stephen. 1996. *Undaunted Courage: Meriwether Lewis, Thomas Jefferson and the Opening of the American West.* New York: Simon & Schuster.

Applegate, Shannon. 1988. *Skookum.* New York: Beech Tree Books.

Dillard, Annie. 1992. *The Living.* New York: HarperCollins.

Duniway, Abigail Scott. 1859. *Captain Gray's Company.* Portland, Ore.: S. J. McCormick.

Fitzgerald, F. Scott. 1925. *The Great Gatsby.* New York: Charles Scribner's Sons.

Foote, Mary Hallock. 1894. *Coeur d'Alene.* Boston: Houghton Mifflin Company.

Gloss, Molly. 1989. *The Jump-Off Creek.* Boston: Houghton Mifflin Company.

Goetzman, William. 1986. *New Lands, New Men: America and the Second Great Age of Discovery.* New York: Viking Penguin.

Irving, Washington. [1836] 1976. *Astoria or Anecdotes of an Enterprize beyond the Rocky Mountains.* Reprint, Lincoln and London: University of Nebraska Press.

Jefferson, Thomas. 1801. *Notes on the State of Virginia.* Philadelphia: R. T. Rawle.

Lewis, Meriwether, and William Clark. [1806] 1989. *The Journals of Lewis and Clark*. Edited by Frank Bergon. Reprint, New York: Viking Penguin.

Nisbet, Jack. 1994. *Sources of the River: Tracking David Thompson across Western North America*. Seattle: Sasquatch.

Raban, Jonathan. 1999. *Passage to Juneau: A Sea and Its Meanings*. New York: Pantheon Books.

Swan, James. [1857] 1972. *The Northwest Coast or Three Years' Residence in the Washington Territory*. Reprint, Seattle and London: University of Washington Press.

Thompson, David. 1916. *David Thompson's Narrative*. Edited by J. B. Tyrrell. Toronto: The Champlain Society.

Vancouver, George. [1798] 1984. *The Voyage of George Vancouver*, Volume II. Edited by W. Kaye Lamb. Reprint, London: The Hakluyt Society.

Victor, Frances Fuller. 1870. *The River of the West*. Hartford, Conn.: R. W. Bliss.

West, David, trans. 1990. *The Aeneid of Virgil*. New York: Penguin Books.

Whitman, Narcissa. [1836] 1937. *The Coming of the White Women, 1836, as told in Letters and Journal of Narcissa Prentice Whitman*. Compiled by T. C. Elliott. Portland: Oregon Historical Society.

3 / ROMANTIC MOVEMENT

Balch, Frederick Homer. [1890] 1965. *The Bridge of the Gods: A Romance of Indian Oregon*. Reprint, Portland, Ore.: Binfords & Mort.

Cantwell, Robert. 1972. *The Hidden Northwest*. Philadelphia: J. B. Lippincott Company.

Egan, Timothy. 1990. *The Good Rain: Across Time and Terrain in the Pacific Northwest*. New York: Alfred A. Knopf.

Emerson, Ralph Waldo. [1841] 1957. "Self-Reliance." *Selections from Ralph Waldo Emerson*. Edited by Stephen E. Whicher. Cambridge: The Riverside Press.

Frost, O. W. 1967. *Joaquin Miller*. New York: Twayne Publishers.

Miller, Joaquin. 1868. *Specimens*. Portland, Ore.: Carter Hines.

———. 1871a. *Pacific Poems*. London: Whittingham and Wilkins.

———. [1871b] 1915. *Songs of the Sierras. Joaquin Miller's Poems*, Volume II. Reprint, San Francisco: Whitaker and Ray.

———. 1873. *Unwritten History: Life Amongst the Modocs*. London: Richard Bentley & Son.

Nash, Roderick. 1982. *Wilderness and the American Mind*. 3rd ed. New Haven and London: Yale University Press.

Rousseau, Jean Jacques. 1761. *Julie ou La Nouvelle Héloïse*. Dublin: printed for James Hunter.

———. 1762. *Emile*. London: printed for R. Griffiths, T. Becket, and P. A. Hondt.

Thoreau, Henry David. 1863. "Walking." *Excursions*. Boston: Ticknor and Fields.

Winthrop, Theodore. 1861. *Cecil Dreeme*. Boston: Ticknor and Fields.

———. 1861. *John Brent*. New York: Dodd, Mead.

———. [1862a] 1986. *The Canoe and the Saddle*. Nisqually edition, reprint. Portland, Ore.: Binfords & Mort.

———. 1862b. *Edwin Brothertoft*. Boston: Ticknor and Fields.

4 / REALISTIC WRITING

Bryant, Paul T. 1978. *H. L. Davis*. Boston: Twayne Publishers.

Blunt, Judy. 2002. *Breaking Clean*. New York: Alfred A. Knopf.

Clearman-Blew, Mary. 1991. *All But the Waltz: Essays on a Montana Family*. New York: Viking Press.

Davis, H. L. 1919. *Primapara. Poetry* 14 (April).

———. 1929. "Old Man Isabell's Wife." *American Mercury* 14.

———. 1929. "Back to the Land—Oregon, 1907." *American Mercury* 16.

———. 1930. "A Town in Eastern Oregon." *American Mercury* 19.

———. [1935] 1984. *Honey in the Horn*. Reprint, New York: Avon.

———. 1952. *Winds of Morning*. New York: William Morrow & Company.

———. 1953. *Team Bells Woke Me*. New York: William Morrow & Company.

———. 1954. "A Walk in the Woods." *Holiday* 15.

———. 1959. *Kettle of Fire*. New York: William Morrow & Company.

Davis, H. L., and James Stevens. [1927] 1986. "Status Rerum: A Manifesto, Upon the Present Condition of Northwest Literature." *Collected Essays and Short Stories*. Moscow: University of Idaho Press.

Doig, Ivan. 1978. *This House of Sky: Landscapes of a Western Mind.* New York: Harcourt Brace Jovanovich.

———. 1980. *Winter Brothers.* New York: Harcourt Brace Jovanovich.

———. 1982. *The Sea Runners.* New York: Atheneum.

———. 1984. *English Creek.* New York: Atheneum.

———. 1987. *Dancing at the Rascal Fair.* New York: Atheneum.

———. 1990. *Ride with Me, Mariah Montana.* New York: Atheneum.

———. 1995. Personal interview. March 2.

———. 1996. *Bucking the Sun.* New York: Simon & Schuster.

———. 1999. *Mountain Time.* New York: Charles Scribner's Sons.

Fisher, Vardis. 1928. *Toilers of the Hills.* Boston: Houghton Mifflin Company.

———. 1931. *Dark Bridwell.* Boston: Houghton Mifflin Company.

———. 1932. *In Tragic Life.* Caldwell, Idaho: Caxton Printers.

———. 1939. *Children of God.* New York: Harper and Brothers.

Flora, Joseph. 1965. *Vardis Fisher.* New York: Twayne Publishers.

Guthrie, A. B. Jr. [1947] 1975. *The Big Sky.* Reprint, New York: Bantam Books.

———. 1949. *The Way West.* New York: Sloane.

———. 1953. Screenplay for *Shane.* Hollywood, Calif.: Paramount.

———. 1955. Screenplay for *The Kentuckian.* Hollywood, Calif.: Hecht-Lancaster Productions and James Productions.

———. 1956. *These Thousand Hills.* New York. Boston: Houghton Mifflin Company.

———. 1960. *The Big It.* Boston: Houghton Mifflin Company.

———. 1970. *Arfive.* Boston: Houghton Mifflin Company.

———. 1975. *The Last Valley.* New York: Simon & Schuster.

———. 1988. *Big Sky, Fair Land.* Flagstaff, Ariz.: Northland Press.

———. 1991. *A Field Guide to Writing Fiction.* New York: HarperCollins.

Haig-Brown, Roderick. [1939] 1982. "If Armageddon's On." *Writings and Reflections: The World of Roderick Haig-Brown.* Seattle: University of Washington Press.

———. [1942] 1993. *Timber.* Reprint, Corvallis: Oregon State University Press.

———. 1946. *A River Never Sleeps.* New York: William Morrow & Company.

———. 1949. *On the Highest Hill.* New York: William Morrow & Company.

———. [1959] 1982. "The Writer in Isolation." *Writings and Reflections: The World of Roderick Haig-Brown.* Seattle: University of Washington Press.

———. 1961. *The Living Land: An Account of the Natural Resources of British Columbia.* New York: William Morrow & Company.

Hardy, Thomas. 1856. *The Mayor of Casterbridge.* London: Smith, Elder & Co.

Hemingway, Ernest. 1924. "Big Two-Hearted River." *In Our Time.* Paris: Three Mountins Press.

———. 1952. *The Old Man and the Sea.* New York: Charles Scribner's Sons.

Kesey, Ken. 1962. *One Flew Over the Cuckoo's Nest.* New York: New American Library.

———. [1964] 1978. *Sometimes a Great Notion.* Reprint, New York: Bantam Books.

———. 1986. *Demon Box.* New York: Viking Press.

———. 1992. *Sailor Song.* New York: Viking Press.

Kittredge, William. 1992. *Hole in the Sky: A Memoir.* New York: Alfred A. Knopf.

Limerick, Patricia Nelson. 1988. *The Legacy of Conquest: The Unbroken Past and the American West.* New York and London: W. W. Norton.

London, Jack. 1900. *The Son of the Wolf.* London: Mills & Boon.

———. [1903] 1960. *The Call of the Wild.* Reprint, New York: New American Library.

MacDonald, Betty. [1945] 1987. *The Egg and I.* Reprint, New York: Harper and Row.

———. 1948. *The Plague and I.* Philadelphia: J. B. Lippincott Company.

———. 1950. *Anybody Can Do Anything.* Philadelphia: J. B. Lippincott Company.

———. 1955. *Onions in the Stew.* Philadelphia: J. B. Lippincott Company.

Maclean, Norman. 1976. *A River Runs Through It and Other Stories.* Chicago: University of Chicago Press.

———. 1988. "The Hidden Art of a Good Story: Wallace Stegner Lecture." *Norman Maclean.* Edited by Ron McFarland and Hugh Nichols. Lewiston, Idaho: Confluence Press.

————. 1992. *Young Men and Fire.* Chicago: University of Chicago Press.

Maguire, James H. 2000. "The Dim Immense Terror: Literary Naturalism in *Toilers of the Hills, Dark Bridwell* and *In Tragic Life.*" *Rediscovering Vardis Fisher: Centennial Essays.* Edited by Joseph M. Flora. Moscow: University of Idaho Press.

O'Connell, Nicholas. 1998. *At the Field's End: Interviews with 22 Pacific Northwest Writers.* Seattle: University of Washington Press.

Simpson, Elizabeth. 1992. *Earthlight, Wordfire: The Work of Ivan Doig.* Moscow: University of Idaho Press.

Stevens, James. 1948. *Big Jim Turner.* Garden City, N.Y.: Doubleday & Company.

Thoreau, Henry David. 1854. *Walden.* Boston: Ticknor and Fields.

Twain, Mark. 1884. *The Adventures of Huckleberry Finn.* New York: C. L. Webster.

Wolfe, Thomas. 1956. *The Letters of Thomas Wolfe.* Edited by Elizabeth Nowell. New York: Charles Scribner's Sons.

————. 1968. *The Electric Kool-Aid Acid Test.* New York: Farrar, Straus & Giroux.

5 / THE NORTHWEST SCHOOL

Broughton, Irv. 1975. *Mill Mountain Review.* Volume II-2. Seattle: Mill Mountain Press.

Carlson, Roy, ed. 1979. *Contemporary Northwest Writing.* Corvallis: Oregon State University Press.

Gerstenberger, Donna. 1983. *Richard Hugo.* Boise, Idaho: Boise State University Press.

Gloss, Molly. 1981. "The Doe." *The World Begins Here.* Oregon Literature Series. Corvallis: Oregon State University Press.

Haines, John. 1966. *Winter News.* Middletown, Conn.: Wesleyan University Press.

————. [1989] 1992. *The Stars, the Snow, the Fire: 25 Years in the Alaska Wilderness.* Reprint, New York: Washington Square Press.

————. 1996. *Fables and Distances.* St. Paul, Minn.: Graywolf Press.

Hugo, Richard. 1961. *A Run of Jacks.* Minneapolis: University of Minnesota Press.

————. 1965. *Death of the Kapowsin Tavern.* New York: Harcourt, Brace & World.

————. 1969. *Good Luck in Cracked Italian.* New York: World Publishing Company.

————. 1973. *The Lady in Kicking Horse Reservoir.* New York: W. W. Norton.

————. 1979a. *Selected Poems.* New York: W. W. Norton.

————. 1979b. *The Triggering Town: Lectures and Essays on Poetry and Writing.* New York: W. W. Norton.

————1986. *The Real West Marginal Way: A Poet's Autobiography.* Edited by Ripley S. Hugo, Lois Welch, and James Welch. New York: W. W. Norton.

Kitchen, Judith. 1999. *Writing the World: Understanding William Stafford.* Corvallis: Oregon State University Press.

Kizer, Carolyn. 1956. "Poetry: School of the Pacific Northwest." *The New Republic* (July 16).

————. 1961. *The Ungrateful Garden.* Bloomington: Indiana University Press.

————. 1965. *Knock Upon Silence.* Garden City, N. Y.: Doubleday & Company.

————. 1971. *Midnight Was My Cry: New and Selected Poems.* Garden City, N.Y.: Doubleday & Company.

————. 1984a. *Mermaids in the Basement: Poems for Women.* Port Townsend, Wash.: Copper Canyon Press.

————. 1984b. *Yin: New Poems.* Brockport, N.Y.: Boa Editions.

————. 1986. *The Nearness of You.* Port Townsend, Wash.: Copper Canyon Press.

————. 1995. *Harping On.* Port Townsend, Wash.: Copper Canyon Press.

Mills, Ralph Jr. 1968. *Selected Letters of Theodore Roethke.* Seattle: University of Washington Press.

O'Connell, Nicholas. 1998. *At the Field's End: Interviews with 22 Pacific Northwest Writers.* Seattle: University of Washington Press.

Roethke, Theodore. 1948. *The Lost Son.* Garden City, N.Y.: Doubleday & Company.

————. 1953. *The Waking.* Garden City, N.Y.: Doubleday & Company.

————. 1958. *Words for the Wind.* Garden City, N.Y.: Doubleday & Company.

————. 1965a. "An American Poet Introduces Himself." *On the Poet and His Craft.* Seattle: University of Washington Press.

————. 1965b. *The Far Field.* Garden City, N.Y.: Doubleday & Company.

————. 1965c. "Some Remarks on Rhythm," *On the Poet and His Craft.* Seattle: University of Washington Press.

————. 1965d. "Some Self-Analysis." *On the Poet and His Craft.* Seattle: University of Washington Press.

————. 1965e. "On Identity." *On the Poet and His Craft.* Seattle: University of Washington Press.

————. 1975. *Collected Poems of Theodore Roethke.* New York: Anchor Books.

Seager, Allan. 1975. *The Glass House: The Life of Theodore Roethke.* New York: Anchor Books.

Skelton, Robin, ed. 1964. *Five Poets of the Pacific Northwest.* Seattle: University of Washington Press.

Stafford, William. 1947. *Down in My Heart.* Elgin, Ill.: The Brethren Press.

————. 1960. *West of Your City.* Los Gatos, Calif.: Talisman Press.

————. 1962. *Traveling Through the Dark.* New York: Harper and Row.

————. 1966. *The Voices of Prose.* New York: McGraw-Hill Book Company.

————. 1973. *Someday, Maybe.* New York: Harper and Row.

————. 1977. *Stories that Could Be True: New and Collected Poems.* New York: Harper and Row.

————. 1978. *Writing the Australian Crawl: Views on the Writer's Vocation.* Ann Arbor: University of Michigan Press.

————. 1982. *A Glass Face in the Rain.* New York: Harper and Row.

————. 1987. *An Oregon Message.* New York: Harper and Row.

————. 1993. *The Darkness Around Us Is Deep: Selected Poems of William Stafford.* New York: HarperPerennial.

Vanderbilt, Kermit. 1979. "Theodore Roethke as a Northwest Poet." *Northwest Perspectives: Essays on the Culture of the Pacific Northwest.* Edited by Edwin R. Bingham and Glen A. Love. Seattle and London: University of Washington Press.

Wagoner, David. 1976. *Collected Poems 1956–1976*. Bloomington: Indiana University Press.

———. 1978. *Who Shall Be the Sun?* Bloomington: Indiana University Press.

———. 1987. *Through the Forest: New and Selected Poems: 1977–1987*. New York: Atlantic Monthly Press.

———. 1999. *Travelling Light*. Urbana: University of Illinois Press.

6 / CONTEMPORARY NORTHWEST LITERATURE

Alexie, Sherman. 1995. *Reservation Blues*. New York: Atlantic Monthly Press.

Bass, Rick. 1992. *The NineMile Wolves*. Livingston, Mont.: Clark City Press.

Berry, Don. 1960. *Trask: A Novel*. New York: Viking Press.

———. 1962. *Moontrap: A Novel*. New York: Viking Press.

Brown, Bruce. 1983. *Mountain in the Clouds: A Search for the Wild Salmon*. New York: Simon & Schuster.

Callenbach, Ernest. 1975. *Ecotopia*. Berkeley: Banyan Tree Books.

Crane, Stephen. 1898. *The Open Boat and Other Tales of Adventure*. New York: Doubleday & McClure.

Craven, Margaret. 1973. *I Heard the Owl Call My Name*. Garden City, N.Y.: Doubleday & Company.

Dickens, Charles. [1853] 1964. *Bleak House*. Reprint, New York: New American Library.

Duncan, David James. 1983. *The River Why*. San Francisco: Sierra Club Books.

Guterson, David. 1994. *Snow Falling on Cedars*. San Diego: Harcourt Brace & Company.

———. 1999. *East of the Mountains*. New York: Harcourt Brace & Company.

Hamill, Sam. 1995. *Destination Zero: Poems 1970–1995*. Fredonia, N.Y.: White Pine Press.

Herbert, Frank. 1984. *Dune*. New York: Putnam.

Johnson, Charles. 1982. *Oxherding Tale*. Bloomington: Indiana University Press.

Kroeber, Theodora. 1961. *Ishi in Two Worlds: A Biography of the Last*

Wild Indian in North America. Berkeley: University of California
Press.

Le Guin, Ursula K. 1972. *The Word for World Is Forest.* New York: Berkeley
Publishing Corp.

———. 1974. *The Dispossessed.* New York: Harper and Row.

———. 1985. *Always Coming Home.* New York: Harper and Row.

———. 1991. *Searoad: Chronicles of Klatsand.* New York: HarperCollins.

———. 1994. *A Fisherman of the Inland Sea: Science Fiction Stories.* New
York: HarperPrism.

———. 1996. *Unlocking the Air.* New York: HarperCollins.

Lesley, Craig. 1984. *Winterkill.* Boston: Houghton Mifflin Company.

———. 1989. *River Song.* Boston: Houghton Mifflin Company.

Lopez, Barry. 1976. *Desert Notes: Reflections in the Eye of a Raven.* New
York: Avon.

———. 1978. *Of Wolves and Men.* New York: Charles Scribner's Sons.

———. 1979. *River Notes: The Dance of the Herons.* Kansas City: Andrews
& McMeel.

———. 1981. *Winter Count.* New York: Charles Scribner's Sons.

———. 1986. *Arctic Dreams: Imagination and Desire in a Northern
Landscape.* New York: Charles Scribner's Sons.

———. 1989. "Landscape and Narrative." *Crossing Open Ground.* New
York: Vintage Books.

———. 1990. *The Rediscovery of North America.* Lexington: University
of Kentucky Press.

———. 1994a. *Field Notes: The Grace Note of the Canyon Wren.* New York:
Alfred A. Knopf.

———. 1994b. Personal interview. December 4.

———. 1998a. *About This Life.* New York: Alfred A. Knopf.

———. 1998b. Personal interview.

———. 2000. *Light Action in the Caribbean.* New York: Alfred A. Knopf.

Mech, L. David. 1970. *The Wolf: The Ecology and Behavior of an Endangered
Species.* New York: Natural History Press.

Melville, Herman. 1851. *Moby Dick.* New York: Harper and Brothers.

Mitsui, James. 1986. *After the Long Train: Poems.* Minneapolis, Minn.:
The Bieler Press.

Mowat, Farley. 1963. *Never Cry Wolf.* Boston: Little, Brown.

Murie, Adolph. 1966. *The Wolves of Mount McKinley*. Washington, D.C.: U.S. Dept. of the Interior, Fauna and National Parks, Fauna Series 5.

Nelson, Richard K. 1989. *The Island Within*. San Francisco: North Point Press.

Newhouse, Sewell. 1869. *Trapper's Guide*. New York: Oakley, Mason & Company.

O'Connell, Nicholas. 1998. *At the Field's End: Interviews with 22 Pacific Northwest Writers*. Seattle: University of Washington Press.

Okada, John. 1981. *No-No Boy*. Seattle: University of Washington Press.

Peterson, Brenda. 1990. *Living by Water: Essays on Life, Land and Spirit*. Anchorage: Alaska Northwest Books.

Pyle, Robert Michael. 1988. *Wintergreen: Listening to the Land's Heart*. Boston: Houghton Mifflin Company.

Robinson, Marilynne. 1981. *Housekeeping*. New York: Farrar, Straus & Giroux.

———. 1989. *Mother Country*. New York: Farrar, Straus & Giroux.

———. 1998. *The Death of Adam: Essays on Modern Thought*. Boston: Houghton Mifflin Company.

Skinner, B. F. 1948. *Walden II*. New York: Macmillan.

Snyder, Gary. 1951. "He Who Hunted Birds in His Father's Village: The Dimensions of a Haida Myth." Undergraduate thesis. Portland, Ore.: Reed College.

———. 1957. *Earth Household*. New York: New Directions.

———. 1959. *Riprap*. Asland, Mass.: Origin Press.

———. 1967. *The Back Country*. London: Fulcrum Press.

———. 1970. *Regarding Wave*. Iowa City: Windhover Press.

———. 1974. *Turtle Island*. New York: New Directions.

———. 1983. *Axe Handles*. Port Townsend, Wash.: Copper Canyon Press.

———. 1992. *No Nature: New and Selected Poems*. New York: Pantheon.

———. 1995a. "Reinhabitation." *A Place in Space*. Washington, D.C.: Counterpoint.

———. 1995b. "The New Wind." *A Place in Space*. Washington, D.C.: Counterpoint.

———. 1996. *Mountains and Rivers Without End*. Washington, D.C.: Counterpoint.

Stafford, Kim. 1986. *Having Everything Right.* Lewiston, Idaho: Confluence Press.

Sund, Robert. 1983. *Ish River: Poems.* San Francisco: North Point Press.

Tisdale, Sallie. 1991. *Stepping Westward: The Long Search for Home in the Pacific Northwest.* New York: H. Holt.

Twain, Mark. 1884. *The Adventures of Huckleberry Finn.* New York: C. L. Webster.

Wallace, David Raines. 1983. *The Klamath Knot: Explorations of Myth and Evolution.* San Francisco: Sierra Club Books.

Welch, James. 1986. *Fools Crow: A Novel.* New York: Viking Press.

ADDITIONAL SOURCES

1 / EARLY NATIVE AMERICAN STORIES

Herbert, Frank. 1972. *Soul Catcher*. New York: Putnam.

McNickle, D'Arcy. 1936. *The Surrounded*. New York: Dodd.

Niatum, Duane. 1991. *Drawings of the Song Animals: New and Selected Poems*. Duluth, Minn.: Holy Cow! Press.

Owens, Louis. 1999. *Dark River*. Norman: University of Oklahoma Press.

2 / JOURNALS OF EXPLORATION AND SETTLEMENT

Wilkes, Charles. 1852. *Narrative of the United States Exploring Expedition, during the years 1838, 1839, 1840, 1841, 1842*. London: Ingram, Cooke.

3 / ROMANTIC MOVEMENT

Burney, W. T., ed. 1910. *The Gold-Gated West: Songs and Poems by Samuel L. Simpson*. Philadelphia and London: J. B. Lippincott Company.

4 / REALISTIC WRITING

Haycox, Ernest. 1952. *The Earthbreakers*. Boston: Little, Brown.

5 / THE NORTHWEST SCHOOL

Aliesan, Jody. 1998. *Desperate for a Clearing*. Sedro-Woolley, Wash.: Grey Spider Press.

Barnard, Mary. 1979. *Collected Poems*. Portland, Ore.: Breitenbush Publications.

Barrington, Judith. 1985. *Trying to Be an Honest Woman: Poems*. Portland, Ore.: Eighth Mountain Press.

Bentley, Beth. 1976. *Country of Resemblances*. Athens: Ohio University Press.

Bentley, Nelson. 1981. *Snoqualmie Falls Apocalypse*. Lewiston, Idaho: Confluence Press.

Bierds, Linda. 1988. *The Stillness, the Dancing: Poems*. New York: H. Holt.

Birney, Earle. 1975. *The Collected Poems of Earle Birney*. Toronto, Canada: McClelland and Stewart.

DeFrees, Madeline. 2001. *Blue Dusk: New and Selected Poems, 1951–2001*. Port Townsend, Wash.: Copper Canyon Press.

Gallagher, Tess. 1987. *Amplitude: New and Selected Poems*. St. Paul, Minn.: Graywolf Press.

Hanson, Kenneth O. 1983. *Lighting the Night Sky: Poems*. Portland, Ore.: Breitenbush Books.

Kenney, Richard. 1993. *The Invention of the Zero: Poems*. New York: Alfred A. Knopf.

McElroy, Colleen. 1990. *What Madness Brought Me Here: New and Selected Poems 1968–1988*. Middletown, Conn.: Wesleyan University Press.

McHugh, Heather. 1999. *The Father of the Predicaments*. Hanover, N.H.: Wesleyan University Press.

McPherson, Sandra. 1996. *Edge Effect: Trails and Portrayals*. Hanover: University Press of New England for Wesleyan University Press.

Mitsui, James. 1997. *From a Three-Cornered World: New and Selected Poems*. Seattle: University of Washington Press.

Mueller, Melinda. 1998. *Apocrypha: Poems*. Sedro-Woolley, Wash.: Grey Spider Press.

Rutsala, Vern. 1985. *Backtracking*. Santa Cruz, Calif.: Storyline Press.

Swift, Joan. 1999. *The Tiger Iris: Poems*. Rochester, N.Y.: BOA Editions.

Wrigley, Robert. 1999. *Reign of Snakes*. New York: Penguin Books.

6 / CONTEMPORARY NORTHWEST LITERATURE

Alexie, Sherman. 1993. *The Lone Ranger and Tonto Fistfight in Heaven.* New York: Atlantic Monthly Press.

Carver, Raymond. 1988. *Where I'm Calling From: New and Selected Stories.* New York: Atlantic Monthly Press.

Hyde, Dayton O. 1986. *Don Coyote: The Good Times and the Bad Times of a Much-Maligned American Original.* New York: Ballantine Books.

Levertov, Denise. 1992. *Evening Train.* New York: New Directions.

Moore, Kathleen Dean. 1995. *Riverwalking: Reflections on Moving Water.* New York: Lyons and Burford.

Murie, Margaret. [1962] 1978. *Two in the Far North.* Reprint, Anchorage: Alaska Northwest Publishing Company.

Robbins, Tom. 1971. *Another Roadside Attraction.* Garden City, N.Y.: Doubleday & Company.

Silko, Leslie Marmon. 1997. *Ceremony.* New York: Viking Press.

Wolff, Tobias. 1989. *This Boy's Life: A Memoir.* New York. Atlantic Monthly Press.

INDEX

The Adventures of Huckleberry Finn,
    59, 64
Alexie, Sherman, 143
Always Coming Home, 151–56
Ambrose, Stephen E., 23
Applegate, Shannon, 30
Arctic Dreams, 165, 176–78
A River Runs Through It, 83–90
A Run of Jacks, 119
Axe Handles, 149–50

Balch, Frederick Homer, 43–46
Barcott, Bruce, xviii
Barnard, Mary, 99
Barrington, Judith, 99
Bass, Rick, 142
Bentley, Beth, 99
Bentley, Nelson, 99
Bergon, Frank, 21
Berry, Don, 143
Bierds, Linda, 99

The Big Sky, 71–74
Birney, Earle, 99
Blunt, Judy, 91
Boas, Franz, 5
The Bridge of the Gods, 44–46
Brown, Bruce, 142
Bryant, Paul T., 64
Buell, Lawrence, xix

The Call of the Wild, 48–52
The Canoe and the Saddle, 34–39
Cantwell, Robert, xvi
Carlson, Roy, xvii
Carr, Emily, 71
Carver, Raymond, 141
Children of God, 52, 57
Chittick, V.L.O., xvi
Clark, Ella, 5
Clark, William, 20–24
Clearman-Blue, Mary, 91
Crane, Stephen, 167

Craven, Margaret, 143
Cultee, Charles, 9

Dark Bridwell, 55–56
Davis, H. L., 57–65
DeFrees, Madeline, 99
Desert Notes, 169–71
Dickens, Charles, 157
Dillard, Annie, 30
Doig, Ivan, 47, 90–96
Down in my Heart, 128
Drucker, Philip, xii, 6, 9
Duncan, David James, 143
Duniway, Abigail Scott, 30

Earth Household, 145–46
Egan, Timothy, 38
The Egg and I, 76–79
Eliot, T. S., 112
Emerson, Ralph Waldo, 38, 167
English Creek, 94–95
Etulain, Richard, xvi
Everson, William, xvi

The Far Field, 111–17
Field Notes, 178–79
Finne, Ron, xvii
Fisher, Vardis, 52–57
Foote, Mary Hallock, 30
Frost, O. W., 42

Gallagher, Tess, 99
Gerstenberger, Donna, 121
Gloss, Molly, 30
Goetzman, William, 17

Guterson, David, 143
Guthrie, A. B., 71–75

Haig-Brown, Roderick, 66–71
Haines, John, 131
Hamill, Sam, 142
Hanson, Kenneth O., 99
Hardy, Thomas, 70
Hemingway, Ernest, 85–86
Herbert, Frank, 14, 141
Hilbert, Vi, 4
Hogkins, Jack, 71
Holbrook, Stewart, xvi
Honey in the Horn, 59–65
Horner, John B., xv
Housekeeping, 156–64
Hugo, Richard, 117–24
Hyde, Dayton O., 142

Indians of the Northwest Coast,
   xii
Irving, Washington, 27

Jefferson, Thomas, 20
Johnson, Charles, 142

Kazin, Alfred, xix
Kenney, Richard, 99
Kesey, Ken, 79–82
Kitchen, Judith, 129
Kittredge, William, xviii-xix
Kizer, Carolyn, 98, 124–27

The Lady in Kicking Horse Reservoir,
   121

Le Guin, Ursula K., 150–56
Lerner, Andrea, 14
Lesley, Craig, 143
Levertov, Denise, 141
Lewis, Meriwether, 20–24
Light Action in the Caribbean, 179
Limerick, Patricia Nelson, 65
London, Jack, 48–52
Lopez, Barry, 140–43, 164–79
The Lost Son, 102
Love, Glen A., xviii
Lucia, Ellis, xvi

MacDonald, Betty, 75–79
Maclean, Norman, 82–90
Maguire, James H., 54
McElroy, Colleen, 99
McHugh, Heather, 99
McNickle, D'Arcy, 13
McPherson, Sandra, 99
Meany, Edmond, xv
Mech, L. David, 172
Melville, Herman, 167
Mencken, H. L., 58
Midnight Was My Cry, 126
Miller, Joaquin, 39–43
Mitsui, James, 99, 142
Moore, Kathleen Dean, 142
Mount Rainier, x, 36–37
Mowat, Farley, 172
Murie, Adolph, 172
Murie, Margaret, 142

Nash, Roderick, 35
Nelson, Richard K., 142

Newhouse, Sewell, 175
Niatum, Duane, 14
Nisbet, Jack, 24
No Nature, 150
Northwest region, definition
    of, xi, xii

O'Connell, Nicholas, xvii
O'Connor, Flannery, xi
Of Wolves and Men, 171–76
Okada, John, 142
One Flew Over the Cuckoo's Nest,
    80–81
Owens, Lewis, 13

Peterson, Brenda, 142
Phinney, Archie, 12
Powers, Alfred, xv
Pyle, Robert Michael, 142

Ramsey, Jerold, 7–10
The Rediscovery of North America,
    178
Ricou, Laurie, xviii
Ride with Me, Mariah Montana,
    95
Robbins, Tom, 141
Robinson, Marilynne, 156–64
Roethke, Theodore, 98–117
Rutsala, Vern, 99

Saint Francis, 174
Schama, Simon, xix
Seattle, Chief, 3–4
Simonson, Harold P.,

Simpson, Elizabeth, 93
Skelton, Robin, 124
Smith, Annick, xviii
Snyder, Gary, 143–50
Sometimes a Great Notion,
    79–82
Songs of the Sierras, 40–43
Stafford, Kim, 143
Stafford, William, xi, 127–31
The Stars, the Snow, the Fire, 133–35
"Status Rerum," 57
Stegner, Wallace, 72
Stevens, Isaac, 3
Stevens, James, 57
Sund, Robert, 142
Swan, James, 30–31

This House of Sky, 47, 90–92
Thompson, David, 24–26
Thoreau, Henry David, 43
Timber, 66–71
Tisdale, Sallie, 143
Toilers of the Hills, 54–55
Traveling Through the Dark, 128–30

Travelling Light, 139
Turtle Island, 147–49

The Ungrateful Garden, 125

Vancouver, George, 15–20
Venn, George, xvii
Victor, Frances Fuller, 30

Wagoner, David, 97–99, 135–39
Wallace, David Raines, 142
The Way West, 74–75
Welch, James, 143
Whitman, Marcus, 28
Whitman, Narcissa, 28–30
Who Shall Be the Sun?, 138–39
Wilson, Ethyl, 71
Winter News, 132–33
Winthrop, Theodore, 33–39
Wolfe, Thomas, 52–53
Wolff, Tobias, 141
Wrigley, Robert, 99

Young Men and Fire, 84